Situating Shakespeare Pedagogy in US Higher Education

Situating Shakespeare Pedagogy in US Higher Education

Social Justice and Institutional Contexts

Edited by
Marissa Greenberg and Elizabeth Williamson

EDINBURGH
University Press

Edinburgh University Press is one of the leading university presses in the UK. We publish academic books and journals in our selected subject areas across the humanities and social sciences, combining cutting-edge scholarship with high editorial and production values to produce academic works of lasting importance. For more information visit our website: edinburghuniversitypress.com

We are committed to making research available to a wide audience and are pleased to be publishing an Open Access ebook edition of this title.

© editorial matter and organization Marissa Greenberg and Elizabeth Williamson 2024, under Creative Commons Attribution-NonCommercial licence CC-BY-NC
© the chapters their several authors 2024

Published with the support of the University of Edinburgh Scholarly Publishing Initiatives Fund.

Edinburgh University Press Ltd
13 Infirmary Street, Edinburgh, EH1 1LT

Typeset in 11/13pt Sabon LT Pro
by Cheshire Typesetting Ltd, Cuddington, Cheshire

A CIP record for this book is available from the British Library

ISBN 978 1 3995 1664 8 (hardback)
ISBN 978 1 3995 1665 5 (paperback)
ISBN 978 1 3995 1666 2 (webready PDF)
ISBN 978 1 3995 1667 9 (epub)

The right of Marissa Greenberg and Elizabeth Williamson to be identified as the editors of this work has been asserted in accordance with the Copyright, Designs and Patents Act 1988, and the Copyright and Related Rights Regulations 2003 (SI No. 2498).

Contents

List of Figures	vii
Acknowledgments	viii
Abstracts	x
Notes on Contributors	xvi

Introduction   1
Marissa Greenberg and Elizabeth Williamson

1. On Shakespeare, Anticolonial Pedagogy, and Being Just   23
   Amrita Dhar

2. Deeply Engaged Protest: Social Justice Pedagogy and Shakespeare's "Monument"   44
   Elisa Oh

3. Teaching Shakespeare at an Urban Public Community College: An Equity-Driven Approach   62
   Victoria M. Muñoz

4. Teaching Shakespeare as a Killjoy Practice in a White Dominant Institution   77
   Mary Janell Metzger

5. Shakespeare and Environmental Justice: Collaborative Eco-Theater in Yosemite National Park and the San Joaquin Valley   94
   Katherine Steele Brokaw

6. Where Curriculum Meets Community: Teaching Borderlands Shakespeare in San Antonio   111
   Katherine Gillen and Kathryn Vomero Santos

7. Dressing to Transgress: Aesthetic Matching, Historical Costumers of Color, and the Restorying of Institutional Spaces   126
   Penelope Geng

8. Shakespeare in a Catholic University: (Re)creating Knowledge in a Divided Landscape   144
   Kirsten N. Mendoza

9. Shakespeare's Mixed Stock: Biracial Affect in the Field   159
   Roya Biggie and Perry Guevara

10. Who Shot Romeo? And How Can We Stop the Bleeding? Urban Shakespeare, White People, and Education Beyond the Neoliberal Nightmare   180
    Eric L. De Barros

Afterword   196
Wendy Beth Hyman

Bibliography   203
Index   224

List of Figures

2.1	Robert E. Lee statue, Richmond, Virginia. August 29, 2020. MediaPunch Inc./Alamy Stock Photo.	52
2.2	*Louise de Kéroualle, Duchess of Portsmouth with an unknown female attendant*. Pierre Mignard, oil on canvas, 1682. 47½ × 37½ inches. © National Portrait Gallery, London.	55
2.3	*Seeing Through Time 2*. Titus Kaphar, oil on canvas, 2018. 92 × 72 inches. © Titus Kaphar, courtesy Gagosian.	56
5.1	The stage at Curry Village on which Shakespeare in Yosemite performs, with Half Dome in the background. Photo: Shawn Overton.	98
5.2	Lee Stetson, Sofia Andom, and Ángel Nuñez on set in Yosemite. Photo: Katherine Steele Brokaw.	101
5.3	Cat Flores singing in *Love's Labor's Lost*. Photo: Darah Carrillo Vargas.	102
5.4	Tonatiuh Newbold (Leo) and Dennis Brown (Cymbeline) embrace. Still from *Imogen in the Wild*.	103
5.5	Andrew Hardy, Tonatiuh Newbold, Sofia Andom, Cat Flores, Bella Camfield, and Bethy Harmelin in *Love's Labor's Lost*. Photo: Grace Garnica.	108
7.1	*Portrait of an African Woman Holding a Clock*, c. 1583–5. Annibale Carracci (attributed), oil on canvas, 23¾ × 15½ inches. © Department of Culture and Tourism, Abu Dhabi. Photo by Ismail Noor, Seeing Things. Reproduced with permission.	132
7.2	*The Carracci Project*, 2021. Shasta Schatz, digital photography. © Shasta Schatz. Reproduced with permission.	133

Acknowledgments

The spark for this collection arose from a long-standing collaboration between the editors. We were both fortunate to attend the University of Pennsylvania's doctoral program, where peer-to-peer collaboration was explicitly fostered by pathbreaking feminist scholar Phyllis Rackin. Thanks in large part to this aspect of our training, we continued to receive intellectual inspiration and collegial support from Urvashi Chakravarty, Jane Hwang Degenhardt, Jennifer Higgenbotham, Erika T. Lin, and many others long after we graduated. Our professional friendship and the principles that continue to fuel it owe so much to these generous and talented scholars.

As we matured into our roles as scholar-teachers, both of us became increasingly committed to integrating our research with our pedagogical praxis, and we began experimenting with using identity-based caucusing in the classroom. Perhaps because we taught at two very different institutions, we developed an appreciation both for our common ground and for the uniqueness of our teaching situations. Throughout this process of experimentation, we were buoyed first, last, and always, by the bravery and wisdom of our students. One of the great joys of our collaboration was sharing our delight in our students' achievements and our appreciation for all the ways they continually taught us about their lives, their communities, and their needs as learners.

The breath that turned our spark into a fire was, without question, the Shakespeare Association of America (SAA) plenary panel we convened during the second tumultuous year of the COVID-19 pandemic. Despite the profound pressures bearing down on all of us, our co-panelists (Eric De Barros, Kirsten Mendoza, and Mary Janell Metzger) graciously agreed to meet with us prior to the session itself so that we could share our work and our stories with each other. We will never find enough ways to express our gratitude for those vulnerable, dynamic, and generative conversations. We also wish to thank the SAA trustees for turning a spotlight on our panel, "Walking the Talk: Embodied Pedagogies of Social Justice," during a politically charged moment when our students were (rightfully) clamoring for more equitable and inclusive classroom practices.

Research funding to support our work on this volume, highlighted in the introduction, was provided by a University of New Mexico ASSURE (Arts & Sciences Support for Undergraduate Research Experience) grant. We wish to offer a special thanks to Brigid A. Shaski for her role in supporting the project. The Center for Regional Studies at the University of New Mexico provided vital subvention funding for image permissions and color reproductions. Our caucusing research also received support from The Evergreen State College's summer undergraduate research fellowship program, and we would be remiss if we did not mention the crucial ways that Sylvia Chowdhury contributed to and shaped our thinking.

We are grateful to the entire editorial team at Edinburgh University Press for their support of this volume, including Michelle Houston for shepherding it through peer review and advocating for open access, Susannah Butler for supporting our revision process, and Elizabeth Fraser and Emily Sharp for bringing the work to completion.

Most of all, we wish to thank the co-authors of this volume for their brilliance and their passion. Because we wanted this collection to provide a space for meaningful conversation, we made extraordinary asks of them from start to finish—hosting several live virtual gatherings and asking authors to provide peer feedback to each other on early versions of their chapters. We hope that readers will find in the finished product traces of these urgent and impactful discussions. Equally important, we hope readers—whether they are teachers or administrators—will carry its spark into their classrooms and committee rooms and support each other in making our institutions of higher education spaces where all our students can learn and thrive.

Abstracts

1. On Shakespeare, Anticolonial Pedagogy, and Being Just
Amrita Dhar

Midwest | Public state university system | Decolonization

It was in 1822 at the Hindu College in Calcutta that Shakespeare first entered a university curriculum, anywhere in the world. Shakespeare's presence in India, and his integration into the academy in Calcutta, were both directly a result of colonialism. Recognizing that the massive presence of Shakespeare in the world of letters and theater today is a direct result of imperialism, and meditating on my pedagogy of Shakespeare, race, and disability across campuses of a large Midwestern state university today, this essay asserts the urgent need for anticolonial Shakespeare scholarship, performance, and pedagogy in our current moment of the twenty-first century. Bringing an ethic of decolonization to my professional life in the US, this essay examines the possibilities and impossibilities of anticolonial curricula, and justice-oriented pedagogy more broadly, at my institution and in the global North academy.

2. Deeply Engaged Protest: Social Justice Pedagogy and Shakespeare's "Monument"
Elisa Oh

Washington, DC | Historically Black College or University (HBCU) | Race and intersectionality

This chapter proposes an approach to social justice pedagogy at a Historically Black College or University (HBCU) through identifying and working against traditional institutional power structures and colonial legacies of literary canon formation. In response to my students' desire to choose a principled intellectual boycott of Shakespeare's work due to the racism in it, I created a protest assignment to render students' arguments equal to the professor's and to model creative critical challenges to traditional authorities on English language and literature. We study visual protest art, Titus Kaphar's revisions of the early modern portrait tradition, and Black Lives Matter protests on and around Confederate monuments. The students then create their own protest art on and around Shakespeare texts for display in the English department and beyond.

3. Teaching Shakespeare at an Urban Public Community College: An Equity-Driven Approach

Victoria M. Muñoz

New York City | Public community college | Socioeconomics and race

At an urban public community college, Shakespeare threatens to alienate students experiencing various conditions of precarity. Addressing the material elitism of Shakespeare is especially paramount for those working within lower-income communities of color, where preexisting inequities in higher education have been further intensified by the COVID-19 pandemic. This essay presents practical recommendations for faculty seeking to meet the needs of minoritized students through such measures as: privileging students' responses to the material; adopting free and open educational materials; incorporating visual and audio performances; and meeting students where they are, such as by differentiated instruction. While prompting faculty to address unacknowledged inequities in the Shakespeare classroom, this essay also calls on institutions to support faculty seeking to revolutionize the curriculum.

4. Teaching Shakespeare as a Killjoy Practice in a White Dominant Institution

Mary Janell Metzger

Pacific Northwest | Large public university | Ethics and race

Metzger explores the challenges and opportunities of developing an antiracist community of 'killjoy' Shakespeareans within a predominantly white institution founded on unceded Native land. Via the study of tragic action, racialization, and adaptation in—and of—Shakespeare, Metzger offers specific practices for developing students' capacity for dialogue and analysis of the production of whiteness in Shakespeare's work. Drawing on critical race theory, human geography, and the history of normal schools in the American west, Metzger argues for a place-based approach to Shakespeare that draws on the tragic power of human vulnerability to suffering, loss, and death while illuminating the particular violence of absolute social hierarchies and their institutional advancement.

5. Shakespeare and Environmental Justice: Collaborative Eco-Theater in Yosemite National Park and the San Joaquin Valley

    Katherine Steele Brokaw

    West Coast | Mid-sized public university and Hispanic Serving Institution (HSI) | Ecocriticism and eco-performance

At the University of California, Merced, environmental injustice is keenly felt by students, many of whom are from farmworker families and have grown up in highly contaminated areas. My interest in how adaptations of Shakespeare might address issues of environmental justice led me to co-found Shakespeare in Yosemite, which performs free, ecologically inflected shows in Yosemite for Earth Day. This essay details student work on our film adaptation of *Cymbeline*, *Imogen in the Wild*, and briefly describes our 2022 *Love's Labor's Lost* stage show. I center the voices of my students, who explain how collaborative, practice-based learning allows them to engage creatively with both Shakespeare and environmental justice issues, benefiting them intellectually, socially, and emotionally.

6. Where Curriculum Meets Community: Teaching Borderlands Shakespeare in San Antonio

    Katherine Gillen and Kathryn Vomero Santos

    South-Central/Southwest | Public university and private liberal arts college | Community-based research

In this essay, we share our experiences negotiating the ethical implications of teaching Shakespeare at two very different institutions in San Antonio, Texas, as well as our efforts to do so in culturally sustaining ways that mitigate colonial and white supremacist violence. We also advocate for the pedagogical value of engaging with Shakespeare through the lens of Borderlands theories, histories, and cultural production and of teaching works of adaptation, translation, and appropriation that are part of a body of work that we term Borderlands Shakespeare. As we discuss, moreover, our work teaching Shakespeare and Shakespeare appropriations in the US–Mexico Borderlands has revealed the importance of curricular revisions on a larger scale and of collaborating with communities outside our academic institutions. Teaching Shakespeare responsibly, we suggest, demands holistic engagement not only with students but also with the communities in which our institutions are located.

7. Dressing to Transgress: Aesthetic Matching, Historical Costumers of Color, and the Restorying of Institutional Spaces

Penelope Geng

Midwest | Small private college | Race and fandom

In culturally white spaces such as the university or the museum, non-white readers and viewers are assumed to be less than culturally competent on the basis of a perceived mismatch between their race and the (white) field of study, a phenomenon of "aesthetic matching" that recalls critical race studies' critique of "whiteness as property." The British literature survey, with its strong emphasis on canonicity, has the potential to reproduce this very harm. This essay explores how to oppose aesthetic matching through a "restorying" of the canon. In fan culture, a community of self-trained historical costumers like Shasta Schatz show the power of restorying when they combine research, crafting, and theatrical performance to expose the racializing logics inherent in European Renaissance art. Their stunning creations provide a model for students to attempt their own critical and creative interventions. The essay concludes with a description of a simple yet highly effective curation assignment that asks students to practice restorying an object in the Minneapolis Institute of Art.

8. Shakespeare in a Catholic University: (Re)creating Knowledge in a Divided Landscape

Kirsten N. Mendoza

Midwest | Private Marianist university | Ethics and race

This chapter reflects on my experiences teaching Shakespeare at a predominantly white, Catholic institution as one of five nonwhite full-time faculty members in the Department of English. I share my pedagogical approaches that center modes of inquiry on the politics of knowledge (re)creation as part of my commitment to inspire liberatory action and social change. Specifically, I have students think deeply in order to unsettle the religious "truths" and the history we think we know about Shakespeare and the early modern past, assumptions, norms, and expectations that have been and continue to be yoked to gender and race violence.

9. Shakespeare's Mixed Stock: Biracial Affect in the Field
Roya Biggie and Perry Guevara
West Coast and Midwest | Private institutions | Mixed-race identity

This chapter attends to the increase in mixed-race faculty and students in higher education from the vantage of early modern studies. Specifically, we bring together affect theory with critical race studies to examine structures of biracial feeling in Shakespeare, and in so doing, critique the institutional politics of racial inscrutability, unbelonging, and exclusion that continue to replicate ideological patterns of settler colonialism. As a response to this institutional failure, we propose an upper-level course, Shakespeare's Mixed Stock, that traces biraciality in Shakespearean drama and the early modern archive to offer insight into the affective lives of a scant yet nonetheless documented population in early modern England. Central to the course is the experience of biracial silence and the premise that silence can be more than archival absence; instead, it may function, in drama, as an opportunity for resistance, ambiguity, and affective possibility. In confronting these silences, we attempt to cultivate an ethos of wonder and a practice of reparative reading through which students may apprehend more fully a literary history of race that has thus far received little critical attention. Ultimately, the course aspires to model how universities might begin to encounter racial inscrutability and to acknowledge the affective labor of diversity and inclusion.

10. Who Shot Romeo? And How Can We Stop the Bleeding? Urban Shakespeare, White People, and Education Beyond the Neoliberal Nightmare

Eric L. De Barros

International | Urban institutions | Adaptation and activism

In Jason Zeldes's *Romeo Is Bleeding*, a 2015 documentary film about an urban adaptation of *Romeo and Juliet*, the two questions of my chapter's primary title are the governing, largely unspoken ones driving the narrative. In the process of identifying a pedagogy of figurative denial—what I term "Shakespeare-as-poetry"—mystifying and thereby perpetuating the ugly realities of urban (Black and Brown) suffering as well as the neoliberal policies of paternalistic white people, I argue that the point of the film and the play was never to offer any real answers. By contrast, I argue that, if it is possible for us to answer these questions, it will require our courage to be rude, unpleasant, and, yes, unpoetic enough to reject "Shakespeare-as-poetry" and to call out all those committed to perpetuating it. And furthermore, if there is any hope of saving the Romeo of the titular questions, it will require our sacrificial willingness—our tireless and courageous willingness—to fight against the neoliberal policies destroying our educational institutions.

Notes on Contributors

Roya Biggie is Assistant Professor of English at Knox College. She is currently working on two book projects: one on cross-species sympathetic bonds in early modern tragedy, and another on the racialized rhetoric surrounding plants in the period's travel writing and horticultural texts. She has received grants and fellowships from the Folger Shakespeare Library, the Mellon Foundation, the Associated Colleges of the Midwest, and the National Endowment for the Humanities. Her work has appeared in *Renaissance Drama*, *Early Theatre*, *Early Modern Literary Studies*, *Lesser Living Creatures of the Renaissance*, and *Race in the European Renaissance: A Classroom Guide*.

Katherine Steele Brokaw is Associate Professor of English at University of California, Merced, and co-founding artistic director of Shakespeare in Yosemite. She authored *Staging Harmony: Music and Religious Change in Late Medieval and Early English Drama* (2016) and has published articles and reviews in several journals and essay collections. With Jay Zysk she co-edited *Sacred and Secular Transactions in the Age of Shakespeare* (2019), and she edited *Macbeth* (2019). Her most recent book is *Shakespeare and Community Performance* (2023).

Eric L. De Barros is an Assistant Professor of English at American University of Sharjah, United Arab Emirates. His research centers on the politics of embodied subjectivity in early modern literary and educational texts. He has authored several articles on the topic, and his main book project, *Shakespeare and the Pedagogy of Sexual Violence: Race, Class, and the Redefinition of Masculinity*, will endeavor to rethink Shakespeare as an ethically oriented educational theorist with much to teach us about how education reflects, shapes, and interrogates cultural norms. In that spirit, he has developed and taught a range of cross-historical, politically responsive courses over a period of twenty years at several institutions of higher learning.

Amrita Dhar is Assistant Professor of English at The Ohio State University. She is completing her first monograph, *Milton's Blind Language*, which examines the workings of blindness towards the making of Milton's long poetry. Her next project, on the crossings of disability, race, and empire, examines the relationship between the cultural production of disability and the intertwined phenomena of early modern global contact, race-making, and belonging. With Amrita Sen, she is co-editing the collection *Shakespeare in the "Post" Colonies: Legacies, Cultures and Social Justice* and a special issue of *Borrowers and Lenders* on the topic of Shakespeare in Bengal. She also writes on world mountaineering literatures.

Penelope Geng is Associate Professor of English at Macalester College, where she teaches courses on early modern literature, Shakespeare, law and literature, and disability. She is the author of *Communal Justice in Shakespeare's England: Drama, Law, and Emotion* (2021). Her articles have appeared in *Studies in Philology, The Sixteenth Century Journal, The Ben Jonson Journal*, and *Law, Culture and the Humanities*. She is working on her second monograph, provisionally titled *Disabled by Law: Literature, Property, and Ablenationalism in an Age of Empire*, which explores the deep influence of property law on early modern ideas of racial difference, disability, and able-bodied citizenship. A beginner improviser and serial hobbyist, she lives in St. Paul, Minnesota, USA.

Katherine Gillen is Associate Professor of English at Texas A&M University–San Antonio. She is the author of *Chaste Value: Economic Crisis, Female Chastity and the Production of Social Difference on Shakespeare's Stage* (Edinburgh University Press, 2017) and several essays on race, gender, and economics in early modern drama. She is working on a monograph called *Shakespeare's Racial Classicism: Whiteness, Slavery, and Humanism*, which examines Shakespeare's use of classical sources within the context of emerging racial capitalism. With Kathryn Vomero Santos and Adrianna M. Santos, she co-founded the Borderlands Shakespeare Colectiva, which has received funding from the Mellon Foundation and the National Endowment for the Humanities.

Marissa Greenberg is Associate Professor of English at the University of New Mexico. She is the author of *Metropolitan Tragedy: Genre, Justice, and the City in Early Modern England* (2015) and the co-editor (with Rachel Trubowitz) of *Milton's Moving Bodies* (forthcoming). She has published widely on Shakespeare and his contemporaries, theatrical adaptation, social justice pedagogy, and bodily motions in early modern English literature and culture. She is currently writing a book about the ways contemporary authors and artists adapt John Milton's works to advance today's movements for gender equity, racial justice, disability rights, and religious freedom.

Perry Guevara writes on early modern literature, cognitive science, and the history of medicine. He has authored essays and reviews for *Public Books, Shakespeare Studies, Renaissance Quarterly, Early Modern Studies*, and *Configurations*. Most recently, he has contributed chapters to *Lesser Living Creatures of the Renaissance* and *Inclusive Shakespeares: Identity, Pedagogy, Performance*. While at Dominican University of California, he co-founded and directed the program in Performing Arts and Social Change in partnership with Marin Shakespeare Company's prison-theater program. He was also a Visiting Scholar at the University of California, Berkeley's Center for Science, Technology, Medicine, and Society.

Wendy Beth Hyman is Professor of English and Comparative Literature at Oberlin College. She is the author of *Impossible Desire and the Limits of Knowledge in Renaissance Poetry* (2019), co-editor of *Teaching Social Justice Through Shakespeare: Why Renaissance Literature Matters Now* (Edinburgh University Press, 2019), and editor of *The Automaton in English Renaissance Literature* (2011). She has published widely on Shakespeare, Renaissance literature, lyric poetry, social justice, and the history of science and technology in the early modern era. She is currently writing a book on Shakespearean romance, optical technology, and the global history of stage magic, and collaborating with an artist on a project called *How to Read Shakespeare: A Visual Learner's Companion*. She is the Knowledge editor for Routledge Resources Online: The Renaissance World, and Trustee of the Shakespeare Association of America.

Kirsten N. Mendoza is Assistant Professor of English and Human Rights at the University of Dayton. Her first book project, *A Politics of Touch: The Racialization of Consent in Early Modern English Literature*, examines the conceptual ties that link shifting sixteenth- and seventeenth-century discourses on self-possession and sexual consent with England's colonial endeavors, involvement in the slave trade, and global mercantile pursuits. Her work has appeared or is forthcoming in *Renaissance Drama, Shakespeare Bulletin, The Oxford Handbook of Shakespeare and Race,* and *Teaching Social Justice Through Shakespeare: Why Renaissance Literature Matters Now.* She has been supported with research grants from the Huntington Library, Folger Shakespeare Library, and the American Council of Learned Societies.

Mary Janell Metzger is a scholar of early modern English literature and critical theory and an award-winning teacher. Her work as an educator committed to a social justice pedagogy has taken shape in classrooms in Iowa, Mississippi, and the Pacific Northwest, and bridged the academic spaces of the university with its surrounding communities. She is the author of *Shakespeare Without Fear: Teaching for Understanding* (2004) and numerous critical and pedagogical essays in journals and edited volumes such as *Feminist Teacher, PMLA, Mosaic, Genre, The Sundial,* and *Teaching Social Justice Through Shakespeare: Why Renaissance Literature Matters Now.* Her recent work explores the ethical demands of and strategies for teaching Shakespeare in the context of one's institution's regional racial history.

Victoria M. Muñoz is Assistant Professor in the English Department at the City University of New York's Eugenio María de Hostos Community College and a 2022 Mellon Foundation/American Council of Learned Societies Community College Faculty Research Fellow. Her research explores Anglo-Spanish imperial relations in Renaissance literature and drama. Her first book, *Spanish Romance in the Battle for Global Supremacy: Tudor and Stuart Black Legends* (2021), illustrates how early modern Spanish romance literature inspired the aspirational imperialism of Shakespeare and his contemporaries, particularly informing the exceptionalist, anti-Spanish logics that promoted Britain's overseas colonization. Her current project concerns the representation of Spanish imperialism and race in early modern English revenge tragedies written in the style of the classical Hispano-Roman dramatist Lucius Annaeus Seneca.

Elisa Oh is Associate Professor in the English Department at Howard University. Her current book project is entitled *Choreographies of Race and Gender: Dance, Travel, and Ritual in Early Modern*

English Literature 1558–1668, which investigates kinetic discourses in early modern court masques, liturgies, drama, and colonial propaganda. She has published on early modern women's silences in *King Lear*, *The Tragedy of Mariam*, the speeches of Elizabeth I, *Measure for Measure*, and Wroth's *Urania*; constructions of race and gender in Jonson's *The Masque of Blackness* and early modern English representations of Pocahontas; and the racialized movements of the witches in *Macbeth*. Her research has received support from the Folger Shakespeare Library, the Arizona Center for Medieval and Renaissance Studies, and the National Endowment for the Humanities.

Kathryn Vomero Santos is Assistant Professor of English and co-director of the Humanities Collective at Trinity University. She is currently completing a book entitled *Shakespeare in Tongues*, which situates Shakespeare and his legacy within conversations about imperialism, multilingualism, and assimilation in the United States. She is also co-editing a collection of essays for Edinburgh University Press entitled *The Ethical Implications of Shakespeare in Performance and Appropriation* with Louise Geddes and Geoffrey Way. With Katherine Gillen and Adrianna M. Santos, she co-founded the Borderlands Shakespeare Colectiva, which has received funding from the Mellon Foundation and the National Endowment for the Humanities. Together, they are editing *The Bard in the Borderlands: An Anthology of Shakespeare Appropriations en La Frontera*.

Elizabeth Williamson has served as both a faculty member and an academic dean at The Evergreen State College. She is the author of *The Materiality of Religion in Early Modern English Drama* (2009) and the co-editor (with Jane Hwang Degenhardt) of *Religion and Drama in Early Modern England: The Performance of Religion on the Renaissance Stage* (2011). Her work has appeared in the *New Companion to Renaissance Drama*, *Medieval and Renaissance Drama in England*, *Journal of American Drama and Theatre*, *Borrowers and Lenders*, *English Literary Renaissance*, and *Studies in English Literature*.

Marissa and Elizabeth are co-authors of "Caucusing in the Online Literature Classroom," in *Teaching Literature in the Online Classroom* (2022).

Introduction
Marissa Greenberg and Elizabeth Williamson

The role of faculty in social justice-oriented education is, in one sense, immediately apparent. Our job is to do the necessary work of unlearning the hierarchical forms of instruction that were used to teach us, so that we can provide the learning experiences our students actually need. In another sense, however, our role as faculty goes well beyond the classroom itself. In order to sustain the difficult work of constant pedagogical innovation, we must first achieve a sustainable relationship with the colleges and universities where we teach. Our situation as educators and as employees is made even messier by our affiliation with Shakespeare, whose position atop literary canons and cultural hierarchies is both what we ask students to critique and unlearn and the driving force justifying our employment. It is only after we acknowledge the reality of these ideological and material conditions and consequences that we can begin to transform institutions of higher education in the United States through activist teaching.

In "On Entrenched Inequalities in the Research University," Jorge Coronado targets three especially problematic elements of the status quo in US colleges and universities: the disconnect between scholarship and teaching; the effect of scarcity on working conditions; and the seeming inability of administrators to pair discourse with action.[1] While Coronado focuses on the research university, his comments apply across the gamut of higher education in the US, including minority-serving institutions (MSI)—like Historically Black Colleges and Universities (HBCU), Hispanic-Serving Institutions (HSI), and Native American-Serving Non-Tribal Institutions (NASNTI)—as

---

[1] Jorge Coronado, "On Entrenched Inequalities in the Research University: Activism and Teaching for Tenured Faculty Members," *PMLA/Publications of the Modern Language Association of America* 136, no. 3 (2021): 441–46.

well as community colleges and liberal arts colleges.[2] Institutions whose missions prioritize the classroom experience often do a better job of supporting students' well-being and success. That said, political, cultural, and financial pressures have led many to adopt practices historically associated with the research university in hopes of remaining competitive in an increasingly crowded sector, resulting in a glaring set of gaps between institutions' stated equity commitments and their willingness to make meaningful policy change. At the same time, the COVID-19 pandemic and social movements such as Black Lives Matter and MeToo have brought global awareness to the structural inequities that disproportionately impact communities of color, trans and queer communities, people with disabilities, and women, not to mention all the individuals who live at the intersection of these identities. In the fierce urgency of this present moment, when the cracks in the foundation of higher education in the US have never been more apparent, Coronado urges faculty to push back against "the culture of the research university [that] encourages tenure-line faculty members to consider teaching as secondary, a task that must be attended to (but avoided if at all possible)."[3] This resistance is the first part of a process of faculty becoming—or perhaps resuming their roles as—custodians and "*producers* of the university itself" by "insist[ing] on their activities within their classrooms as the core of the institution itself."[4] For faculty at institutions with better track records of supporting inclusive teaching and learning, resistance involves sharing disciplinary expertise in, and experiential knowledge of, how to help students survive and thrive in higher education.

Situating Shakespeare Pedagogy picks up this call for change and contributes to the archive of strategies and tactics for resistance, paying particular attention to the institutional contexts that shape our equity-focused classroom activities. Its contributors contend that a focus on teaching is primary to our work as scholar-pedagogues and that any attempt to reform higher education must include a recognition of this primacy. We also agree with Coronado that faculty are interpolated by their institutions, and while that interpolation may galvanize revolutionary pedagogies, it may also be a source of pushback. University and college administrators and boards of trustees alternatively make possible, nurture, necessitate, frustrate, interrupt,

---

[2] For a list of the categories of minority-serving institutions (MSI), consult the US Department of Education: https://www2.ed.gov/about/offices/list/ocr/edlite-minority-inst-list-tab.html
[3] Coronado, "Entrenched," 443.
[4] Coronado, "Entrenched," 444–45, original emphasis.

or shut down radical approaches to teaching—often influenced by both internal and external political groups. Accordingly, a strategic response to Coronado's essay must take into consideration the institutional contexts that have the power to either bolster or hinder a focus on student-centered teaching as the core of what faculty do.

This is also a fortuitous moment to be talking about social justice pedagogy in the field of Renaissance literary studies, thanks to the robust body of work that has already been written. A selective rehearsal of this work is necessary: first, because it is likely unfamiliar to the department heads and other administrators best positioned to support faculty toward institutional transformation; and, second, because we want to lift up the often-unrecognized work of the scholars—many of them women of color—whose research, teaching, and activism make possible the conversations we are pursuing in this volume. The impact of Kim F. Hall's *Things of Darkness: Economies of Race and Gender in Early Modern England* cannot be overstated. Published a quarter-century ago, Hall's revolutionary monograph laid the groundwork for what Margo Hendricks has dubbed premodern critical race studies (PCRS) and, along with later writings on pedagogy and the discipline, galvanized generations of researchers in Shakespeare and early modern literature and culture to interrupt white patriarchal supremacy through their teaching and scholarship.[5] Following Hall's lead, volumes such as *Teaching Shakespeare with Purpose*, edited collections focused on teaching for social justice, and special journal issues on premodern literature and education have skillfully paired evidence-based literary history with student-centered best practices.[6] Open-access resources,

---

[5] Kim F. Hall, *Things of Darkness: Economies of Race and Gender in Early Modern England* (Ithaca: Cornell University Press, 1995); Kim F. Hall, "Beauty and the Beast of Whiteness: Teaching Race and Gender," *Shakespeare Quarterly* 47, no. 4 (1996): 461–75, https://doi.org/10.2307/2870958; Peter Erickson and Kim F. Hall, "'A New Scholarly Song': Rereading Early Modern Race," special issue, *Shakespeare Quarterly* 67, no. 1 (2016), 1–13, https://doi.org/10.1353/shq.2016.0002; Kimberly Anne Coles, Kim F. Hall, and Ayanna Thompson, "BlacKKKShakespearean: A Call to Action for Medieval and Early Modern Studies," *The Profession*, November 2019, https://profession.mla.org/blackkkshakespearean-a-call-to-action-for-medieval-and-early-modern-studies/. For one set of examples of the impact of Hall's work, consult the recent festschrift published in *The Sundial*, a public-facing digital publication of the Arizona Center for Renaissance and Medieval Studies: Brandi K. Adams, ed. "We Acknowledge Ours: Celebrating Kim F. Hall and *Things of Darkness* at 25," special issue, *The Sundial*, March 30, 2021, https://medium.com/the-sundial-acmrs/we-acknowledge-ours-celebrating-kim-f-hall-and-things-of-darkness-at-25-5db6bd623f6b.

[6] Ayanna Thompson and Laura Turchi, *Teaching Shakespeare with Purpose: A Student-Centred Approach* (London: Bloomsbury, 2016); Hillary Eklund and Wendy Beth Hyman, eds., *Teaching Social Justice Through Shakespeare: Why Renaissance*

such as the multimedia educational tools Farah Karim-Cooper spearheaded at the Globe Theatre and the digital, public-facing publication of the Arizona Center for Medieval and Renaissance Studies, *The Sundial*, provide materials and methods to teach to students' complex positionalities.[7] Usually understood principally in terms of identity, students' positionalities are complicated by location, as Jonathan Burton's collaborative project *The Qualities of Mercy* and Ruben Espinosa's radical interventions on Shakespeare in the US–Mexico borderlands have shown.[8] Disrupting injustice in and beyond Shakespeare studies requires that we meet students where they are both figuratively ("Who are our students?") and literally ("Where are our classrooms?").

What distinguishes our volume is an attention to the situations—geographical, embodied, and structural—in which *faculty* take up the work of social justice-oriented teaching.[9] Our focus on situation allows us to address the political realities we face as scholar-pedagogues, while simultaneously highlighting the fact that these realities are not totalizing, or at least not uniformly so. US universities and colleges share material and conceptual histories of settler colonialism, enslavement, incarceration, and sexual assault that first established higher education as a site of exclusion. The unique situation

---

Literature Matters Now (Edinburgh: Edinburgh University Press, 2019); Sharon O'Dair and Timothy Francisco, eds., *Shakespeare and the 99%: Literary Studies, the Profession, and the Production of Inequity* (Switzerland: Palgrave Macmillan, 2019); David Ruiter, ed., *The Arden Research Handbooks of Shakespeare and Social Justice* (London: Bloomsbury, 2021); Emma Smith, ed., "Shakespeare and Education," special issue, *Shakespeare Survey* 74 (2021); Sarah Davis-Secord, ed., "Teaching a Diverse and Inclusive Premodern World," special issue, *Studies in Medieval and Renaissance Teaching* 27, no. 2 (2020); and Rebecca Olson and Stephanie Pietros, eds., "First-Generation Shakespeare," *Early Modern Culture* 14 (2019): articles 2–13.

[7] "Teaching Resources," *Shakespeare's Globe*, https://www.shakespearesglobe.com/learn/teaching-resources/; *The Sundial*, The Arizona Center for Medieval and Renaissance Studies (ACMRS), https://medium.com/the-sundial-acmrs.

[8] Jonathan Burton, project lead, *The Qualities of Mercy*, https://www.youtube.com/playlist?list=PLEcX8YVMVUzMF3r3hUo2Kl8BGOqacYYZg; Geoffrey Way, ed., "*The Qualities of Mercy* Dispatches," *The Sundial*, August 12, 2020, https://medium.com/the-sundial-acmrs/introducing-the-qualities-of-mercy-dispatches-3a2682f98585; Ruben Espinosa, "Chicano Shakespeare: The Bard, the Border, and the Peripheries of Performance," in Eklund and Hyman, *Teaching Social Justice*, 76–84; "Shakespeare and Your Mountainish Inhumanity," *The Sundial*, August 16, 2019, https://medium.com/the-sundial-acmrs/shakespeare-and-your-mountainish-inhumanity-d255474027de; "Stranger Shakespeare," *Shakespeare Quarterly* 67, no. 1 (2016): 51–67, https://doi.org/10.1353/shq.2016.0012; and "Traversing the Temporal Borderlands of Shakespeare," *New Literary History* 52, no. 3–4 (2021): 605–23.

[9] Notable exceptions include several of the contributions to O'Dair and Francisco, eds., *Shakespeare and the 99%*.

in which each of us engages with our students, however, informs whether and how we heed the call of writers like Sandy Grande to refuse the university.[10]

Following the lead of Black and Indigenous scholars, and eschewing long-standing traditions of self-promotion and resource hoarding, each of the contributors to this volume has chosen to navigate the path toward refusal by forging relationships of collectivity and reciprocity with their students. Equally important, they are also cultivating such relationships with one another: *Situating Shakespeare Pedagogy* developed through the mutual support of contributors who are committed to the hard work of disrupting their institutions. Even as their chapters bear witness to different zones of personal and professional risk in different parts of the US, they constitute what Grande calls the "common ground" where social justice-oriented pedagogies may form "a corpus of shared ethics."[11] The not-so-modest aim of this collection is to engage readers in these relationships, as well. In what follows, we offer readers an orientation to the key concepts that animate this collaborative endeavor. First and foremost, what connects these essays is their deliberate mapping of the authors' unique relationships to sites of teaching.

Situation

So, what does it mean to situate Shakespeare pedagogy? For the contributors to this volume, it means acknowledging how their teaching of Shakespeare and Renaissance English literature emerges at the intersection of one's immediate, present conditions with a set of shared, future-oriented, and actionable commitments. This sense of "situation" originates in premodern England, where its most basic meaning was "location or physical position" (*OED*). But it is energized by more current usage that denotes personal and social circumstances. Tracing these meanings will bring us to *Shakespeare*, whose name we use as a shorthand to refer to the corpus of sixteenth- and seventeenth-century English literature and performance and its modern, global appropriation and critique, and to *pedagogy*, specifically the social justice-oriented classrooms in which contributors to this volume

---

[10] Sandy Grande, "Refusing the University," in *Toward What Justice? Describing Diverse Dreams of Justice in Education*, ed. Eve Tuck and K. Wayne Yang (New York: Routledge, 2018), 47–65.

[11] Grande, "Refusing," 61. The editors are grateful to Victoria Muñoz for helping us to think through the dynamics between Grande's concept of refusal and ours of situation.

conspire with students, communities, and, sometimes, administrators. We then conclude with a roadmap of *Situating Shakespeare Pedagogy*, including its origins, organization, and ultimate objectives.

Shakespeare uses "situation" rarely and in the context of bodies and places. His usage thus aligns with the earliest recorded instances, which refer to surgery (e.g., setting a broken bone) and locality (e.g., setting up a town). In Shakespeare's *Sonnet 128* the speaker imagines his lips "chang[ing] their state / And situation with those dancing chips" of his beloved's harpsicord keys (ll. 9–10), and in *The Comedy of Errors* Luciana explains the constraint of women's "liberty" in terms of the "bound[s]" that constrain everything "situate under heaven's eye" (2.1.15–17).[12] The word takes on a more topographical connotation in Shakespeare's history plays: in *Henry V*, Fluellen compares "the situations" of Macedon and Monmouth (4.7.26–27), and in *Henry IV, Part II* Bardolph compares going to war to "survey[ing] / The plot of situation and the model" of a house (1.3.52–53). What emerges from Shakespeare's lyric and dramatic poetry is *situation* as relational. Because these relations are embodied and spatial, they direct attention to structures of race, religion, gender, sexuality, and ability—structures that we recognize today as white supremacy.[13] After all, the harms perpetuated by supremacist ideology are not limited to racist violence against Asian, Black, Indigenous, Latinx, and people of color; they extend to, and intersect with, other forms of discrimination, including religious intolerance, sexism, and ableism.[14]

Shakespeare's less famous contemporary George Puttenham also propels our understanding of situation toward the arena of higher education. Puttenham's *The Art of English Poesy* (1589), designed

---

[12] In support of open-resource editions, we cite Barbara Mowat, et al., *Shakespeare's Plays, Sonnets and Poems* (Washington, DC: Folger Shakespeare Library, n.d.), https://shakespeare.folger.edu.

[13] Among other recent salient conversations about the dynamics between premodern race formations and modern white supremacy, we refer readers to the articles in Urvashi Chakravarty and Ayanna Thompson, eds., "Race and Periodization," special issue, *New Literary History* 52, no. 3/4 (2021).

[14] Here we refer, of course, to Kimberlé Crenshaw's definition of intersectionality as "an analytic sensibility, a way of thinking about identity and its relationship to power. Originally articulated on behalf of Black women, the term brought to light the invisibility of many constituents within groups that claim them as members but often fail to represent them." Kimberlé Crenshaw, "Why Intersectionality Can't Wait," *Washington Post*, September 24, 2015, https://www.washingtonpost.com/news/in-theory/wp/2015/09/24/why-intersectionality-cant-wait [https://perma.cc/HGD7-TKCP], qtd. Cheryl I. Harris, "Reflections on *Whiteness As Property*," *Harvard Law Review Forum* 134 (2020): 2n3.

to help ambitious courtiers understand this crucial mode of elite communication, is a part of the western history of pedagogy that has shaped how we understand the act of teaching. Importantly, the text presents *situation* as not only relational but also structural, placing it among the principles of "proportion," or verse arrangement, where he defines it as the "plac[ement]" of "measure" (meter) and "concord" (rhyme).[15] Puttenham explains that separately meter and rhyme are not ineffectual, but that they work best together: "both proportions concurring together as they needs must" makes a poem "breedeth a variable and strange harmony not only in the ear, but also in the conceit of them that hear it."[16] By aligning situation with the structural dynamics that make a poem powerful, *The Art of English Poesy* draws early modern embodied and spatial sensibilities into dialogue with the concerns of scholar-pedagogues committed to teaching Renaissance literature for positive social change.

This commitment returns us to Coronado and, more broadly, to scholars of critical university studies who call for the reformation (or abolition) of US institutions of higher education.[17] The contributors to this volume recognize that making space in their classrooms for social justice pedagogy may put them at professional and personal risk. Rather than accept this crisis as ordinary, or indulge what Lauren Berlant calls "cruel optimism", they work to nurture affective, aesthetic, and social relations that constitute institutional action and generate political action.[18] This work is done within their situation, which Berlant defines as "a genre of social time and practice in which a relation of persons and worlds is sensed to be changing but the rules for habitation and the genres of storytelling about it are

---

[15] George Puttenham, *The Art of English Poesy: A Critical Edition*, ed. Frank Whigham and Wayne A. Rebhorn (Ithaca: Cornell University Press, 2007), 174. "Of proportion by situation" appears in book 2, chapter 11.

[16] Puttenham, *Art*, 174.

[17] E.g., Grande, "Refusing"; Fred Moten and Stefano Harney, *The Undercommons: Fugitive Planning and Black Study* (Brooklyn: Minor Compositions, 2013); la paperson, *A Third University Is Possible* (Minneapolis: University of Minnesota Press, 2017); and Eli Meyerhoff, *Beyond Education: Radical Studying for Another World* (Minneapolis: University of Minnesota Press, 2019).

[18] "A relation of cruel optimism exists when something you desire is actually an obstacle to your flourishing." This includes a desire for everyday life not characterized by crisis that leads "people [to] find themselves developing skills for adjusting to newly proliferating pressures to scramble for modes of living on" as an ordinary rather than a crisis situation. Lauren Berlant, *Cruel Optimism* (Durham: Duke University Press, 2011), 1, 8. Faculty's efforts to accommodate to supposed crises in higher education and in the humanities, such as pronounced by institutional leaders and popular media alike, are forms of cruel optimism.

unstable, in chaos."[19] In the context of higher education, Berlant's definition of situation represents a recognition of the precarious conditions of academic life and work and a choice to determine amid the uncertainty how we will live and work as scholar-pedagogues.

In her groundbreaking *On Being Included: Racism and Diversity in Institutional Life*, Sara Ahmed provides us with a powerful framework for situating ourselves within institutional life—illuminating both "how we experience life within institutions" and "how institutions acquire a life of their own."[20] Of particular importance to us, given our emphasis on social justice, is the way Ahmed explores the problems of institutional life in terms of relationality and/as exclusion: "Institutions are kinship technologies: a way of 'being related' [that] is a way of reproducing social relations" with the effect of "*restrict[ing] to whom an institution is open.*"[21] A university may extend hospitality, for instance, through diversity statements; but this is not the same as committing and taking action to foster belonging. Institutional leaders are often reluctant to take action, however, because it unsettles what we know about the university, including its structures of power. To know the university differently, to create new relations, would require and constitute a transformation of institutional life.[22]

In *Living a Feminist Life*, Ahmed returns to the quotidian exclusions and violence of institutional life for women, people of color, disabled, trans, and queer folks and sets out practical tools for transformation. Among these tools are "sweaty concepts" that describe and conceptualize a situation, which Ahmed defines "as something that comes to demand a response."[23] Ahmed uses

> the idea of sweaty concepts ... to show how descriptive work is conceptual work. A concept is worldly, but it is also a reorientation to a world, a way of turning things around, a different slant on the same thing. More specifically, a sweaty concept is one that comes out of a description of a body that is not at home in the world . . . . A sweaty concept might come out of a bodily experience that is trying. The task is to stay with the difficulty, to keep exploring and exposing this difficulty.[24]

---

[19] Berlant, *Cruel Optimism*, 5–6.
[20] Sara Ahmed, *Living a Feminist Life* (Durham: Duke University Press, 2017), 22.
[21] Ahmed, *Living*, 38–39, original emphasis.
[22] Ahmed, *Living*, 174–87.
[23] Sara Ahmed, *On Being Included: Racism and Diversity in Institutional Life* (Durham: Duke University Press, 2012), 13.
[24] Ahmed, *On Being Included*, 13.

The situation of not being at home in the world, whether experienced by a teacher or by a student, is not something that we should expect to resolve. Rather, the condition of being not at home—far from being a problem to be fixed—can instead provide the necessary fuel for transformation, if we are willing to engage in ongoing, strenuous effort. This effort, which is the work of sweaty concepts, makes possible a fuller knowledge of the institution through our reorientation of the relations between *where* (and *when*) we find ourselves and where and when we find *ourselves*. Put another way, situations for Ahmed emerge at the juncture of position (spatial and temporal) and positionality (structural and embodied), and sweaty concepts are how teachers and students may use their situations to transform their relations to the institution. Undertaking the work of sweaty concepts, then, constitutes a refusal to accept personal and institutional crises as ordinary (Berlant's cruel optimism); and even as Ahmed acknowledges that sometimes we need to break our bonds with the university—to "snap"—she advocates for mobilizing lived experiences of an unlivable situation toward the creation of positive personal and institutional bonds.[25] In situating Shakespeare pedagogy, we follow Ahmed in focusing our attention on, and leveraging the insights of, those who have never been "at home" in the modern university yet persistently labor toward its transformation.

Shakespeare

For those of us committed to teaching Shakespeare through the lens of social justice, James Baldwin's sonorous, provocative essays provide a valuable set of critical tools and models. As a Black intellectual, Baldwin is uniquely positioned to help students explore what Jason Demeter calls "the apparent contradictions and tensions occasioned by the necessity of operating within a cultural and linguistic field that has been employed historically in the service of exclusion and white supremacy."[26] And as an artist, he offers us a radically inclusive vision of the poet as witness—a vision that invites us, as Adhaar Noor Desai shows, to democratize our classrooms in order

---

[25] Ahmed, *On Being Included*, esp. 194–95.
[26] Jason Demeter, "'To appropriate these white centuries': James Baldwin's Race-Conscious Shakespeare," in *The Routledge Handbook of Shakespeare and Global Appropriation*, ed. Christy Desmet, Sujata Iyengar, and Miriam Jacobson (London and New York: Routledge, 2020), 59–68, quote 60.

to privilege "the context of students' own lives."[27] His insights are also uniquely suited to grappling with the complex sense of situation that we have introduced. Baldwin was both a fierce critic of European literature's role in reproducing systemic inequities and a grudging admirer of the works themselves, especially insofar as they can lead us to a better understanding of our shared history. By putting his famous essay "Why I Stopped Hating Shakespeare" in dialogue with his writing about the aims of education itself, we hope to articulate why we believe Renaissance literature can serve our exploration of social justice, so long as it is combined with a critical analysis of the white supremacist institutions that have propped up the Shakespeare industry for so many centuries.

In his 1963 essay "A Talk to Teachers," Baldwin investigates the role of the educator living in what he calls "a revolutionary situation."[28] Here he is evoking the social movements devoted to the cause of freedom, both within the US and across the world, but he also wants to warn his audience that they cannot escape the current reality, in which the lives of the people matter less than the symbols of their historical oppression, and in which the monuments of colonialism and slavery have not yet been reduced to rubble. The purpose of education, he argues, is to socialize a child, to open up their access to everything that their culture has to offer. At the same time, however, the goal of teaching is "to perpetuate the aims of society," including the racist ideologies that have driven public policy ever since African slaves were first brought to the Americas to work the land stolen from Indigenous peoples.[29] The difficulty for a teacher who believes in education as the practice of freedom is that they cannot welcome their students to a liberated society that does not yet exist. And until antiracist pedagogy "becomes part of what an institution is already doing," as Ahmed explains, there is always the risk—the likelihood—that those scholar-pedagogues who call out racism as a problem become perceived, and targeted, as the problem.[30]

Indeed, of equal importance, and equal difficulty, for Baldwin is the ever-present threat of counterrevolutionary violence. "You must understand," he tells his audience, "that in the attempt to correct

---

[27] Adhaar Noor Desai, "Topical Shakespeare and the Urgency of Ambiguity," in Eklund and Hyman, *Teaching Social Justice*, 27–35, quote 29.
[28] James Baldwin, "A Talk to Teachers" (1963), in *Collected Essays* (New York: Library of America, 1998), 678.
[29] Baldwin, "A Talk to Teachers," 678.
[30] Ahmed, *On Being Included*, 27 and ch. 5.

so many generations of bad faith and cruelty, when it is operating not only in the classroom but in society, you will meet the most fantastic, the most brutal, and the most determined resistance."[31] In the US in 2022, the brunt of that resistance is being felt by our colleagues working in the K–12 system. But although few of us working in higher education regularly experience a lack of physical safety at work, we routinely experience the university "*as* resistance."[32] Resistance comes from university policies, reactionary students, and political groups invested in maintaining the status quo, and it leads many faculty—for understandable if tragic reasons—to silence themselves and their students. In order to combat this silencing, which is one of the core characteristics of white supremacy culture, *Situating Shakespeare Pedagogy* aims to give faculty a set of specific, realistic models for engaging with both the constraints and opportunities offered by the institutions in which they teach.[33] Equally important, we hope that this volume will be read by academic administrators and boards of trustees who have the power to change the conservative policies and practices that prioritize institutional stability over and above the needs of students, staff, and faculty.

Both educators and those who determine their working conditions will be interested in our contributors' nuanced and meaningful answers to the question of why faculty who believe deeply in Baldwin's view of education still ask students to engage with Shakespeare's work. In "Why I Stopped Hating Shakespeare" (1964), Baldwin provides his own answer to that question, explaining how he first began to identify with this figurehead of the European canon as a fellow witness. This essay makes a case for Shakespeare's value not by affirming traditional (i.e., colonial) claims to universality but, quite the opposite, by asserting that Shakespeare's vivid portraits of the world around him can illuminate the link between the injustices of the past and those suffered by our contemporaries:

> The greatest poet in the English language found his poetry where poetry is found: in the lives of the people. He could have done this

---

[31] Baldwin, "A Talk to Teachers," 678. One need only look to the 1619 Project and the racist attacks on its editor, Nikole Hannah-Jones, for fresh evidence of Baldwin's claim. L.Z. Granderson, "Nikole Hannah-Jones Became a Political Target: What She's Learned from the 'Hurtful' Attacks," *Los Angeles Times*, November 14, 2021, https://www.latimes.com/entertainment-arts/books/story/2021-11-14/nikole-hannah-jones-the-1619-project-book.
[32] Ahmed, *On Being Included*, 26, original emphasis.
[33] Tema Okun, "White Supremacy Culture" (1999), http://www.whitesupremacyculture.info.

> only through love—by knowing, which is not the same thing as understanding, that whatever was happening to anyone was happening to him. It is said that his time was easier than ours, but I doubt it—no time can be easy if one is living through it. I think it is simply that he walked his streets and saw them, and tried not to lie about what he saw: his public streets and his private streets, which are always so mysteriously and inexorably connected; but he trusted that connection.[34]

The syntax here is confusing—does "them" refer to "the people" or to the streets in which they lived their lives?—but the answer ceases to matter when we realize that there is no difference between loving the people and loving the places where their dramas play out. And just as Baldwin was only ever able to love the United States by fleeing to Paris, it was in France where he carved out a "new relationship" with English itself, realizing that any language, from jazz to iambic pentameter, contains within it vital information about the experience of a people, situated within a particular time and place.[35]

In other words, the geography of Shakespeare's witnessing matters, but so too does the situation of his readers and audience members. If they can achieve physical or cognitive distance from the poet's presumed greatness, they can make his language "bear the burden of [their] experience."[36] This is the foothold Baldwin offers us as educators: if we want all our students to find a place for themselves in Shakespeare's poetry, they must first plant their feet on new ground, apart from that "loveless education" which demands that all children love Shakespeare merely because of his iconic whiteness.[37] So too we, scholar-pedagogues, may find new relations with Shakespeare when we find our feet literally on new ground. Demeter, citing Baldwin, reminds us that "an artist must meet the people where they stand."[38] What does it mean for us, as educators, to meet our students where they stand? "Meeting students where they are" has become shorthand for welcoming students' experiences, interests, and concerns. It also signals the importance of rejecting deficit thinking about historically marginalized student groups, especially students of color and first-generation students, and instead placing their funds of cultural knowledge on the same footing as scholar-pedagogues'

---

[34] James Baldwin, "Why I Stopped Hating Shakespeare" (1964), in *The Cross of Redemption* (New York: Pantheon, 2010), 56.
[35] Baldwin, "Why I Stopped Hating Shakespeare," 55.
[36] Baldwin, "Why I Stopped Hating Shakespeare," 55.
[37] Baldwin, "Why I Stopped Hating Shakespeare," 53.
[38] Demeter, "'To appropriate,'" 65.

subject expertise. *Situating Shakespeare Pedagogy* fully endorses these goals, even as it seeks to amplify how higher education leaders can support this vital work by meeting faculty where *they* are. For it is not only students who may find themselves displaced within the university, let alone the literature classroom; faculty too face obstacles to belonging, especially when their activist teaching makes them vulnerable to erasure or overt targeting.

Pedagogy and Institutionality

Like the contributors to *Situating Shakespeare Pedagogy*, we (the editors) share a commitment to activist teaching in and beyond the Shakespeare classroom. Significantly, our disparate situations nurtured our earliest collaborations by expanding our research to best practices in the online environment where Marissa has taught since before the COVID-19 pandemic and by learning from one another about how to build alliances with students in the absence of affinities, such as Marissa experiences working remotely at a HSI as a white-passing Jewish woman with a chronic illness. Orienting ourselves toward one another, across geographical, experiential, and structural distance and difference, helped us to assume ideological positions of refusal, such as this collection aims to foster. It also brought us face to face with the kinds of institutional supports and resistance that makes refusal necessary. The Center for Teaching and Learning and the Center for Teaching Excellence at the University of New Mexico provided formal accolades and funding for Marissa's activist teaching.[39] By contrast, Elizabeth taught for many years at a college committed to social justice that nonetheless struggled to live up to that commitment. Turning to her situation, we seek to acknowledge, especially for readers in administrative and other leadership roles, the realities and challenges of this work, even at well-meaning institutions of higher education.

The Evergreen State College (Evergreen), where Elizabeth worked for almost two decades, provides a salient example of what happens when the need to preserve the institution at all costs trumps pedagogical innovation and faculty and staff welfare. This is surprising

---

[39] The editors wish to thank Brigid Shaski for her research assistance, which was funded by the Arts and Sciences Support for Undergraduate Research Experience (ASSURE) fellowship from the Office of the Vice President for Research at the University of New Mexico.

(and disappointing) given the institution's origins in the principled refusal of some of the most inequitable elements of higher education. Evergreen began as an experiment in student-centered teaching in the 1970s and was designed around a rejection of many aspects of traditional academic hierarchy, including competition between students (in the form of grades) and competition between faculty (in the form of rank). Thanks to visionary leadership at the state level, it was founded as a public university, and many of the students who have thrived at Evergreen over the years have been those who were drawn to, but could not afford, similarly experimental private institutions.

From its inception, Evergreen has attempted to commit itself to social justice, including racial justice. Located in one of the whitest states in the country, whose not-too-distant history includes sundown towns and racial quotas, Evergreen has benefited from the presence of innovative staff and faculty of color who have challenged that history through events like the annual Day of Absence. This tradition, named for Douglas Turner Ward's 1965 play of the same name, gave students, staff, and faculty of color the opportunity to gather off campus in order to have open, comparatively safe conversations in protected spaces referred to as *caucuses*. The popularity of this practice, which creates a sense of belonging for students most likely to be excluded by the conventional white supremacist structures of the institution, is one of many that inspired us (the editors) to experiment with caucusing in our own classrooms.[40]

As part of Evergreen's Day of Absence, white members of the campus community were asked to reflect on how much they would lose if their colleagues and peers of color were to disappear permanently. In practice, however, there were so few people of color on campus that their absence was barely felt. Moreover, inviting white community members to consider the impact of people of color only in their absence had the unintentional effect of emphasizing a relatively superficial understanding of diversity focused on visible differences. Accordingly, in 2016 the planning committee rewrote the protocol for the Day of Absence. Off-campus sessions were organized for white students, staff, and faculty, while their peers and colleagues of color stayed on campus. This change was intended

---

[40] Consult Marissa Greenberg and Elizabeth Williamson, "Caucusing in the Online Literature Classroom," in *Teaching Literature in the Online Classroom*, ed. John Miller and Julie Wilhelm (New York: The Modern Language Association of America, 2022), 124–39.

as a kind of refusal, to remake existing structures toward more meaningful inclusion; but by recognizing interpretations of the Day of Absence as a "'gift' of belonging," the planning committee did not simply reject it but also created new "conditions of precarity" for the college's most vulnerable populations.[41] One especially vocal white faculty member began speaking out against the revised protocol, despite the fact that off-campus sessions were entirely optional. The reactions of this white faculty member echoed a familiar pattern of resistance among white undergraduates, who often bristle at being excluded, even temporarily, from any discussion space. In the end, it proved far more damaging, especially in the aftermath of the presidential election and the high-profile shooting of two young African American men by a local police officer.[42]

It was in this hyper-charged political environment that Evergreen students learned about the white faculty member's attacks on the Day of Absence. The result was a nonviolent racial uprising, including a confrontation between the faculty member and a group of student leaders, the temporary occupation of the college president's office, and the issuing of a list of demands from BIPOC students. The backlash against those involved, or perceived to be involved, in the uprising was both predictable and horrifying, exacerbated by the white faculty member's appearance on Tucker Carlson's wildly popular Fox News show. During that appearance, he labeled student activists a "mob"—language that, predictably, enraged Carlson's audience, which was already primed to go on the attack against "woke culture."[43] As a result, student leaders received death threats and several staff and faculty (all African American women) were barraged by obscenity-laden emails and phone calls.[44] All the while, Evergreen's administration, with one eye on the state legislature, opted for damage control—mostly in the form of radio silence, though it also expelled two queer African American student activists.

---

[41] Grande, "Refusing," 59.
[42] Mike Carter, "Brothers' Lawsuit against Olympia Police Officer Who Shot Them Can Move Forward, Judge Rules," *Seattle Times*, February 12, 2019, https://www.seattletimes.com/seattle-news/law-justice/federal-judge-allows-lawsuit-alleging-excessive-force-by-olympia-officer-in-2015-shooting-to-move-forward/.
[43] Anne Fischel, Zoltan Grossman, and Lin Nelson, "Another Side of the Evergreen State College Story," *Huffington Post*, August 11, 2017, https://www.huffpost.com/entry/evergreen-state-college-another-side_b_598cd293e4b090964295e8fc.
[44] Ana Sofia Knauf, "'Go Back to the Zoo': How Evergreen State College Became a Target for Right-Wing Trolls," *The Stranger*, June 14, 2017, https://www.thestranger.com/news/2017/06/14/25216539/go-back-to-the-zoo-how-evergreen-state-college-became-a-target-for-right-wing-trolls.

But this defensive strategy has largely failed; at every turn, Evergreen was outspent and underprepared.

In the wake of the uprising, Evergreen's administration has discontinued the Day of Absence, and its legal counsel has warned faculty against any activities that appear to deprive students of educational opportunities, guidance which has had a chilling effect on instructors' willingness to engage in caucusing and other experimental practices. Seen from a risk management perspective, this advice is altogether logical; the job of college and university counsel is to help avoid lawsuits, and in the era of organizations such as Turning Point USA that strategically target liberal-leaning colleges and universities, that threat is not inconsiderable. What we are interested in here, however, is the ethical responsibility of academic administrators, who, in our view, have an obligation to base their decisions not just on the risks to the institution's budget, but on the need to foster the well-being of students, staff, and faculty.

In fact, it is our assertion that supporting "risky" pedagogical tactics is actually what higher education leaders most need to do in order to ensure the long-term survival of their institutions. If they do not take dramatic steps to increase the sense of belonging experienced by those whose bodies and voices have been excluded from US colleges and universities, students will continue to vote with their feet and enrollments will continue to plummet. Even faculty lucky enough to have earned tenure have demonstrated that they are not unwilling to leave their institutions or the profession itself.[45] We believe that faculty have a key role to play in creating learning environments that are responsive to student needs; we also believe that academic administrators have an equally pressing task before them—to create the institutional situations in which social justice-oriented practices can flourish.

Roadmaps

Situating Shakespeare Pedagogy originated in a plenary panel on just such social justice-oriented practices for the annual conference of the Shakespeare Association of America (SAA).[46] In recent years SAA has

---

[45] Unsurprisingly, this trend is particularly dramatic among faculty of color. Colleen Flaherty, "Calling It Quits," *Inside Higher Ed*, July 5, 2022, https://www.insidehighered.com/news/2022/07/05/professors-are-leaving-academe-during-great-resignation.

[46] The panel included the editors and three of the contributors to this volume: Eric L. De Barros, Kirsten N. Mendoza, and Mary Janell Metzger.

made commitments to the same priorities as this volume: championing social justice-oriented scholarship and teaching that focus on race, sexuality, gender, and disability; lifting up early career researchers, especially Black, Indigenous, and other scholar-pedagogues of color; recognizing innovative pedagogy as academic work and field-specific expertise on par with traditional scholarship; and bringing attention to, and supporting collaboration with, artists and organizations beyond higher education as partners in these efforts.[47] When the SAA conference committee selected a panel on inclusive pedagogy as its conference plenary, it sent a clear message to members, new and established, that teaching and/for justice must be part of institutional decision-making, including policies and practices around hiring, promotion, and funding.

This message took on unexpected urgency in 2020, as the murder of George Floyd mobilized people of color and many white people to protest anti-Black state violence and to raise awareness of its intersectional histories in the US. Meanwhile, COVID-19 forced conversations about these histories, including classroom conversations, into online spaces. Because the pandemic wave reached the US weeks before the 2020 SAA annual conference, our plenary panel was postponed to the following year, which gave us an opportunity to meet periodically online. The result was not only closer collaboration than any of us had experienced previously on a panel but also a new community of scholar-pedagogues with whom to share our struggles. Our situations could not have been more distinct—we occupied different timezones, taught at different kinds of institutions, and held different professional ranks—but each situation, in its own way, was increasingly noxious, torturous, even unlivable. Yet talking about our teaching became a powerful route to alliance, allowing us to support one another more fully through the academic, institutional, societal, and familial challenges we were experiencing. Reluctant to lose the supportive network that our panel had made possible, we began to brainstorm ways to extend and expand it.[48] Our informal

---

[47] In addition to SAA, organizations that are leading the struggle for equity, inclusion, and justice are the Arizona Center for Medieval and Renaissance Studies, the Folger Shakespeare Library, and the Globe Theatre. University and commercial presses are following suit, creating series dedicated to pedagogy, including Edinburgh University Press, Cambridge University Press, and Bloomsbury/Arden Shakespeare.

[48] The chat transcript from our post-SAA debrief meeting pinpoints the moment of this volume's inception:

> 12:47:04 From Kirsten Mendoza to Everyone: Our identity positions come in contact with students

community of practice continued to evolve as more contributors joined the conversation and as some of us changed roles and affiliations, left the country, or left higher education for other ventures. What remained constant was a commitment to explore the murky and generative space between inclusive teaching methods and historically inequitable academic environments. Equally important, we all shared the goal of providing scholar-pedagogues of Renaissance literature with practical, detailed models they could use to analyze and act within the constraints of their particular institutional contexts, especially as those contexts continue to be shaped by the deeply politicized nature of academia in the US today.

Seeking to tell the truth about the classrooms and neighborhoods we share with our students, the contributors to *Situating Shakespeare Pedagogy* locate their teaching at the interstices of geography, identity, and institution. The book's front matter draws attention to these situational factors. Abstracts of the ten chapters in this volume are tagged with keywords identifying the authors' regional, institutional, and thematic perspectives. We include these labels in an effort to help readers identify those essays that relate most closely to their own situations, although we believe that readers will benefit from essays that describe and conceptualize responses to the work of social justice pedagogy in less relatable situations. The organization of essays is likewise designed to encourage readers to witness others' public streets and private streets, to borrow Baldwin's turns of phrase. Opening and closing chapters foreground the experiences of scholar-pedagogues who have witnessed institutional life both inside and outside the US. Amrita Dhar reminds us that the first university to adopt Shakespeare as part of its curriculum was the Hindu College in Calcutta, and uses this fact to make a case for embedding a decolonial perspective into every Shakespeare classroom, while Eric De Barros uses his position as an American scholar teaching abroad to argue for a politically responsive, pedagogically oriented alternative to the false universality of white humanism.

Within this perspectival frame, the remaining chapters take readers on a roadtrip of sorts to a selection of US colleges and

> 12:47:49 From Elizabeth Williamson to Everyone: yes, exactly, Kirsten—this is where intersectionality gets, um, exciting
> 12:50:31 From Kirsten Mendoza to Everyone: How our identities come in contact with our students in the institution/the institution in communities

universities. This geographical organization makes explicit the politics and cultures of localities and regions that powerfully shape our lives in academia, including but not only our teaching. Put another way, our sense of belonging in our classrooms is often determined by the synergy or lack thereof between who and where we are—that is, between our positionalities and our positions. Institutional type, course assignments, and career status are factors, as well; but the emphasis on physical location in early modern meanings of "situation" continues to characterize the personal and professional experiences of many Shakespeare and early modern English literature scholar-teachers in the US. So, even as the strategies and tactics outlined in the volume may be adapted to a wide range of teaching and learning environments, they emerge from local pressures and regional contexts in tandem with the writers' hard-won embodied knowledge of the academy. Indeed, several contributors to this volume are already performing significant work in the realm of critical geographical practice.

We begin in Washington, DC with Elisa Oh, who explores the terrain of activist teaching by attending to what it means to bring the spirit of protest into the HBCU classroom. We then proceed north to New York City, where Victoria Muñoz exposes the material barriers that often alienate first-generation and working-class students from Shakespeare even before they enter our classrooms. From there we travel across the country to the Pacific Northwest, where Mary Janell Metzger confronts the ethical implications of adopting an antiracist pedagogical framework in one of the whitest states in the country. Turning south, we journey along the length of California, where Katherine Steele Brokaw provides a model for ecologically inflected, community-based teaching in the inter-institutional space between her university and Yosemite National Park. Next we travel to the US–Mexico borderland, arriving at Katherine Gillen and Kathryn Vomero Santos's Borderlands Shakespeare Collective, which lifts up students' cultural wealth through the process of participatory research. Moving to the Midwestern heartland of America, Penelope Geng shows us how to mobilize the power of disidentification and fan culture to make the European canon "bear the burden of [students'] experience," and Kirsten N. Mendoza probes the link between her students' religious identities and their desire to find totalizing moral lessons in the plays. In so doing, Mendoza brings us nearly full circle, offering another carefully situated alternative to the hollow promise of a monolithic Shakespeare. Finally, we come to Roya

Biggie and Perry Guevara's intranational collaboration, which spans the distance between their West Coast and Midwest institutions, mapping the complex space of racial hybridity they share with their students.

Throughout this virtual journey, readers will encounter a range of issues unique to the authors' situations. Overviews of these issues appear in the abstracts that introduce this volume. But a few concerns transcend differences in geography, identity, and institution, and demand our attention as problems for social justice-oriented teachers working in higher education:

- When we teach Shakespeare, where do we find multiple access points—physical locations, virtual resources, regional and global communities—and how do we use them to resist universality, especially presumptive whiteness?
- As scholar-pedagogues of Renaissance literature, how do we attend to our institutions' unique demographics, in particular students' cultural backgrounds, without discounting our own genealogies, both educational and embodied?
- What are the advantages of leaning into the affective dimensions of our classrooms? That is, how do we attend to students' physical and mental well-being without pulling away from powerful stories and storytelling that elicit positive feelings and pose emotional risks?
- How can we create learning environments that meet the needs of marginalized students—that is, students who have been not only omitted from public imaginings of who is, can, or "should" attend college, but also forcibly excluded from higher education due to discriminatory practices in admissions, enrollment, coursework, professionalization, and graduation?
- How can administrators support inclusive teaching by addressing inequitable economic, technological, and other material conditions for first-generation, immigrant, and disabled students as well as students who are cut off from familial support because of their gender identity, sexuality, or religious observance?

These questions privilege the students in our Shakespeare and early modern English literature classrooms. Yet our volume also intervenes in the field of social justice pedagogy by illuminating the situation of the scholar-teachers who create these classrooms for students. Accordingly, we are committed to pursuing questions that emphasize faculty members' (often adverse) experiences:

- What is the obligation of administrators to acknowledge the challenges facing faculty who don't look, sound, or move "right" for their classrooms or the material they teach?[49]
- How can administrators mediate the risks of truth-telling—especially for untenured faculty, contingent faculty, and faculty who are vulnerable to institutional power because of their identities and/or embodiments? When administrations are increasingly preoccupied with reputation management around matters of diversity yet refuse to commit the necessary resources to advancing equity, how can faculty safely "call out" their institutions without fear of reprisal?
- And just as important and most difficult: What is the cost of striving to create institutions to which we *want* to belong? What occurs when the efforts of students and faculty are not reciprocated by administrations or the larger communities of which our institutions are often vital parts?[50]

Situating Shakespeare Pedagogy does not offer easy solutions to these problems, as if any single volume could. Instead, it explores these sweaty concepts, aiming to bolster our readers' resilience for dealing with the most challenging aspects of their particular situations. Its contributors, some of whom are already well-known voices in social justice-oriented Shakespeare pedagogy, share their institutional lives in the hope of transforming how others experience life within their institutions and possibly the life of the institution itself—which, as Ahmed reminds us, has its own inertia that must be overcome in order to make equity a reality in our classrooms.[51] *Situating Shakespeare Pedagogy* thus follows field-redefining work on social justice-oriented Shakespeare pedagogy focused on teaching strategies and societal conditions, even as it marks a new path through the increasingly fraught terrain of institutional power dynamics that have historically contributed to systemic injustice and continue to affect our work lives on a daily basis.

In this effort to know a better future by bringing it into being, we return again to the trail markers left for us by James Baldwin. For while Baldwin frequently plays the role of a truth-telling historian, he is just as often a prophetic voice crying out in the wilderness of

---

[49] Rather than self-serving, this question returns us to the students, especially but not just minoritized students, who benefit when faculty mobilize their "wrongness."

[50] The editors are grateful to the contributors to this volume, and especially Roya Biggie and Perry Guevara, for shaping and providing language for these questions.

[51] Ahmed, *On Being Included*, 22.

the present moment. And it is this form of witnessing that shapes the final lines of his 1964 essay, which promises his readers that if the poet has done his work honestly, "the people—all people!—who search in the rubble for a sign or a witness will be able to find him there."[52] What moves us most about this passage is its implication that we can uncover Shakespeare's true witness *only* in the wreckage of the past. It is a profoundly hopeful act to imagine a future history in which the names of enslavers have been stripped from all the public monuments and all the street signs. And it is precisely because those edifices are still firmly in place, because freedom cannot yet be taught as a fundamental characteristic of our society, that we must give our students the tools to imagine what their world might look like if and when the Shakespeare monument has been demolished and only the living, breathing reality of his testament remains.

---

[52] Baldwin, "Why I Stopped Hating Shakespeare," 56.

Chapter 1

On Shakespeare, Anticolonial Pedagogy, and Being Just
Amrita Dhar

This essay is written from my conviction that there is no point to Shakespeare in the twenty-first century if the stakes of Shakespeare performance, scholarship, and pedagogy are not firmly anchored in the anticolonial (as opposed to the colonial), the reparative (as opposed to the exploitative), and the just (as opposed to the overtly or covertly accepting of the injustice of imperialism). The outsize presence of Shakespeare in the world of letters and theater today is a direct result of English imperialism, and I must begin by stating that fact without reservation. Just as I take Shakespeare's worldwide presence today as a given, I also take the fact that our world's interlocked history is an ongoing outcome of colonialism as a given. Any discussion of anticolonial pedagogy must first take into account that we are living in continuously colonial conditions.[1] Thus, everything that I write here comes from my commitment to anticolonial thought and action, and from acknowledging that there is no way to work toward justice in and through Shakespeare studies without taking into account the matter of European and especially English colonialism and the aftermaths of that colonialism, which include Indigenous genocide, chattel slavery, and profiteering war. Meditating on anticolonialism as an ethic brought to my professional life in the United States—an ethic that I have been compelled to explicitly develop because of my third-world and

---

[1] The scholarship of Ibram X. Kendi teaches us that racism is a naturally learned behavior within a racist society no matter one's intentions, and the only way for one to not be racist is to be deliberately antiracist. See *Stamped from the Beginning: The Definitive History of Racist Ideas in America* (New York: Nation Books, 2016) and *How to Be an Antiracist* (New York: Random House, 2019). I would argue, in the same vein, that a basic colonialism is part of our learned behavior in any mainstream twenty-first-century society irrespective of background and intention, and that the only way for a person to not be colonial in mindset and actions is to be deliberately anticolonial. If this is a politics of opposition, it is so because it is a politics of survival.

immigrant identity in the global North—and examining my pedagogy of Shakespeare, anticolonialism, race, and disability across campuses of a large Midwestern state university, this essay assesses the possibilities and impossibilities of decolonizing curricula, and justice-oriented pedagogy more broadly, at my institution and in the academy at large.

I open this essay with an account of my trajectory to the current moment, analyzing specific formative moments in my ongoing education. Thus, in the next section of this essay, I discuss primarily my journey as a student, a learner. In the subsequent section, I discuss curriculum-oriented strategies that I use in the present to engage my students—whom I see as my companions and fellow-citizens in the world we inhabit together—in the discovery, examination, and interrogation of literature's capacities to hurt and heal, exclude and include, do harm and promote justice. Throughout, I write about my love of the literature I teach, and my love of teaching, while I fully understand that other and more urgent matters, such as simple survival and subsistence, increasingly occupy many of us who are Black, Indigenous, or Persons of Color in the corporatized and capitalist, settler-colonialist and heteronormatively patriarchal, global North academy. A pursuit of the literary humanities, you might say, is a pleasure of peacetime. And does it really feel like peace in the United States, today, when pregnant persons' bodily autonomy has been legally attacked, especially in a way that will disproportionately affect poor and disabled communities of color; when our collective ability to regulate the earth-draining fossil fuel sector has been curtailed; when mandating effective and scientific disease-prevention measures such as vaccines has been ridiculed and called unlawful; when Indigenous rights have been trampled anew by the settler state; and when arms proliferation is at a high, even as children die in terrifyingly frequent acts of gun violence and domestic terrorism?[2] Yet the living cannot in good conscience escape the duty of continued thought, pedagogy, and action. And I would argue that if a pursuit of the literary humanities is a pleasure of peacetime, it

---

[2] See, for instance, Ann E. Marimow, Aadit Tambe, and Adrian Blanco, "How the Supreme Court Ruled in the Major Decisions of 2022," *Washington Post*, June 21, 2022, https://www.washingtonpost.com/politics/interactive/2022/significant-supreme-court-decisions-2022/, and the National Public Radio special series "Uvalde Elementary School shooting," May 24, 2022–September 10, 2022, https://www.npr.org/series/1101183663/uvalde-elementary-school-shooting.

is nothing less than an urgency in a time of resistance and action. Poetry, after all, is not a luxury.[3]

Learning

I did my schooling and undergraduate studies in Calcutta, West Bengal, India. My undergraduate work—English Honours, as it is called—was at Jadavpur University. It was there, in lectures and seminars led by my teachers in India, that I had my first in-depth encounters with some of the biggest names in literature, world literature, premodern literature, and English literature. For instance, Shakespeare and Milton, both of whom I would continue to study in graduate school, first came to me through my brilliant teachers in my hometown, teachers who were simultaneously dedicated instructors at the university level and commentators on civic life.[4] Through my teachers' example (and I could not be a teacher today had I not had the teachers I did), I came to see a position in the literary humanities as one that is necessarily publicly engaged, socially responsive, and activist in the full sense of rigorous-thinking-must-lead-to-responsible-and-meaningful-action.

My hometown, incidentally, is also where Shakespeare first entered a university program anywhere. By 1822, he was part of the English curriculum at Hindu College, which is now Presidency

---

[3] Audre Lorde establishes gloriously the need for poetry in our day-to-day lives of resistance and survival. "[I]t is through poetry that we give name to those ideas which are—until the poem—nameless and formless, about to be birthed, but already felt." See "Poetry Is Not a Luxury," in *Sister Outsider: Essays and Speeches* (Berkeley: Crossing Press, 2007), 36–39.

[4] For a small sampling, confined to writing in English, see Sukanta Chaudhuri, "Development vs Environmental Security: How to Kill an Ecosystem," *Economic Times*, July 12, 2016, https://economictimes.indiatimes.com/blogs/et-commentary/development-vs-environmental-security-how-to-kill-an-ecosystem/, and "Knowledge Seekers: The Pursuit of Knowledge for Human Welfare," *Telegraph* (India), July 4, 2022, https://www.telegraphindia.com/opinion/knowledge-seekers-the-pursuit-of-knowledge-for-human-welfare/cid/1873033; Supriya Chaudhuri, "Rolling in the Stuff of Magic," *Telegraph* (India), August 26, 2000, https://www.telegraphindia.com/opinion/rolling-in-the-stuff-of-magic/cid/891864, and "Day and Life in the City," *Telegraph* (India), December 4, 2010, https://www.telegraphindia.com/opinion/day-and-night-in-the-city/cid/456115; Swapan Chakravorty, "Imminent Ruin and Desperate Remedy: Calcutta and Its Fragments," *Eurozine*, May 25, 2007, https://www.eurozine.com/imminent-ruin-and-desperate-remedy-calcutta-and-its-fragments/. See also Abhijit Gupta's weekly "Only Connect" column in the *Telegraph*, 2004–6, and Sukanta Chaudhuri's fortnightly column in the *Asian Age*, 1993–2001. Chaudhuri's columns have been collected into a book, *View from Calcutta* (New Delhi: Chronicle Books, 2002).

University, in north central Kolkata.[5] Shakespeare's current inhabitation of the subcontinent's school and college curricula in general, and Bengal in particular, has come about through a complex, centuries-old history—embodying, at once, profound if conflicted Anglophilia (itself often a product of male upper-caste privilege) and radical anticolonial resistance (especially in the hands of twentieth-century practitioners). While scholars such as Gauri Viswanathan, Gayatri Chakravorty Spivak, and Jyotsna Singh, working in the US, variously and generatively theorized the impact of colonial English education systems (including and especially involving Shakespeare) for the subcontinent's political postcolonial reality, my teacher Swapan Chakravorty, for instance, wrote in Calcutta about the ways and byways of Bengalis' engagement with English literary studies (often with special emphases on Shakespeare).[6]

In my heady undergraduate days, early in the twenty-first century, my friends and I were reading everything we could lay hands on, and certainly reading all these scholars—such as Viswanathan, Spivak, Singh, Chakravorty—for all the stories they had to tell. (They are storytellers.) At the same time, we were also attending and often participating in productions of plays by Shakespeare, Euripides, Girish Karnad, Ntozake Shange, Kalidasa, Bertolt Brecht, Aimé Césaire, and Mahasweta Devi, among others. An important upshot, for me, of this promiscuous and almost indiscriminate consumption

---

[5] For an accessible introduction to Indian Shakespeare, especially popular Shakespeare, see Jonathan Gil Harris, *Masala Shakespeare: How a Firangi Writer Became Indian* (New Delhi: Aleph, 2018). See also Gauri Viswanathan, *Masks of Conquest: Literary Study and British Rule in India* (New York: Columbia University Press, 1989) and Vikram Singh Thakur, *Shakespeare and Indian Theatre: The Politics of Performance* (New Delhi: Bloomsbury India, 2020). I should note that the city of Calcutta, which was the capital of the British government in India until 1911, had its name formally changed to Kolkata in 2001. (In 1911, Delhi was named the capital city of India; New Delhi remains the capital of India to this day.) Like so many of my contemporaries, I use "Calcutta" for talking about my city pre-2001 and "Kolkata" for talking about geographically the same city in more recent years.

[6] See, for instance, the wave of scholarship produced in the 1980s and 1990s, including Viswanathan, *Masks*; Gayatri Chakravorty Spivak, *The Post-Colonial Critic: Interviews, Strategies, Dialogues* (London: Routledge, 1990), and *Thinking Academic Freedom in Gendered Post-Coloniality* (Cape Town: University of Cape Town, 1992); Jyotsna Singh, "Different Shakespeares: The Bard in Colonial/Postcolonial India," *Theatre and Hegemony* 41, no. 4 (1989): 445–58, and *Colonial Narratives/Cultural Dialogues: "Discovery" of India in the Language of Colonialism* (London: Routledge, 1996); and Swapan Chakravorty's essays collected in the volume *Bangalir Ingreji Sahitya Charcha* [*The Study of English Literature by Bengalis*] (Kolkata: Anushtup, 2011). See also Singh's recent work *Shakespeare and Postcolonial Theory* (London: Bloomsbury, 2019) and Akshya Saxena, *Vernacular English: Reading the Anglophone in Postcolonial India* (Princeton: Princeton University Press, 2022).

of literature and theater from across periods and cultures—yet materially produced within the context of our chaotic but beloved city, in our specific moment—was that I came to see all these writers as part of my own coming of age; as part of my inalienable intellectual inheritance; and as part of the exhilarating blend of portable magic that I would now always own.[7] Shakespeare, no less than Mahasweta Devi (then living and writing in my city) or Aimé Césaire (certainly not then living and writing in my city, but nevertheless writing about many of my realities), was indisputably mine. Like other writers who were forming my sense of belonging within the literary traditions of the world, Shakespeare was mine to think with, think about, have opinions about, discuss, teach, perform, write on. And as far as my Shakespeare was concerned, a production's merits or a classroom discussion's virtues had nothing to do with any parochial "accuracy" of the material in merely historical terms, but everything to do with what was rendered as a true and invested observation of the world, and with what came through in the plays as luminously in service to the people who were the theater's inspiration in the first place.[8]

Imagine my surprise, then, during my first year of teaching as a Graduate Student Instructor at the University of Michigan, when one of my students, a young white woman, casually mentioned to me one day that I was her "first Shakespeare professor who's not white." I was surprised, and then surprised at my surprise.[9] What had I been expecting? That a white North American undergraduate student at Michigan had been so far taught her Shakespeare by a bunch of multilingual Bengalis? Or that various multicultural teachers in schools and colleges in the United States made nonwhite Shakespeare professors commonplace in the global North? I, who had never had a white Shakespeare teacher until graduate school, and who had certainly never thought of myself as a "Shakespeare professor who's not white," learned something important that day: that I indeed was, in my current context, a person of color (in a way

---

[7] See Emma Smith, *Portable Magic: A History of Books and Their Readers* (London: Penguin, 2022) and Stephen King, *On Writing: A Memoir of the Craft* (New York: Scribner, 2000).

[8] "The greatest poet in the English language found his poetry where poetry is found: in the lives of the people." James Baldwin, "Why I Stopped Hating Shakespeare," *The Cross of Redemption: Uncollected Writings*, ed. Randall Kenan (1964; New York: Vintage, 2010), 65–69. I mention plays because, at the time, our main engagement was with the plays of Shakespeare much more than with his poetry.

[9] I have later heard this comment from students also elsewhere, including at my current institution, The Ohio State University.

that I was and am not among other Bengalis and Indians and South Asians), an instructor of color (in a white-majority setting), an immigrant instructor of color (and therefore perceivably foreign in my current setting), and an immigrant instructor of color teaching one of the great bequests of English colonial capital, Shakespeare, in a still-colonized, settler-colonized, land, this country that calls itself the United States.

My student and I had a lively and genial exchange. She had done some Shakespeare in school but was hoping to "deepen her understanding of Shakespeare" now. She had not considered *The Tempest* as a tale of colonization but could see why someone like me, someone with an obviously postcolonial background, might, and she was intrigued that one really could "look at Shakespeare in all these different ways." The conversation stayed with me, intriguing me with what I had learned about my own identity where I was now. But it wasn't until much later, while listening to a lecture by Kim F. Hall a few years ago, that I started to understand the vaguely surprised tone of my student's remark, and that I started to grasp another dimension of why my being her instructor of Shakespeare was remarkable (she did, after all, remark on it).

Hall did a hauntingly beautiful lecture at the Folger Shakespeare Library in 2016. She mentioned in it that "[p]eople of color, but particularly Black people, are not free to love Shakespeare."[10] As I listened, I was struck by how much I could relate to what Hall said and how equally much her truth was not my truth. During my education, with the general privileges and ambiguous advantages of a post-refugee-status Bengali middle-class and muddled-caste upbringing, I had never considered that I was not free to love my Shakespeare—and even more, my Milton.[11] In a manner that now seems to me miraculous, I had never doubted that my opinions of these writers were as good and as valuable as anyone else's.[12] I was

---

[10] Kim F. Hall, "Othello Was My Grandfather: Shakespeare in the African Diaspora," Shakespeare's Birthday Lecture at the Folger Shakespeare Library, June 27, 2016; see a full transcript at https://folgerpedia.folger.edu/Shakespeare%27s_Birthday_Lecture:_%22Othello_Was_My_Grandfather:_Shakespeare_in_the_African_Diaspora%22

[11] As a girl, I knew very well what was expected of women in my section of life. A little ambition, within decorous bounds, was acceptable, even good. But the ambition had to be genteelly exhibited for, and approved by, a generally patriarchal and caste-oriented "we-stay-within-our-bounds" system. So it is not that I did not know that I was transgressing—but I had rebellion enough to also know that anyone wishing to place me in my "safe" role/box/home/marriage/kitchen should meet resistance.

[12] Thinking about it now, I must conclude that language had something to do with it. I had encountered Shakespeare first not in his language, but in mine, Bengali. Just as representation matters, translation matters. There is perhaps something always

certain that I had every right to love my Shakespeare and to speak my love. But now, after years of living in the United States, years also of scholarly activism toward justice-oriented pedagogy in a country where white supremacy and settler supremacy remain the underlying current animating every formal institution, I knew somewhere deep in my bones what Hall meant. Hall tells of her study in "encounters between Shakespeare and race from the 18th to the 21st century":

> [T]he initial evidence suggests that my own experiences have many precedents: much in [the] combined history of Blackness and Shakespeare makes claiming three things at once—a Black identity, a desire for freedom, and an appreciation of Shakespeare's plays—a more formidable task than you might imagine.

Hall could be talking about me, my friends back home, my students at Jadavpur. Much in the combined history of colonialism/postcolonialism and Shakespeare makes claiming three things at once—a postcolonial identity, a desire for freedom, and an appreciation of Shakespeare's plays—a more formidable task than you might imagine. This was brought forcefully home to me when I started my current faculty position.

On my first day as an assistant professor, my first class was The Ohio State University's English 2201, "Selected Works of British Literature, Medieval through 1800," to be taught at the regional campus of Newark, Ohio. (The main campus of Ohio State is in the city of Columbus, Ohio.) As I walked in and went to the front of the class, four students stood up and walked out. I said my greetings and started to pass out copies of the syllabus. Some ten minutes later—we were still talking about the syllabus—four students came in. I noted, to my surprise, that they were the same four students—all white, all male—who had left a little while ago. When I looked up at them, one of them volunteered, uncertainly: "We thought this was a British literature class." So it is, I said, please come in and take your seats, here are copies of the syllabus, these are the texts we shall be using. The following year, one student, again on the first day of the semester (English 2220, "Introduction to Shakespeare"), told me that I didn't "look like a Shakespeare professor." There are variations of these sentiments and comments every year. Where I teach, it seems usual to question a junior Brown female immigrant academic's ability to teach and discuss The Greats, and especially A Great Like

inalienable about what is first encountered through one's very own (such as a mother tongue), and as one's very own.

Shakespeare. Because of who I am, my teaching the early English literature survey or a Shakespeare class or a Milton class is frequently a bit suspect—if not outright an "agenda" that takes away from the "real" Shakespeare, say, from that "lofty" language, the "universal" themes, the "timeless" poetry, and the "true" understanding of human character.[13]

But in the course of my teaching in white-majority classrooms in large schools of the US Midwest, I have also come to know that most of my students arrive with a genuine thirst for knowledge and are only looking for opportunities to learn about the wide expanses of the world that they do not have firsthand experience of. It is one of the great privileges of my life to work with young people; people who *want* to learn to think critically and live responsibly; people who never, ever, dismiss an idea out of hand and can always be relied on to examine what has been proposed to them. In both the cases mentioned in the last paragraph, the students who said what they did spoke out of a frankness that I respect. And it was their candidness and their openness that allowed them, in both cases, not only to continue in my classes but to complete them with high grades. I thus cannot but be open myself, cannot but see my teaching as a form of care for my students and for the world that we occupy together.

I say out loud, always in the first few meetings of any given semester, that I teach the premodern material I do because this is history and literature that we need to know in order to understand—really understand—where we are today: capitalism, colonialism, racism, ableism, and heteronormative patriarchy. I also spell out that I research and teach early modern English literature because this is where I go to talk about the things that I want urgently to talk about: gender, race, sexuality, disability, and language. I clarify that I am not offering an uncritical "safe place" in my classes. I say, too, that I care more about my students' learning than about their short-term comfort. That said, I also point out that in our learning community, as long as we respect one another and remain open to learning from our mistakes, we cannot say the "wrong" thing. Just as nothing solidifies race so much as race-*making*, or race-*ism*, nothing disrupts racism so much as our willingness to acknowledge our learned and

---

[13] Like Felice Blake, I too have heard numerous times the statement: "I study Shakespeare; I don't do race." See Blake's "Why Black Lives Matter in the Humanities," in *Seeing Race Again: Countering Colorblindness across the Disciplines*, ed. Kimberlé Crenshaw, Luke Charles Harris, Daniel Martinez HoSang, and George Lipsitz (Berkeley: University of California Press, 2019), 307–26.

structural racisms and commit to doing better.[14] Since it is impossible, living in the world we do, to *not* have bias, we need to commit to grappling honestly with our biases. What is at stake is not praise or blame but solidarity and our collective obligation to create a more equal world.[15] I also say out loud that I am indeed a Brown woman from the postcolonial third world and that I absolutely prioritize the voices of the historically disenfranchised. So, for instance, a race-conscious reading of a text and a race-ist reading of a text are not both of equal validity. I acknowledge that the discipline of English literature, and certainly my subdiscipline in premodern English literature, has a white supremacy problem.[16] That is: white supremacists profess a liking for premodern English literature, and some, indeed, train in white-majority fields precisely in order to make claims for the superiority of a culture that produces "great" literature—such as Shakespeare.[17] Even as we study what we do, therefore, we need

---

[14] For a very accessible formulation of what interrupts racism, see Ibram X. Kendi's children's boardbook *Antiracist Baby* (New York: Kokila, 2020). See also my essay "When They Consider How Their Light Is Spent: On Intersectional Race and Disability Theories in the Classroom," in *Race in the European Renaissance: A Classroom Guide*, ed. Matthieu Chapman and Anna Wainwright (Tempe: Arizona Center for Medieval and Renaissance Studies Press, 2023), 161–86.

[15] See Priyamvada Gopal, *Insurgent Empire: Anticolonial Resistance and British Dissent* (London: Verso, 2019).

[16] For instance, in 2019, my campus was one of several in the US to receive white-supremacist flyers (The Ohio State University, Anti-Hate Resources and Action Network, "Campus Attacks," https://u.osu.edu/fighthate/assault-on-u-s-campuses/). My department, in particular, received many—ostensibly because it is seen as a possible haunt for those who are likely to believe in the superiority of white people or English people or European people. See also Luke O'Brien's article on a past student of The Ohio State University's Department of English, "The Making of an American Nazi," *The Atlantic* (2017), https://www.theatlantic.com/magazine/archive/2017/12/the-making-of-an-american-nazi/544119/. As I now write, in autumn 2022, the main campus of Ohio State is again host to hard-right campaigns. On November 15, 2022, this campus was visited by Jack Posobiec, anti-democracy speaker and collaborator with white nationalists and antigovernment extremists: https://www.splcenter.org/fighting-hate/extremist-files/individual/jack-posobiec.

[17] The problem is especially pronounced in the field of medieval literature, of which many tropes, signs, symbols, and catchy excerpts are made to directly serve violent and white-supremacist ends. See Jennifer Schuessler, "Medieval Scholars Joust with White Nationalists. And One Another," *New York Times*, May 5, 2019, https://www.nytimes.com/2019/05/05/arts/the-battle-for-medieval-studies-white-supremacy.html; Hannah Natanson, "'It's all white people': Allegations of White Supremacy Are Tearing Apart Prestigious Medieval Studies Group," *Washington Post*, September 19, 2019, https://www.washingtonpost.com/education/2019/09/19/its-all-white-people-allegations-white-supremacy-are-tearing-apart-prestigious-medieval-studies-group/; and Kristin Romey, "Decoding the Hate Symbols Seen at the Capitol Insurrection," *National Geographic*, January 23, 2021, https://www.nationalgeographic.co.uk/history-and-civilisation/2021/01/decoding-the-hate-symbols-seen-at-the-capitol-insurrection.

to reckon with how the field of premodern English literature has historically driven out Black, Brown, Hispanic, third-world-immigrant, and postcolonial subjects—especially those who place the past they study in critical dialogic relationship with our unequal present.[18] I finally emphasize what my background, and my studying what I did from within that background, has meant for me: that an anticolonial sensibility was so centrally the point of my intellectual efforts that I didn't even call it by that name.[19] And that I do what I do because I believe in the classroom as one of the last truly meaningful places of possibility in the world, and because I love what I do.

That word returns: love. Hall talks about her love of Shakespeare, a Black love, a complex love that sustains her scholarship in premodern literature, and a love that allows her to make connections, across centuries, between the literary legacy of Shakespeare, African-descent performers from the eighteenth century to the present, and transformative scholarship and performance today.[20] But she too asks why this love of Shakespeare should even matter in the time of the New Jim Crow and in our relentless hour of racial discrimination

---

See also Helen Young, "Why the Far-Right and White Supremacists Have Embraced the Middle Ages and Their Symbols," *The Conversation*, January 13, 2021, https://theconversation.com/why-the-far-right-and-white-supremacists-have-embraced-the-middle-ages-and-their-symbols-152968. While some medievalists opposed to white supremacist ideals like to claim "This is not who we are," other medievalists opposed to white supremacist ideals point out that it is precisely as a result of this kind of smugness and complacency (the this-is-not-who-we-are kind) within the white-majority field of medieval studies that medieval studies has been co-opted in violent white supremacy. Early modern studies—again, with an unmarked Eurocentrism even in the name of our field of study—is not without its own problems. Wendy Beth Hyman and Hillary Eklund write how "Shakespeare, perhaps more than any other literary figure, has been trotted out as a symbol of white cultural supremacy" and why it is incumbent on us, as scholars, to address and correct this notion ("Introduction: Making Meaning and Doing Justice with Early Modern Texts," *Teaching Social Justice Through Shakespeare: Why Renaissance Literature Matters Now*, edited by Eklund and Hyman [Edinburgh: Edinburgh University Press, 2019], 2). To reiterate, then: premodern English literature has a white supremacy problem.

[18] See, for instance, Kathy Lavezzo's article documenting Stuart Hall's departure from medieval studies: "New Ethnicities and Medieval 'Race,'" *Addressing the Crisis: The Stuart Hall Project* 1 (2019): 1–5, https://doi.org/10.17077/2643-8291.1003.

[19] I still hesitate to, because like so much in our corporatized global North, even terms such as "decolonization" can be bent out of all meaning through being co-opted by administrators, public relations cadres, and politicians. See also the critique by Olúfẹ́mi Táíwò, *Against Decolonisation: Taking African Agency Seriously* (London: Hurst, 2022).

[20] Among Kim F. Hall's many pieces of transformative scholarship, see particularly the critical landmark *Things of Darkness: Economies of Race and Gender in Early Modern England* (Ithaca: Cornell University Press, 1996).

and violence.²¹ Her answer, convincingly, is toward demonstrating "Shakespeare's role in racial formation in this country and the resultingly profound relationship between Shakespeare and Black freedom" and thus also about positing a "Shakespeare usable for the next 400 years." This resonates deeply with me. I have written elsewhere about why the very ubiquity of Shakespeare in erstwhile-colonized or still-colonized places is reason to take decolonial and anticolonial Shakespeare studies seriously.²² Shakespeare's generative affordances in the decolonial/anticolonial program is precisely why my love for Shakespeare matters. All my pedagogical strategies for justice-oriented Shakespeare studies—as outlined in the next section—are geared not only toward creating the world that I want to live in, but also toward creating an academy that I can love enough to continue working within.²³

I recognize that my institution wants to be seen to be changing; it wants to be perceived as truly transforming itself from a stronghold of white male cisgender able-bodied belonging into an institution authentically welcoming for persons of all races, genders, sexual orientations, abilities, religions, and nationalities, among other categories.²⁴ There is not a week that goes by without missives from our

---

[21] See Michelle Alexander, *The New Jim Crow: Mass Incarceration in the Age of Colorblindness* (New York: The New Press, 2010). For other work at the intersection of race and the US legal system, especially the criminal justice system, see also Bryan Stevenson, *Just Mercy: A Story of Justice and Redemption* (New York: Spiegel & Grau, 2014); Beth E. Richie, *Arrested Justice: Black Women, Violence, and America's Prison Nation* (New York: New York University Press, 2012); Carol Anderson, *The Second: Race and Guns in a Fatally Unequal America* (New York: Bloomsbury, 2021); Margaret A. Burnham, *By Hands Now Known: Jim Crow's Legal Executioners* (New York: Norton, 2022); and the "NAACP Criminal Justice Factsheet," https://naacp.org/resources/criminal-justice-fact-sheet.

[22] Amrita Dhar, "*The Invention of Race* and the Postcolonial Renaissance," *The Cambridge Journal of Postcolonial Literary Inquiry* 9, no. 1 (2022): 132–38; https://doi.org/10.1017/pli.2021.38.

[23] I am indebted to Margaret Price, who has undertaken multiple mixed-methods studies in disabled faculty life, for this formulation. See especially her book *Crip Spacetime* (forthcoming from Duke University Press in 2024). See also Sara Ahmed, *Complaint!* (Durham: Duke University Press, 2021).

[24] My university's documentation of its own history leaves unremarked the race, for instance, of its first students: "In 1870, The Ohio State University was founded as a land-grant university. Its original name was the Ohio Agricultural and Mechanical College due to its location in a farming community. The first classes were held on September 17, 1873 with the first class of six men graduating in 1878. The first woman, an engineering major, graduated in 1879. The college's name was changed to The Ohio State University in 1878." See https://ehistory.osu.edu/topics/ohio-state-university. As Richard Dyer points out: nonwhite people are raced, white people are just people. See Dyer's "The Matter of Whiteness," *White* (New York: Routledge, 1997): 1–40. Today, my university professes an aspiration toward equitable opportunities

administration about our "Shared Values," or our ostensible passage "On Seas of Care," or our upholding of "inclusive excellence."[25] We even have an entire Office of Diversity and Inclusion.[26] Buffeted as I am on those "seas of care," however, I must also recognize that this urgency of public-image-curation on the part of my institution is a function of its very real anxieties about whether it is possible—or even ultimately desirable—for it to change. There is a difference between wanting to be seen to be changing and actually changing. I therefore recognize, as well, that if an institution habitually and proactively supported its members of nonwhite, non-cisgender, non-able-bodied, non-US-citizen backgrounds, and so on, that is, if an institution in fact supported its diverse community, it would become an inclusive place and take a real step toward equity in the world. But that is not where we are. Yet in the daily life of my institution there remain us, its students and teachers and learners. And we still have our classrooms, our desks, our libraries, our discussions—all of which we can use to imagine necessary transgressions, places of genuine hope, and a world where the mind is without fear and the head is held high.[27] It is to my classroom that I now want to turn in this discussion of anticolonial Shakespeare pedagogy.

---

for all: "Ohio State does not discriminate on the basis of age, ancestry, color, disability, gender identity or expression, genetic information, HIV/AIDS status, military status, national origin, race, religion, sex, gender, sexual orientation, pregnancy, protected veteran status, or any other bases under the law, in its activities, academic programs, admission, and employment." See the statement by the university's Office of Institutional Equity: https://equity.osu.edu/.

[25] See the statements on the institutional web pages https://oaa.osu.edu/shared-values-initiative and https://oaa.osu.edu/vision-mission-values. The College of Engineering at Ohio State even offers a certificate in "Inclusive Excellence": https://engineering.osu.edu/diversity-inclusion/inclusive-excellence-certificate. Many in the Ohio State community, including Andreá N. Williams, Director of The Women's Place at Ohio State (https://womensplace.osu.edu/), have pointed out the tautology inherent within the term "inclusive excellence"—for if a university culture is *not* inclusive, it is by definition not excellent. It should suffice to say "excellence," and mean it, precisely by baking inclusion and equity into all aspects of university life. But mentions and even protestations of "inclusive excellence" are everywhere in my institution's rhetoric.

[26] See https://odi.osu.edu/.

[27] I deliberately note the resonances between bell hooks's and Rabindranath Tagore's pedagogical philosophies. See particularly Tagore's "Where the Mind Is without Fear" (published in English as poem "35" by Tagore in *Gitanjali*, 1912; https://www.poetryfoundation.org/poems/45668/gitanjali-35) and hooks's idea of "Education as the Practice of Freedom" in *Teaching to Transgress* (New York: Routledge, 1994).

Teaching

I teach Shakespeare across undergraduate and graduate career stages of students at my institution, The Ohio State University. At the regional campus of Newark, Ohio, which serves undergraduates in an open-admission four-year program, the most common Shakespeare offerings are "Introduction to Shakespeare" (English 2220) and "Shakespeare's Major Plays" (English 4520). Another frequent offering is English 3378, "Special Topics in Film and Literature," which I have taught as a Shakespeare and film class, either "World Film Shakespeares" or "Indian Film Shakespeares." All these classes enroll students pursuing both the English Major and the General Education program. Thus, there is a range of preparation that students bring to the classroom. Some students come with significant prior knowledge of premodern literature, including Shakespeare, and for some, this is their first college-level Shakespeare. At the main campus of Columbus, Ohio—and in my classes, we are aware of the profound colonialism embedded within and expressed in the very name of the city—I teach Shakespeare, specifically *Othello*, for the entire first half of a graduate seminar in Disability Studies, "Disability and the Early/Modern" (English 7891). While the unfolding discussions and class materials range in depth and scope depending on the level of the course, I have a few core goals that are common to all these classes: good close reading, a sound grasp of a few plays, and an intersectional and dynamic understanding of how these plays work for us, today, in the twenty-first century.[28]

To that effect, I open every class with a few questions that the community must consider:

1) What do we mean when we say "Shakespeare"?
2) Whose Shakespeare is it anyway? (And who is an "authority" on Shakespeare?)[29]

---

[28] Explicitly and otherwise, my pedagogical, scholarly, and activist understandings of intersectionality are indebted to the germinal work of two legal scholars, Kimberlé Crenshaw and Patricia Williams, especially Crenshaw's "Demarginalizing the Intersection of Race and Sex: A Black Feminist Critique of Antidiscrimination Doctrine, Feminist Theory and Antiracist Politics," *University of Chicago Legal Forum*, Article 8 (1989): 139–66 (available at http://chicagounbound.uchicago.edu/uclf/vol1989/iss1/8) and Williams's *The Alchemy of Race and Rights: Diary of a Law Professor* (Cambridge: Harvard University Press, 1991).

[29] This question was clarified in my mind as a result of a conversation with Arthur L. Little, Jr., who, while a guest of the graduate-student-led Early Modern Colloquium

3) Is it "anachronistic," or historically inaccurate, to "do" Shakespeare with lots of actors of color, of disabilities, of the "wrong" gender, and so on? (And what does it mean to care about historical accuracy, especially if that care occurs at the expense of lived lives of the present?)[30]

And, just to make my provocation fuller, I also sometimes ask:

4) Is Shakespeare white?[31]

In the "Introduction to Shakespeare" class particularly, that fourth question prompts students to read the first question more carefully—once, that is, some especially surprised students get past the point of "Dear lord, is our (Brown female foreigner junior) professor really asking us if Shakespeare was white/English? Has she not heard of the Swan of Avon? The Bard? The poet not of an age but for all time?" Asking "Is Shakespeare white?" is so outlandish and outrageous (I am not, after all, above the occasional gimmick) that students are obliged to wonder what on earth I mean by "Shakespeare." Thus, we get to consider, collectively, that when we say "Shakespeare," we mean, as Kim F. Hall elucidates in her aforementioned lecture, one or more of four things: first, the historical person William Shakespeare; second, the writings of the historical person William Shakespeare; third, four centuries of cultural conversation around the historical person William Shakespeare and his writings; and fourth, a (dubious) metaphor for Englishness and/or white Europeanness.

This unpacking of what we mean when we say "Shakespeare" leads intuitively into a consideration of "whose Shakespeare": "who gets to call Shakespeare theirs" through "what processes of ownership or creative belonging or liberty" and "who gets to be a Shakespearean."

2014 at the University of Michigan, mentioned that "There's racism in Shakespeare" is not the end of the conversation on Shakespeare and race but the beginning of that conversation.

[30] This question is indebted particularly to Ayanna Thompson and Laura Turchi's *Teaching Shakespeare with Purpose: A Student-Centred Approach* (London: Bloomsbury, 2016). See also Sawyer Kemp and Cameron Hunt McNabb's conversation, "Disability and Shakespeare: A Guide for Practitioners and Scholars," *The Sundial*, July 7, 2022, https://medium.com/the-sundial-acmrs/disability-and-shakespeare-a-guide-for-practitioners-and-scholars-c9ebbfef3c0c; Kyle Grady's "'The Miseducation of Irie Jones': Representation and Identification in the Shakespeare Classroom," *Early Modern Culture* 14 (2019): 26–43, https://tigerprints.clemson.edu/emc/vol14/iss1/3; and Laura Seymour's *Shakespeare and Neurodiversity* (forthcoming).

[31] This question was inspired by Emma Smith, "Was Shylock Jewish?" *Shakespeare Quarterly* 64, no. 2 (2013): 188–219.

For this section of our discussion, I find it useful to lead with a mini-lecture on how Shakespeare is embedded within various cultures of the world today, and how different interpretations and adaptations of Shakespeare enrich our understanding of the words and themes of the plays and poetry. The Massachusetts Institute of Technology's *Global Shakespeares* video and performance archive is one of my go-to resources for illustrations of the numerous adaptations and uses of Shakespeare in different parts of the world.[32] Some examples that I love working with include *Bhrantibilash*, a 1963 Bengali film adaptation of *The Comedy of Errors* in which post-Partition Bengal is evoked to poignant effect (to me, *Comedy* remains indubitably a story of the Partition); the 2010 film *Tempest* directed by Julie Taymor, in which Helen Mirren's Prospera becomes a figure of maternal authority that throws into relief the play's absent Sycorax; Toni Morrison and Rokia Traoré's magnificent 2011 play *Desdemona*, which is brief enough that sometimes we can read entire scenes out loud on the first day of class, everyone taking turns; Vishal Bhardwaj's 2006 film *Omkara*, whose Bollywood music numbers magnificently layer the themes of love, jealousy, caste, and power in the play; and Madeline Sayet's deeply introspective 2022 play *Where We Belong*, which documents the author's Mohegan journey in Shakespeare.[33] Even this brief and teaser-ly exposure to a multiplicity of Shakespeares serves as an invitation for students to engage with our "classical" material on their own terms, according to their specific critical and intellectual needs, and with an eye to what this centuries-old literature and theater can do for them, for us, here, now.

Depending on the class, I also like to draw students' attention to the British Library Harley Manuscript 7368, which contains the play *The Book of Sir Thomas More*, and in which the writing on ff. 8r, 8v, and 9r has been identified to be Shakespeare's. The lines contain what has come to be known as Shakespeare's plea for refugees.[34] I then show a performance video of that plea filmed at Shakespeare's

---

[32] See the digital repository at https://globalshakespeares.mit.edu/.

[33] Manu Sen, dir., *Bhrantibilash* (1963); Julie Taymor, dir., *The Tempest* (2010); Toni Morrison and Rokia Traoré, *Desdemona* (London: Oberon Books, 2012); Vishal Bhardwaj, dir., *Omkara* (2006); and Madeline Sayet, *Where We Belong* (London: Bloomsbury, 2022). See also Sayet's interview with Barbara Bogaev, interviewer, "Farewell, Master, Farewell, Farewell," on *Shakespeare Unlimited* (podcast), episode 170, Folger Shakespeare Library, June 22, 2021, https://www.folger.edu/shakespeare-unlimited/where-we-belong-sayet.

[34] Images of manuscript pages from *The Booke of Sir Thomas More* (1601) are available from the British Library, Harley MS 7368, https://www.bl.uk/collection-items/shakespeares-handwriting-in-the-book-of-sir-thomas-more.

Globe Theatre in London. The video makes electrifyingly present the urgency of Shakespeare's 400-year-old words in our own time of unprecedented mass migration on the planet.[35] Focusing attention on Shakespeare's writing-of-a-part simultaneously helps students conceptualize/reconceptualize Shakespeare as as much a writer of plays as a reviser of one, as much a creator of wholes as a writer of fragments, as much an original composer as a collaborator in the theatrical profession.[36] This is also where I get to insert a brief lecture on the conditions of work in Elizabethan and Jacobean professional playhouses, and thus bring into relief for students the quality of popular entertainment in Shakespeare's period and culture. At or toward the conclusion of the first week, I either play clips from or refer students to specific episodes of the Folger Shakespeare Library's *Shakespeare Unlimited* podcast.[37] I have used this podcast series heavily while teaching at the Newark campus because so many regional campus students commute to class. I have found the podcasts wonderfully useful to get students listening on their drive; they function almost as a means of priming students for the classroom discussion.[38] They arrive already warmed up and part of the conversation. Even better: during the term, students invariably listen to many more episodes than are formally assigned.

An immediate and salutary effect of all this zooming out in our view-of-Shakespeare-in-the-world is that students become aware of the parochialism inherent in thinking of Shakespeare as a metaphor

---

[35] "The Stranger's Case: Refugee Week," *Shakespeare's Globe*, June 20, 2018. https://www.shakespearesglobe.com/discover/blogs-and-features/2018/06/20/the-strangers-case-refugee-week/. As Ruben Espinosa points out, however, it is important to discuss *why* the play itself, *Sir Thomas More*—and not just the fact of Shakespeare's handwriting in the manuscript of the play—continues to have particular purchase in our own time: precisely because of an all-too-contemporarily-relevant anti-immigrant sensibility otherwise platformed in the play. "It is the white rioters who are the catalyst for More's speech, and it is these rioters that propel the violent racism in our present moment" ("A 'nation of such barbarous temper': Beyond the White Savior of *Sir Thomas More*," *Shakespeare Bulletin* 39, no. 4 [2021]: 693). Espinosa is also right to caution: "We should consider . . . the pitfalls of centering Shakespeare and allowing his voice to overshadow the on-the-ground realities [actually facing immigrants]" (684).

[36] On Shakespeare's writing-in-parts, see Simon Palfrey and Tiffany Stern's *Shakespeare in Parts* (Oxford: Oxford University Press, 2011).

[37] See the full series at https://www.folger.edu/shakespeare-unlimited.

[38] Another audio series that I use to get students warmed up for class discussions, especially discussions with a focus on Milton or *Paradise Lost*, is *Promiscuous Listening: A John Milton Podcast*, hosted by Marissa Greenberg, https://marissagreenberg.com/promiscuous-listening-a-john-milton-podcast/. See also Greenberg's "Podcast Pedagogy," *The Sundial*, January 12, 2021, https://medium.com/the-sundial-acmrs/podcast-pedagogy-5185e1c1016e.

for Englishness or whiteness or Europeanness or any such colonialist position. It becomes obvious that whatever Shakespeare the person might have been, it is Shakespeare the world literary and theatrical phenomenon that is our proper topic of discussion and engagement today, and that the value of this Shakespeare is in what it has made possible in the world in terms of ownership within specific communities, in resistance to oppression, and in creative and regenerative possibilities of politics and art. I inculcate this ownership of Shakespeare in my students deliberately. It is valuable for what it then allows us, as a class, to achieve: to take things apart and put them back in new and thought-provoking ways; to do our work of close reading and critical thinking without the baggage of nostalgia for some sort of "glorious past" producing "great literature"; and to get on with true learning, which is an undertaking of nervousness and excitement in equal measure. It is right, I tell students, that we should be exhilarated and terrified in turn. I still am, I say—I still am, after two decades of professional study in Shakespeare. The ground we are on is hallowed not because we are treading in the footsteps of a genius, but, much more remarkably, because this is ground that has been traveled for hundreds of years by profoundly disparate peoples for an almost unimaginable range of purposes. To get to study the grain of these journeys, even a small selection of these journeys, is to travel in human history and to take measure of emotional endeavor at the level of individuals' and communities' dreams and tears and elegy and anger and peace. Shakespeare is indeed special, and this is why.

What follows is our plunge into the plays themselves—into close reading, group discussions, mini-lectures interspersed with low-stakes reflective writing in the classroom, role-plays of selected pivotal moments in the plays, viewing and unpacking short theater and film clips of performances and adaptations, and lots of digging in the online *Oxford English Dictionary* for words and their roots and their meanings and their affordances. To model a due diligence with the centuries-old material, I name and encourage what I call a "habit of learning": I acknowledge the challenges posed by Shakespeare's writing or its theatrical representations; I mention that we should not be surprised if reading five lines and thinking-through-writing about them takes an hour; I do bite-sized and chunk-sized lectures; I incentivize online submission of discussion questions and use those questions in classes; I plan hands-on class activities such as a signature-led assembly of the first quarto of *King Lear* from printed sheets; I do plenty of office hours. Then, somewhere near the end of the first month, the switch flips: students' struggle and effort turn into something like exhilaration, and the very quality of engagement changes.³⁹ At that point, I take notes in real time as my students speak to one another.

Thus, in an "Introduction to Shakespeare" (English 2220) class: "Is that administrator person [Angelo, in *Measure for Measure*] actually proposing forced sex?" "He did say that he's relying on her [Isabella's] 'tender shame' not to out him!"⁴⁰ "Why is it *her* shame if *he's* attracted to her in that icky way?" "Oh man, look at this: 'my authority bears of a credent bulk, / That no particular scandal once can touch / But it confounds the breather'. He's actually saying that he expects her [Isabella] not to be believed because he is in a position of authority!"⁴¹ "Well, [Dr. Richard] Strauss didn't come out of nowhere."⁴² "This is quite the Shakespeare lesson in how not to believe survivors." "#MeToo."

Or while talking about "Shakespeare's Major Plays" (English 4520): "Wait a minute, what does she [Portia] mean by 'Which is the merchant here, and which the Jew?' It's not like it's a profession, being a Jew!"⁴³ "Wait for it, they will also point out finally which is the alien and which is the citizen."⁴⁴ "Equal before the law, right!" "Shylock was being pretty bloodthirsty, but she's being violent too." "It's just that she's using the law to do it."

Or in "World Film Shakespeares" (English 3378): "So, the lyrics of the song [the qawwali 'Tu mere rubaru hai,' or 'You are in front of me,' in the film *Maqbool*] do the double work of indicating the

---

³⁹ Susannah B. Mintz calls it "the wild alchemy of students falling in love with a poet I love before my eyes." See her *Love Affair in the Garden of Milton: Loss, Poetry, and the Meaning of Unbelief* (Baton Rouge: Louisiana State University Press, 2021), 28.

⁴⁰ *Measure for Measure*, ed. A. R. Braunmuller and Robert Watson (London: Bloomsbury, 2020), 4.4.21.

⁴¹ *Measure for Measure*, 4.4.24–26.

⁴² As Ohio State now documents through its office of University Compliance and Integrity, "Ohio State released a report from independent investigators that details acts of sexual abuse against at least 177 former students by Dr. Richard Strauss during his employment with the university from 1978 to 1998." See OSU Office of Compliance and Integrity, "Strauss Investigation," https://compliance.osu.edu/strauss-investigation.html. Most students today find it telling—if not surprising—that complaints numbered into the tens and then into the hundreds, across years and then decades, before the university took any action. On May 17, 2019, then-President Michael Drake of Ohio State wrote to students, faculty, and staff: "On behalf of the university, we offer our profound regret and sincere apologies to each person who endured Strauss' abuse. Our institution's fundamental failure at the time to prevent this abuse was unacceptable—as were the inadequate efforts to thoroughly investigate complaints raised by students and staff members." See The Ohio State University Office of the President, "A Message from President Drake: Strauss Investigation Report," May 17, 2019, https://president.osu.edu/story/strauss-investigation-report.

⁴³ *The Merchant of Venice*, ed. John Drakakis (London: Bloomsbury, 2010), 4.1.170.

⁴⁴ *The Merchant of Venice*, 4.1.345–47.

spiritual and the romantic?"[45] "She [Nimmi, based on the Lady Macbeth figure] clearly wants him [Maqbool, the Macbeth figure]." "Why wouldn't she? Abbaji [the Duncan figure] is so much older." "How did they [Nimmi and Abbaji] come to be in a relationship, anyway?" "What did she know? She must have been a minor when he took her in, took her out of the streets." "Is she looking for power? Or just a way out?" "Remember how Nimmi also manipulates Maqbool?" "Does it matter that she *has* no way out? She's a Muslim woman in a Hindu-majority country and she is known in her community as the mistress of a gangster patriarch. Where will she go?"

In the graduate seminar "Disability and the Early/Modern" (English 7891), the eight or so weeks that we devote to *Othello* feels initially like an expansively long time.[46] But our weeks fill quickly as we read adaptations and afterlives of the play in the works of Djanet Sears (*Harlem Duet*, 1997), Toni Morrison and Rokia Traoré (*Desdemona*, 2012), Lolita Chakrabarti (*Red Velvet*, 2014), and Keith Hamilton Cobb (*American Moor*, 2020) and unpack the ongoing enmeshments of race, gender, postcolonial inheritance, enslavement inheritance, nationality, and im/migration status in creating or enforcing conditions of disability.[47] "The *Othello* that we read or see in the twenty-first century is not the same that Shakespeare's audience read or saw in early modern England, or that slave owners saw in nineteenth-century America, or that Afrikaners saw in Apartheid South Africa."[48] Reading in twentieth-century and contemporary disability theory, we know that a physical or mental difference or impairment does not in itself equal disability. It is, instead, a range of social and structural conditions that restrict access by not providing access that makes a disability out of any physical or cognitive non-normativity.[49]

---

[45] Vishal Bhardwaj, dir., *Maqbool* (2003).
[46] I am indebted to my graduate students Kayley DeLong, Sahalie Martin, D'Arcee Charington Neal, Elise Robbins, Mykyta Tyshchenko, and Jamie Utphall for the insights I mention in this paragraph.
[47] See also the series *Exploring Othello in 2020* hosted by the Red Bull Theater, a series of conversations and readings of selected passages from the play by a group of BIPOC theater practitioners, writers, and scholars (October 7, 14, 21, and 28, 2020), https://www.redbulltheater.com/exploring-othello-2020. Like the *Shakespeare Unlimited* podcasts mentioned earlier, this series was a brilliant warm-up for class conversations.
[48] Ayanna Thompson, "Introduction," in *Othello* (London: Bloomsbury, 2016), 3.
[49] The Disability Studies readings for this graduate seminar focus on both contemporary and early modern texts, keeping in mind that "early modern studies that focus on literary character may unintentionally parallel the medical model of disability. By regarding disability as an individual difference that resides within each separate individual character (rather than as a broader social phenomenon that affects readers, audience

Simultaneously, since this course is about "Disability and the Early/Modern," we also study various dimensions of global early modernity, which is the context in which Shakespeare's Venetian play is set: we examine the 1601 "Draft declaration on the expulsion of 'Negroes and Blackamoors'," we go through the entries in the TIDE Project's open-access collection of *Keywords* essays, and we read Kim F. Hall's user-friendly introduction to *Othello* in the Bedford/St. Martin's edition (since this class serves graduate students from multiple humanities, science, and arts disciplines, it is important for me not to presume expertise in literature or premodern topics).[50] Throughout, we thread our discussions of the play and its adaptations and performances with key scholarship in postcolonial theory and critical race theory, such as those offered by Stuart Hall, James Baldwin, Ngũgĩ wa Thiong'o, Saidiya Hartman, and B. R. Ambedkar.[51] Term-end projects and significant student contributions in this class have included critiques of afro-futurism and afro-pessimism through the figure of Othello; a study of Othello's immigrant identity as a maker of radical in-betweenness and non-belonging; and creative-critical considerations of the interracial romantic relationship between Desdemona and Othello.

A final feature of these Shakespeare courses that I want to mention is that of my invitation to my classes, whenever possible,

---

members, and performers), many of these readings foreground disability as an individual condition that one character/figure has as opposed to regarding disability as a social phenomenon that brings certain people together into a disability community." Sonya Freeman Loftis, *Shakespeare and Disability Studies* (Oxford: Oxford University Press, 2021), 4.

[50] See the "Draft declaration on the expulsion of 'Negroes and Blackamoors'," (1601), British Library Historical Manuscripts Commission, Salisbury MSS, xi, 569 (Hatfield Cecil Papers 91/15), https://www.bl.uk/collection-items/draft-proclamation-on-the-expulsion-of-negroes-and-blackamoors-1601; the webpages of the European Research Council project "Travel, Transculturality, and Identity in England, c. 1550–1700" at https://www.tideproject.uk/; Nandini Das, João Vicente Melo, Haig Smith, and Lauren Working, *Keywords of Identity, Race, and Human Mobility in Early Modern England* (Amsterdam: Amsterdam University Press, 2021); and Kim F. Hall, ed., *Othello: Texts and Contexts* (New York: Bedford/St. Martin's, 2006).

[51] See particularly Stuart Hall, *Familiar Stranger: A Life between Two Islands* (Durham: Duke University Press, 2017); James Baldwin, *The Fire Next Time* (London: Penguin, 1964); Ngũgĩ wa Thiong'o, *Decolonising the Mind: The Politics of Language in African Literature* (Portsmouth: Heinemann, 1986); Saidiya Hartman, "Venus in Two Acts," *Small Axe* 12, no. 2 (2008): 1–14; and B. R. Ambedkar, "Waiting For a Visa," *Babasaheb Ambedkar: Writings and Speeches*, vol. 12, part 1, ed. Vasant Moon (Bombay: Education Department, Government of Maharashtra, 1993), 661–91.

of scholars from the postcolonial world or the global South.⁵² My own enthusiasm about these different expert voices comes from my scholarly ethic of collaboration and mutual teaching. My institution does not have much direct or visible support for guests from other institutions to our classrooms, and as such, I must work hard to find the funds to invite external speakers. But I do this work because the visitors make real for my students the presence of teachers and writers and instructors who don't "belong" with optical correctness to the culture under consideration.⁵³ The global-South visitors' virtual appearance—of course from different timezones in the world—re-table for my Midwest-situated students the accumulated grief and anger of generations of postcolonial learners, and similarly make visible for my students something of the postcolonial history of leveraging the power of Shakespeare for talking back to political might. As Arundhati Roy teaches us: "Respect strength, never power. And never, ever, forget."⁵⁴ My students also get to see the strange love that genuinely multilingual scholars bring to the verse of Shakespeare both in his language and in so many other languages.

That word returns: love. There is no way for an anticolonialist to "do" Shakespeare without love—just as there is no way for an anticolonialist to teach, at any level, at any institution, today except toward justice.⁵⁵ I know now that our love has perhaps to be the stronger for our knowing that any full attainment of justice is simply not within our reach: not in our lifetimes, maybe not even in our children's lifetimes. But it is our work still to try, to continue to do the work, to show up every day for our students, to hold our institutions accountable and bring them closer to what they claim they want to be, and to think and write and will things into being as much as ever we can.

---

[52] I am especially grateful to Paromita Chakravarti, Iqbal Khan, Amrita Sen, and Jyotsna Singh, all of whom have been recent visitors to or contributors for my classes, for their insights on pedagogical practice in different parts of the world.

[53] Whenever I have managed to carry out these invitations—always generously received by the scholars I have approached—the visits have been worth every minute of the online sessions.

[54] See Arundhati Roy's many decades of work in *My Seditious Heart: Collected Nonfiction* (London: Haymarket, 2019).

[55] For this sentiment, I am indebted to Natalie Diaz's poetry collection *Postcolonial Love Poem* (Minneapolis: Graywolf Press, 2020).

Chapter 2

Deeply Engaged Protest: Social Justice Pedagogy and Shakespeare's "Monument"
Elisa Oh

In recent years undergraduate student resistance to studying Shakespeare and other canonical white male authors has been fierce and growing, and their insistence that the English literary canon be decolonized is in need of open recognition and negotiation if we want a new generation to engage deeply with Shakespeare rather than drop it from syllabi, curriculum requirements, and textbooks.[1] I welcome the rewriting of literary canons, curricula, and syllabi every academic year. However, my students and I frequently reach an impasse about what the proper response should be to the frank admission that Shakespeare's texts—like many other works in the traditional western literary canon—are plainly filled with anti-Black racism. This fact, for a majority of my students, automatically disqualifies these works from inclusion in any list of "great" art and in any curriculum or syllabus that surveys influential texts in literary history. While I agree that these texts' language and ideologies of race are offensive and unacceptable by today's standards, I do not find it useful to respond with a complete, principled boycott of Shakespeare. Coming from a Korean and white American background, I have always had complicated encounters with western canonical texts as a nonwhite reader, but that experience does not mean I can intuit or dictate my African American students' responses to the same cultural material. My students and I need a critical practice that allows us to analyze the past without perpetuating its harm and a critical stance, particularly as readers of color, that positions us to judge any text that contains aggressively negative representations of our intersectional identities within it.

---

[1] Alison Flood, "Yale English Students Call for End of Focus on White Male Writers," *Guardian*, June 1, 2016, https://www.theguardian.com/books/2016/jun/01/yale-english-students-call-for-end-of-focus-on-white-male-writers.

As a result, I developed a Shakespeare protest assignment—joining political protest, visual art, and expository writing—to engage with my students' understandable desire to "cancel" Shakespeare as the most fitting response to his works' anti-Black bias and legacy in white supremacist claims about European intellectual achievement. Working toward bell hooks's vision of teaching that "collectively imagine[s] ways to move beyond boundaries, to transgress,"[2] I explore how, in the context of a Historically Black College or University (HBCU), a protest lesson might identify and challenge institutional and colonial power structures; build on students' preexisting strengths and knowledge; and draw connections between early modern texts and social justice today.

I take inspiration from Ayanna Thompson and Laura Turchi's assertion that Shakespeare's works in the classroom can be "powerful opportunities to acknowledge and further advance our students' diverse twenty-first-century identities," and I follow Katherine Gillen and Lisa Jennings's suggestions to combine western epistemologies of "individualistic and detached modes of critique . . . with other ways of knowing, including the corporeal [and] the affective."[3] Encapsulating the pedagogical need to share knowledge and equalize power, bell hooks quotes Paulo Freire's assertion that "we cannot enter the struggle as objects in order to later become subjects."[4] My Shakespeare protest assignment values students' critical opinions as equal to and in dialogue with my critical opinion and requires them to hone their rhetorical appeals for different audiences. Rather than mandating acceptance of my authority, it encourages them to analyze their own intellectual relationship to traditionally celebrated language, literature, and education and, with that awareness, to argue for change. This lesson plan for teaching Shakespeare does not try to ignore, contradict, disarm, or appease their resistance to studying it but rather harnesses and amplifies the deep engagement and personal investment of protest. As a critical approach to a text, protest is automatically energized, creative, and driven to be at once

---

[2] bell hooks, *Teaching to Transgress: Education as the Practice of Freedom* (New York: Routledge, 1994), 207.

[3] Ayanna Thompson and Laura Turchi, *Teaching Shakespeare with Purpose: A Student-Centred Approach* (London: Bloomsbury, 2016), 171; Katherine Gillen and Lisa Jennings, "Decolonizing Shakespeare? Toward an Antiracist, Culturally Sustaining Praxis," *The Sundial*, November 6, 2019, https://medium.com/the-sundial-acmrs/decolonizing-shakespeare-toward-an-antiracist-culturally-sustaining-praxis-904cb9ff8a96.

[4] bell hooks, *Teaching Critical Thinking: Practical Wisdom* (New York: Routledge, 2010), 45.

oppositional and powerfully persuasive. Protest assumes an intellectual intervention in a widely accepted status quo with the urgent and future-oriented intent of improvement. In this case, inviting public protest increases social justice for minoritized students who have felt diminished and erased by their encounters with white canonical writers in the classroom.

Justice for All Viewpoints within Educational Institutions

Despite the difficulty of encouraging my students to challenge my authority as well as my decision to put a Shakespeare play on the syllabus, versions of this lesson with three different classes have been electrifying, rigorous, and surprising in their results.[5] I suggest to my students that it is possible to read a historically influential text without accepting that it is "universally" great and then let the debate unfold. My colleague, Thorell Tsomondo, Professor Emerita of English at Howard University, shared her teaching precepts with me from the time I was a new instructor in the Howard English Department. In response to her students who questioned the value of studying white-authored British texts, including Shakespeare, she told them, "It is not *what* you read but *how you read it* that matters!"[6] She then led students through postcolonial readings of canonical texts like *Othello* and *The Tempest,* providing critical tools for unpacking the shaping influences of European political and cultural domination.

However, my students argue persuasively that reading and studying a work grants it a basic measure of respect, which some books and opinions do not deserve. They argue that giving class airtime, curricular space, and expository writing attention to these works—no matter how decolonizing the critical approach, no matter how diverse the commentators or adaptors—still keeps the dead white man Shakespeare in focus, in the center, on his pedestal. Everyday racism is a tangible, exhausting pressure on many of us in

---

[5] With slight variations, I used this assignment as a culminating semester project in an upper-level Shakespeare class, taught online in fall 2020; and as a mid-semester paper assignment in an introduction to literary genres (including *The Tempest*) and in a British literature survey (including selected sonnets and *Titus Andronicus*), both taught in-person in fall 2021. The Shakespeare class was mostly senior English majors, and the other two classes were mostly sophomore English majors and minors.

[6] Dr. Thorell Tsomondo, personal communication to the author via telephone, July 28, 2022.

America today. A primary way to respond to everyday racism is to avoid it, refuse it, starve it of attention, and especially shut out those who produce it. The impulse to "cancel" Shakespeare's work is an understandable reaction to perceiving its resonances with the mental, physical, and cultural attacks on African Americans today. As an Asian American woman, I can never authoritatively tell you what all African American students experience in a Howard University classroom. Therefore, I submit this claim from my limited point of view, intending it to be subject to my students' evaluation: in an HBCU classroom, there is a foundational expectation of empowering intellectual community within a chosen affinity group and, consequently, an expectation of safety from encounters with everyday anti-Black racism. When faced with a Shakespearean text that elevates "fairness" over "darkness" of complexion, reproduces negative racial stereotypes like the hypersexualized and violent Black man, moralizes good and evil with white and black imagery, and interjects racialized slurs against Black women when trying to express how beautiful a white woman is, a necessary spirit of protest boils up, and students articulate it with conviction.[7] The HBCU academic community of their peers encourages and supports the intellectual risk-taking of challenging the traditional white literary canon, and this is the place where we start.

Agreeing to disagree on canceling Shakespeare, my class and I begin this protest assignment by identifying institutional structures of our own educations in which Shakespeare is embedded. Despite discovering an eventual appreciation for Shakespeare's work, James Baldwin writes frankly of going through a period of youth when he "condemned [Shakespeare] as one of the

---

[7] Shakespeare's works celebrate whiteness and denigrate blackness both aggressively and casually, both as a philosophical abstraction and as an embodied human characteristic. See Kim F. Hall, *Things of Darkness: Economies of Race and Gender in Early Modern England* (Ithaca: Cornell University Press, 1995); and Kim F. Hall, "'These bastard signs of fair': Literary Whiteness in Shakespeare's Sonnets," in *Post-Colonial Shakespeares*, ed. Ania Loomba and Mark Orkin (London: Routledge, 1998), 64–83, which unpacks the insidious Shakespearean discourse of "fairness" and "darkness." Beyond aesthetic judgments of human blackness and whiteness, Shakespeare's writing frequently aligns black color imagery with vice, unkindness, and moral depravity, as in Sonnet 131: "In nothing art thou black save in thy deeds" (13), and when Rosalind condemns Phoebe's harsh love letter by racializing it: "Women's gentle brain / Could not drop forth such giant-rude invention, / Such Ethiop words, blacker in their effect / Than in their countenance" (*AYLI* 4.3.33–36). Even the sin of perjured vows is represented through vivid skin color imagery in Laertes's exclamation, "To hell, allegiance! Vows, to the blackest devil! / Conscience and grace, to the profoundest pit!" (*Hamlet* 4.5.132–33).

authors and architects of my oppression."[8] Like Baldwin, my students have experienced what Jason Demeter calls "the way Shakespeare has traditionally been employed as a vehicle for the transmission and replication of white supremacist ideologies within American scholastic culture."[9] Many Howard students have encountered Shakespeare's work in a predominantly white institution (PWI) classroom led by a white teacher who did not mention race. Ian Smith teaches us that academics have long "enable[d] the normative invisibility of whiteness, which is a sign of its hegemony. This critical failure is a form of protectionism, precluding scrutiny of racialized whiteness, refusing to make it visible and subject to critique."[10] Class discussion reveals that almost all of us have a specific memory of Shakespeare's work being presented to us as the "universal" epitome of peerless style, content, and linguistic innovation. For students of color, this kind of subject matter and pedagogical approach fosters the conflicted perception of the self that W. E. B. Du Bois has named "double-consciousness,"

> this sense of always looking at one's self through the eyes of others, of measuring one's soul by the tape of a world that looks on in amused contempt and pity. One feels his two-ness,—an American, a Negro; two souls, two thoughts, two unreconciled strivings; two warring ideals in one dark body, whose dogged strength alone keeps it from being torn asunder.[11]

A more contemporary text by scholar Marcos Gonsalez provides another accessible inroad for a discussion about intersectionality and power in the classroom. Gonsalez writes eloquently and heartbreakingly about encountering Shakespeare in the American school system "as a poor and gay and mentally ill and fat and Mexican-Puerto Rican person existing in the margins of the United States" and how he learned at every level that "the language of Shakespeare is the

---

[8] James Baldwin, "Why I Stopped Hating Shakespeare" (1964), *The Cross of Redemption* (New York: Pantheon, 2010), 53.

[9] Jason Demeter, "African-American Shakespeares: Loving Blackness as Political Resistance," in *Teaching Social Justice Through Shakespeare: Why Renaissance Literature Matters Now*, ed. Hillary Eklund and Wendy Beth Hyman (Edinburgh: Edinburgh University Press, 2019), 63.

[10] Ian Smith, "We are Othello: Speaking of Race in Early Modern Studies," *Shakespeare Quarterly* 67, no. 1 (2016): 107.

[11] W. E. B. Du Bois, "Strivings of the Negro People," *The Atlantic*, August 1897, https://www.theatlantic.com/magazine/archive/1897/08/strivings-of-the-negro-people/305446/.

language of whiteness."[12] My students and I brainstorm what institutional and pedagogical changes are needed to support Gonsalez's desire to learn without code-switching when he asserts,

> I want to read as many dead white writers as I can. I have a voracious appetite to read literature from every historical period and place on this planet. But I must read them from this body. This body built of colonization. This body built from the pillaging and massacring and dispossessing of the indigenous peoples of the Americas. This body hundreds of years in the making which I now read from.[13]

How can we analyze Shakespeare by mobilizing *all* of our preexisting linguistic, experiential, and cultural knowledge?

In teaching Shakespeare, I always provide early modern historical context information about how sixteenth-century constructions of "race" differ significantly from our twenty-first-century concepts of "race," but this lesson plan starts with contemporary art to build on the students' preexisting knowledge of recent social justice issues and their preexisting skills in visual analysis. To scaffold the proactive critical approach I would like them to use in their analysis of Shakespeare, I define "protest art" broadly:

> Protest art is any form of public art produced by artists creating activist messages to effect social change. It is often seen at public demonstrations and carries political demands to change laws or attitudes currently in place. The end goal of protest art is some kind of action rather than passive appreciation.[14]

Then I present examples of twentieth- and twenty-first-century American protest art and ask the students to articulate what change the artists want to effect and how they persuade their audiences to act to make it happen.[15] In particular, we dissect the "SILENCE = DEATH" (1987) poster with the pink triangle on a black background

---

[12] Marcos Gonsalez, "Caliban Never Belonged to Shakespeare: What Shakespeare's 'Thing of Darkness' Tells us about Gatekeeping and Language," *Literary Hub*, July 26, 2019, https://lithub.com/caliban-never-belonged-to-shakespeare/.

[13] Marcos Gonsalez, "Recognizing the Enduring Whiteness of Jane Austen," *Literary Hub*, December 11, 2019, https://lithub.com/recognizing-the-enduring-whiteness-of-jane-austen/.

[14] Class handout and assignment description, Elisa Oh.

[15] Thessaly La Force, Zoë Lescaze, Nancy Hass, and M. H. Miller, "The 25 Most Influential Works of American Protest Art Since World War II," *New York Times*, October 15, 2020, https://www.nytimes.com/2020/10/15/t-magazine/most-influential-protest-art.html, provides good examples of how artists use both visual and verbal rhetoric to protest broad abstractions like belief systems, prejudices, and inequality.

created to raise awareness of the AIDS epidemic and galvanize political action to combat it. The tiny text below the boldface slogan provokes activist questioning of the status quo and calls for specific actions to fight for greater social justice for LGBTQIA+ individuals:

> Why is Reagan silent about AIDS? What is really going on at the Center for Disease Control, the Federal Drug Administration, and the Vatican? Gays and lesbians are not expendable ... Use your power ... Vote ... Boycott ... Defend yourselves ... Turn anger, fear, grief into action.

Chillingly, the pink triangle is a visual reference to the badge the Nazis used to mark homosexuals, but the historical visual "citation" also encodes a subtle message of empowerment in the fact that the Nazi sign is turned upside down.

Artist Dread Scott also cites and builds on a history of social injustice in his creation of a black flag installation, "A MAN WAS LYNCHED BY POLICE YESTERDAY" (2015), which echoes the format, colors, and design of the flag flown outside NAACP headquarters in New York City from 1920 to 1938 in response to the news of each Black American who had been lynched.[16] The original flag read "A MAN WAS LYNCHED YESTERDAY" and galvanized awareness of and action to counter the racial terror campaign that raged while white Americans refused to acknowledge or oppose it. When mainstream white American audiences in 1989 thought about Nazis murdering homosexuals and in 2015 thought about Jim Crow-era lynching of African Americans, their initial response was horrified disbelief that such injustices could ever happen in their supposedly enlightened and tolerant society. However, protest art engages with the past by claiming that historical human rights abuses continue today in new forms.

Using these visual provocations as a critical lens for studying Shakespeare, we must question the active harm that silences can cause and perpetuate, such as the senators who do not speak up to defend Othello; the attempt to erase the existence of Aaron and Tamora's baby; and the words Caliban cannot speak aloud to Prospero for fear of physical punishment. This visual rhetoric also prompts us to break the pedagogical silences about the role that Shakespeare's works played in normalizing anti-Black racial constructions in Anglo-American culture.

---

[16] Dread Scott, "A Man Was Lynched by Police Yesterday," 2015, https://www.dreadscott.net/portfolio_page/a-man-was-lynched-by-police-yesterday/.

Statues, Portraits, and Toxic History: Scaffolding Protest across Different Media

With the activist intentions of protest art in our minds, my students and I then look at the many ways that protesters are currently engaging with public statues of Confederate soldiers and enslavers. The worldwide protests in the summer of 2020, following the death of George Floyd at the hands of Minneapolis police officers, spawned myriad acts of symbolic retribution against the historic perpetrators of anti-Black racism.[17] For our assignment, I focused on the statue of Robert E. Lee in Richmond, Virginia, located only two hours away from our Washington, DC campus. Black Lives Matter protests in favor of taking the statue down developed while I formulated this lesson. This bronze equestrian statue by Antonin Mercié stood on a huge white pedestal on Monument Avenue in Richmond, the capital of the Confederacy between 1861 and 1865 (Figure 2.1). Unveiled in 1890, the statue embodies the post-Reconstruction values of a resurgent white supremacy, which was asserting itself not only through lynching and segregation but also through myth-making nostalgia for the Confederacy's "Lost Cause."

Mayor Levar Stoney had the jurisdiction to remove other Confederate statues in response to protests, but the Lee statue stood on state-owned land, so it remained standing while the case went through lengthy legal battles. Before the Virginia Supreme Court ruled that then-Governor Ralph Northam did have the power to remove the statue and it was finally taken down in September 2021, community protests surged around it, producing demonstrations, graffiti, and nighttime projections of "BLM" above images of African American activists like Frederick Douglass and Angela Davis as well as images of African Americans recently killed by police violence.

The images of these diverse protest interventions, such as the graffiti "annotation" of the monument in Figure 2.1, are thrilling to unpack with students in class. Students analyze the multivocal symbolic struggle to assert the value of African American lives in past

---

[17] Only available after the end of my classes using this lesson plan, the Toppled Monuments Archive collects records of all the worldwide monument protests since 2020 that "toppled, defaced, contested, and removed monuments" (https://www.toppledmonumentsarchive.org/the-collective). Monument Lab's "National Monument Audit" is another resource showing how American monuments are overwhelmingly white and male and celebrate many colonizers and enslavers (https://monumentlab.com/monumentlab-nationalmonumentaudit.pdf).

Figure 2.1 Robert E. Lee statue, Richmond, Virginia. August 29, 2020. MediaPunch Inc./Alamy Stock Photo.

and present-day America. The graffiti on the pedestal challenges the white supremacist ideologies the statue itself stands for. In addition to anger and mourning for those lives lost to racist police violence, it also expresses exuberant pride in Black survivance and defiant rejection of the racist history that raised the monument.[18] The spray paint marks, the makeshift memorials, and the surrounding community gathering space represent the reclamation and reinterpretation of an outdated piece of art that no longer represents public opinion. Further, this protest art shows how every person is entitled to add active, outspoken commentary on the concrete and abstract "monuments" they oppose in their lives.

This lesson asks students to apply this visual metaphor of critical intervention to Shakespeare's work and its cultural legacy. Our discussion wrestles with these questions: what if Shakespeare is a "monument" in literary studies? How did he get to that position? What is the most appropriate and effective response from critics who do not wish to celebrate the ideas that this "monument"

---

[18] Gerald Vizenor coined the term "survivance" to encompass not only Native peoples' survival of white settler colonial violence but also their creative, thriving resistance to it. See Vizenor, *Fugitive Poses: Native American Indian Scenes of Absence and Presence* (Lincoln: University of Nebraska Press, 1998). I am grateful to Marissa Greenberg for this point.

represents? Further, there has not been one, simple answer to what to do with racist monuments after they are taken down. If you think Shakespeare should be "taken down" from the canon, then what? Once the Bard is demoted from universal superiority, should the works be thrown away? Quietly ignored in storage? Put in a critical edition and displayed with a full academic explanation of its historical context? Marked up with public criticism from today's diverse readers?

Another question to ask as the monuments come down is: what is the proper fate of their empty pedestals? As Seeta Chaganti argues, "by the logic of Chaucer's poem [*The House of Fame*], it takes both a statue *and* a pedestal to make a memorial structure: the prop beneath is integral to a memorial's form and function." That is, the pillars under each famous author's figure "uphold the meanings of what is atop them."[19] Class discussion can prompt the students to extend the metaphor: if Shakespeare is the monument statue, is the pedestal the systemic and institutional support that gives the statue its grandeur, height, and status? Every monument is ideologically "held up" by many institutions, and once students start unpacking the land ownership, artist patronage, and cost of the labor and materials, we collectively map out diverse structures of social privilege that converge in every work of monumental public art.[20] In the case of the literary canon, how might we critically apply Chaganti's call to "deny systemic oppression a platform"?[21]

Drawing further on students' preexisting visual analysis skills to galvanize ideological critique of historically celebrated art, this Shakespeare protest assignment turns to the work of artist Titus Kaphar. Kaphar's words and artwork focus audience attention on social justice, and he models complicated, nuanced intellectual engagement with classical western art traditions. Students watch his powerful TED Talk for homework, and we discuss in class the paintings in his *Seeing Through Time* series. His TED Talk recounts not only the marginalization of African American representation in his art history education, but also his challenge of explaining to

---

[19] Seeta Chaganti, "B-Sides: Chaucer's House of Fame," *Public Books*, February 14, 2019 (original emphasis), https://www.publicbooks.org/b-sides-chaucers-the-house-of-fame/.

[20] Former Virginia Governor Ralph Northam has had the statue and pedestal taken down and the land transferred back to city jurisdiction. See Gregory Schneider, "Virginia to Dismantle Pedestal where Robert E. Lee Statue Stood in Richmond," *Washington Post*, December 5, 2021, https://www.washingtonpost.com/dc-md-va/2021/12/05/lee-statue-richmond-virginia-monument-avenue/.

[21] Chaganti, "B-Sides."

his young son why the Native American man and the Black man by the equestrian statue of Theodore Roosevelt that stood in front of the American Museum of Natural History in New York City are walking while the white man rides a horse. He asks, "Is there a way for us to amend our public sculptures, our national monuments? Not erase them, but is there a way to amend them?"[22] He displays a large copy he has made of a seventeenth-century European aristocratic family by Frans Hals and vigorously paints over the white family members with white paint until the viewer's focus shifts to the round, vulnerable face of a young Black boy who is holding the horse. This whiting-out exercise brings the Black experience in western history to the front of our minds and exposes the institutions, white supremacist "vision," and erasures necessary to make this child visible yet invisible at the same time.

Challenging his audience's sense of *justice through time* even further, Kaphar adds linseed oil to his white paint, noting that it will allow the faces of the enslavers to show through again in time. He raises a valuable point for debate: "I'm not saying erase it. We can't erase this history. It's real. We have to know it."[23] For our class discussion of literary scholarship, Kaphar prompts us to ask whether another layer of erasure is the best way to seek social justice for historical acts of injustice. Kaphar professes, "I want to make paintings, I want to make sculptures that are honest, that wrestle with the struggles of our past but speak to the diversity and advances of our present. And we can't do that by taking an eraser and getting rid of stuff."[24] He proposes that we do not attempt to eradicate the past but *amend* it, like the Constitution, which shows the changes that were made through history to the law of the land.

To learn from a contemporary African American artist who engages with and yet talks back to a racist piece of European art, my students and I take in the visual eloquence of Kaphar's *Seeing Through Time 2* (2018) alongside the seventeenth-century portrait it "cites" and radically revises (Figures 2.2 and 2.3). After noting the historical context of the founding of the Royal African Company in

---

[22] Titus Kaphar, "Can Art Amend History?," *TED Talks*, August 1, 2017, https://www.ted.com/talks/titus_kaphar_can_art_amend_history?language=en. Since the time of this talk, widespread criticism of the racism in the Roosevelt statue arose in 2020, and with the support of the museum, the New York City Commission on Controversial Monuments, and the mayor Bill de Blasio, it was contextualized in an exhibit and then taken down in January 2022. See American Museum of Natural History, "Addressing the Statue," https://www.amnh.org/exhibitions/addressing-the-statue.

[23] Kaphar, "Can Art Amend History?"

[24] Kaphar, "Can Art Amend History?"

Social Justice Pedagogy and Shakespeare's "Monument" 55

Figure 2.2 *Louise de Kéroualle, Duchess of Portsmouth with an unknown female attendant.* Pierre Mignard, oil on canvas, 1682. 47½ × 37½ inches. © National Portrait Gallery, London.

1660 and the exponential increase in English perpetration of the transatlantic slave trade through the century, we dissect the cultural values embedded in the 1682 Pierre Mignard portrait of Charles II's mistress Louise de Kéroualle, Duchess of Portsmouth, with a female attendant of African descent. Students immediately recognize the centering of white female beauty and her power and wealth. Further, we notice the objectification and subordination of the African child in the composition and the way the artist uses her to create a skin color contrast with Kéroualle. The girl can be seen as a visual metaphor, the students point out, because Mignard represents her as yet another colonial possession similar to the coral and pearls she offers in her hands.

Kaphar's painting challenges the original work's bitter injustice of the young girl's enslavement by cutting out the white woman and centering a lushly beautiful portrait of a Black woman within the outlines of the enslaver. Her intense, direct gaze from a side-turning angle elicits awe and then overflowing debate among my students: they theorize that, according to the painting's title, she could be the

Figure 2.3 *Seeing Through Time* 2. Titus Kaphar, oil on canvas, 2018. 92 × 72 inches. © Titus Kaphar, courtesy Gagosian.

young girl's mother, whom she is "seeing through time" in the past, or she could be the strong, proud woman the girl will grow up to be in the future. They also consider whether this subject's wary but unflinching gaze could be the clear vision of someone like them, a twenty-first-century woman "seeing through time," to analyze the legacy of enslavement of her ancestors. Kaphar's painting sets up a dynamic dialogue between the past and present, and the reflective viewer takes away the urgent need for Black lives to matter through activist critique of history's harmful paradigms of race.

After thinking together about political protest art, Confederate statue debates, and Titus Kaphar's re-visionary work with the European portrait tradition, I give an assignment for students to create their own work of protest art using a specific Shakespeare sonnet or play that they have read and discussed in class. I aim to promote social justice in the classroom by shifting agency and power from the instructor to the student while still maintaining rigorous expectations for expanding critical thinking, close reading, and written argumentation with a constant attention to audience. Akin to the active and resistant act of "restorying" that Penelope Geng describes in her essay in this volume, students become the critical remakers of oppressive cultural traditions. I emphasize that the students are fully entitled to produce work that is antithetical to what the professor believes and can still receive full marks if they demonstrate deep and responsible engagement with the text and subject matter they choose to protest. I ask them to submit a piece of artwork in any media (digital or hard copy, poem, image, audio file, or video) and a four-page expository essay explaining their project's inspiration, intent, and chosen rhetorical strategies. The written portion must include a definition of "protest art" and specify what they want to provoke their audience to *do* in relation to one particular Shakespeare text. Some students choose to write a longer expository essay on the theme of protest if they feel more skillful in this genre, but most embrace the opportunity to submit a creative work. The choice of genre works to expand what Mary Janell Metzger's essay in this volume calls the students' "increasing sense of educational agency."

The assignment prompt asks the students to apply the collective work we have done interpreting the protest art to their own critical projects:

> The premise of this assignment is that literary art should be subject to the same kind of critical and creative interventions that these artists are doing with the original monuments or celebratory portrait art. Let's consider the works of William Shakespeare a literature "monument" that has been granted value by centuries of cultural approval, but what if that value is arbitrarily constructed and is not absolute or enduring? In your mind, what aspects of Shakespeare's writing and/or legacy need to be questioned, dismantled, or radically reevaluated? Why? Take one sonnet or 14–25 lines from a play, and use them as the basis for a work of protest art that reveals, interprets, wrestles with, dismantles, and protests the sexism, antisemitism, anti-Black racism, or any specific ideology in the text.

I follow this broad description with a list of questions calculated to make each thinker hone an argument through focus on audience and specificity:

- What is the specific audience for your work of protest art based on Shakespeare?
- What objective ideas, emotions, and practical actions do you want to inspire in your artwork's viewers?

- What are the specific points of contact, debate, tension, or protest between the text and your own present-day opinions and demands for action?
- How will you show the original "monument" text (and what it used to stand for) with, under, through, or beside your words and images, as well as how it is reconfigured in your call for action?
- How will you create an intellectual engagement with a painful past that provokes its audience to change its mind and to engage in activist action?
- What is an ideal location, public space, or media in which to publish, circulate, or display your protest art to the public? Can you, your classmates, or I help to make that happen?

In addition to sharing these protest art pieces with each other in class, we also created a bulletin board display of their projects in the English Department for fellow Howard students to see.[25] Alongside their artwork, the students tacked brief handwritten statements of what they wanted to accomplish with their protest art and shared affirming compliments on each other's work as they worked on the bulletin board. I asked for everyone's verbal consent before inviting students to take pictures of the collective work on the bulletin board to post on social media. The sense of audience and impact widened with every choice to publicize the assignment, and students' rhetorical choices shifted depending on whether they wanted to persuade their fellow Howard students, their other English professors, their social media followers, or the world in general.

The students responded with a wide variety of projects, most incorporating visual elements that would not have appeared in a traditional expository essay. Many students wove in deeply personal commentary, particularly about the experience of encountering pressure in PWI classrooms to code-switch and to discover a love of Shakespeare rather than Black authors who reflected their own identities. They also frequently included text components that were presented in visually engaging, unconventional, or irreverent ways. Some based their work on one of the pieces of protest art introduced in class prior to the assignment, and others took new approaches. Following the lead of the graffiti artists, some projects used digital or handwritten media to create textual palimpsests, writing over the top of a Shakespearean text, including crossing out words like anti-Black slurs and tropes that still showed through

---

[25] Students could opt out of displaying or signing their work in either venue.

from the original text. Several students created side-by-side "blackout" poems where a Shakespearean poem or speech was transformed by their selective blacking out of some words. One student poet moved an image of the page from *Titus Andronicus* discussing Aaron's baby to appear half off the page and literally centered her own two poems expressing Black pride: the first poem featured the fictionalized voice of a sixteenth-century Black child, and the second poem featured her own voice as a twenty-first-century Black child. Another poem used crossed-out but still legible lines about Aaron from *Titus Andronicus* to create an acrostic poem spelling BLACK LIVES MATTER.

Powerful visual rhetoric defined other projects that asserted the need for a more diverse high school and university literature curriculum. For example, one student wrote in red "spray paint" the names of great African American writers on top of an image of a Shakespeare statue. Complex collages juxtaposed cut-out words like "moor" with images of Othello, Aaron, and Caliban alongside images of blackface minstrel performance, anti-Black candy advertisements, a racist cartoon of Venus Williams, and photographs of a lynching and of incarcerated African American men. In bringing together these words and images, the project asserted that Shakespeare's language of race participates in a long and continuous history of American anti-Black racism. A brilliant, poster-sized textual collage cut up several used books, creating jagged edges around speeches where Prospero denigrates Caliban or Caliban admits to Prospero's superior power. This piece used a dark highlighter marker to cross out racialized slurs on pages of *Othello*, and the student incorporated the dust jacket from a used copy of Maynard Mack's 1993 monograph *Everybody's Shakespeare* with a line drawn through the word "Everybody's" and using her own handwriting to interject scathing marginal comments that his summary of critical responses to *Othello* was clearly not aimed at Black readers.

In addition to outlining the labor-based grading contract for the class, my grading rubric cites the Conference on College Composition and Communication's July 2020 Demand for Black Linguistic Justice.[26] I also clarify that

> this course does not require, expect, or reward code-switching as a way to succeed. I do expect rigorous attention to *audience* when you

---

[26] April Baker-Bell et al., "This Ain't Another Statement! This Is a DEMAND for Black Linguistic Justice!," *Conference on College Composition and Communication (CCCC)*, July 2020, https://cccc.ncte.org/cccc/demand-for-black-linguistic-justice.

construct arguments, and we will weigh the rhetorical usefulness of establishing common ground in your language choices. However, effective expository writing should never come at the expense of linguistic self-erasure.

Therefore, some of the students' submissions were in African American Vernacular English (AAVE); others, with creative, selective precision, incorporated aspects of the language(s) they speak both inside and outside the classroom. Using their critical vocabulary beyond Standardized English (SE) enriches students' rhetorical confidence and virtuosity, and this process of code meshing acknowledges that all home languages hold equal value to SE and emphasizes that students have a wealth of preexisting knowledge that exceeds their instructor.

Howard students come to the intellectual work of literary criticism in an institutional context that has a proud tradition of social justice protest. Referencing this history allows Howard students to connect their institutional identity to the analytic work they do in a class on Shakespeare. Since Howard's founding in 1867, students and faculty have led notable political protests throughout the last century. For instance, they protested a 1934 crime convention in Washington, DC that was not addressing lynching, job discrimination, or racial segregation in the Capitol region. Howard students' active NAACP chapter demonstrated for civil rights legislation, voting rights, and school integration, and hundreds of students held a sit-in that became an occupation of the Howard University Administration Building in March 1968 to demand fairness in student discipline and a greater curricular focus on African American history.[27] Returning to campus in the fall of 2021 after over a year of pandemic distance learning, Howard students staged a thirty-three-day protest of subpar dormitory conditions and lack of shared governance, since the student, alumni, and faculty voting members of the Board of Trustees had been silently removed during the pandemic.[28] So while my students were producing this protest assignment, they were engaged in their own protest in their particular institutional context, occupying the Blackburn Student Center and camping out in the Yard in variable fall weather.

---

[27] DC Historic Preservation Office, "Civil Rights Tour: Protest—Howard University," DC Historic Sites, https://historicsites.dcpreservation.org/items/show/1009.
[28] Jonathan Franklin, "Howard University Students Reach an Agreement with Officials after a Month of Protest," NPR, November 15, 2021, https://www.npr.org/2021/11/15/1055929172/howard-university-students-end-protest-housing-agreement.

Through this lesson, my students and I found that Shakespeare's work repays deeply engaged attention to unequal power relationships within the texts as well as attention to the unjust institutional structures in academia and American society that grant it canonical exceptionalism. The undergraduate classroom is the gateway to diverse, courageous postdoctoral early modern scholarship, and it has become increasingly urgent to rewrite the pedagogical practices that are pushing students of color away from studying Shakespeare and other early modern literature.[29] At other institutions with different instructors and different student demographics of diversity, both seen and unseen, the protest assignment I have designed could be retooled to incorporate what the students are already interested in protesting. What inequality, what imbalance in power, and what unfair exercise of that power are they already experiencing? What rhetorical moves render the arguments of disempowered subjects more powerful and persuasive?

This pedagogical approach of stirring up awareness of injustice and empathy for characters who have less power than we today believe they naturally merit activates analysis of cultural values that students themselves hold dear. Exploring examples of protest art and formulating their own protest causes students to investigate their own relationship with canonical literature and make their own decisions about literary "greatness" that they have never been invited to weigh or question before. A class discussion about activist art can produce a stimulating synergy of ideas about how to dismantle patriarchy, counteract economic inequality, and persuasively articulate resistance to racism, ableism, and homophobia in literature—and in everyday life. In short, it is a safe way to practice expressing strong opinions in the service of justice and challenging authority at many levels in the future. Amplifying existing student protest not only works toward decolonizing and reformulating our approach to early modern texts but also fosters critical thinking, persuasive writing, and more nuanced understandings of past intellectual connections to our present cultural moment in America.

---

[29] Kimberly Anne Coles, Kim F. Hall, and Ayanna Thompson call for urgent changes across the profession of premodern and early modern studies to diversify the "pipeline" through teaching, mentoring, citing, and hiring of nonwhite scholars. "BlacKKKShakespearean: A Call to Action for Medieval and Early Modern Studies," *MLA Profession*, November 2019, https://profession.mla.org/blackkkshakespearean-a-call-to-action-for-medieval-and-early-modern-studies/.

Chapter 3

Teaching Shakespeare at an Urban Public Community College: An Equity-Driven Approach
Victoria M. Muñoz

The City University of New York (CUNY) has long been a driver of equity in higher education. Nevertheless, many students fall through the cracks in New York's funding systems. Nearly fifty years have passed since the 1976 financial crisis that eliminated CUNY's free tuition program, in place in various forms since 1847. The state's current, full-tuition Excelsior Scholarship does not grant eligibility to everyone. For instance, it excludes students "who began an associate's degree or a bachelor's degree who had a break in attendance."[1] This policy affects many college students who experience life events that interrupt their schooling. In practice, diversity and inclusion programs designed to recruit minoritized students often fail to adequately address their financial needs.[2] For example, in a recent interview with David Letterman, American rapper Cardi B recalled that her education at Borough of Manhattan Community College, CUNY was plagued by financial burdens she carried even as the recipient of a need-based scholarship. The New York State Higher Education Services Corporation, which coordinates need-based financial aid programs, advises students of a number of such "variable costs" that are excluded from financial aid: textbooks, housing, meals, transportation, personal and living expenses.[3] In order to shoulder these variable costs, Cardi B found work as a cashier, but

---

[1] New York State Higher Education Services Corporation (NYS HESC), "Excelsior Scholarship FAQs," https://www.hesc.ny.gov/pay-for-college/financial-aid/types-of-financial-aid/nys-grants-scholarships-awards/the-excelsior-scholarship/excelsior-scholarship-faqs.html (accessed June 2, 2022).

[2] See Erin Castro, "Addressing the Conceptual Challenges of Equity Work: A Blueprint for Getting Started," in *Understanding Equity in Community College Practice*, ed. Castro (San Francisco: Jossey-Bass, 2015), 1–10.

[3] NYS HESC, "Before You Borrow," https://www.hesc.ny.gov/pay-for-college/smart-borrowing/before-you-borrow.html (accessed June 3, 2022). Many CUNY students deal with food and housing insecurity.

her earnings were insufficient. She dropped out of college after a couple of semesters. She concluded that in New York City, "to go to college here, just because they're giving you financial aid, you still need money."⁴

Cardi B's experience points to a largely unacknowledged disconnect between many college students' experiences of financial precarity, which subsumes all aspects of academic life, and the privileged assumptions that guide American higher education. As a field traditionally aligned to privilege, Shakespeare studies has been especially historically susceptible to enacting policies and practices that tacitly ignore the inequitable lived conditions that students bring to the classroom. This essay contributes to the evolving conversation around inclusive Shakespeare pedagogy and social justice by presenting an equity-centered approach inspired by my own experiences as an assistant professor at Eugenio María de Hostos Community College (hereafter Hostos), an urban public community college within CUNY. Hostos is a Hispanic-Serving Institution with strong ties to Latin American colonial liberation and education movements in the revolutionary tradition of its namesake, the Puerto Rican intellectual, abolitionist, and activist Eugenio María de Hostos (1839–1903).⁵ It is the first college in the United States to be named after a Puerto Rican. As Inmaculada Lara-Bonilla observes, since its founding in 1968, Hostos has embodied "the most long-lasting educational rights gain that Puerto Ricans and other Latinas/os have ever attained on the US mainland."⁶ As I describe in this essay, it is in this radical educational tradition pioneered by Hostos that my approach to teaching Shakespeare is anchored.

By way of addressing the multi-situational struggles that many students carry with them into the classroom, a familiar mantra at Hostos is *meet students where they are*.⁷ The philosophy outlines

---

⁴ David Letterman, "Cardi B," *My Next Guest Needs No Introduction with David Letterman* (Netflix Corporation, 2022).

⁵ Born in Puerto Rico, Eugenio María de Hostos devoted his life to abolishing Spanish colonial rule. A vocal advocate for the Antillean Confederation and slavery's abolition, he further condemned the abuse of Chinese indentured servants in Perú and promoted women's educational rights. He founded normal schools for both sexes, a women's teaching school, a kindergarten, and a laborers' night school. Currently buried in Santo Domingo, he instructed prior to his death that his remains be removed to Puerto Rico upon its independence.

⁶ Inmaculada Lara-Bonilla, "Crafting a Latina/o Higher Education Rights Discourse in New York: The Founding and 'Saving' of Eugenio María de Hostos Community College," *New York History* 97, no. 2 (2016): 187.

⁷ Professors learn it during their first week of New Faculty Orientation led by Professor Cynthia Jones.

Hostos's institutional mission "to meet the higher educational needs of people from this and similar communities who historically have been excluded from higher education."[8] Hostos's proud history of student-centered educational activism well embodies CUNY's historic strides in equitable public education at the apogee of late-1960s social justice movements onward. Amid New York's financial crisis of 1976, in fact, Hostos was nearly shut down, but in a historic feat, students and community leaders organized a series of campus occupations to keep its doors open. "Save Hostos" brought together "local grassroots organizing, intense struggle, and a network of complex, multi-directional discourses and alliances," and the college endured.[9] Today, Hostos continues its equity mission in service to the college's majority-global-majority, predominantly Black and Latinx/e student population, rooted in the multilingual, multicultural, and multinational identities of New York's South Bronx.[10]

Erin Castro defines higher education equity as "the idea that students from historically and contemporarily marginalized and minoritized communities have access to what they need in order to be successful."[11] Each section of this essay accordingly expresses ways that I meet Hostos students where they are in situations cultural/ideological, financial, and technical so that they may excel in their study of Shakespeare. In reflecting upon my own classroom instruction, this essay also confronts larger institutional forces that disadvantage lower-income students of color in higher education, and it offers practiced pedagogical tools for scholar-educators to negate such exertions of privilege and power. By tackling the unspoken assumptions that inform practices in the traditional Shakespeare classroom and course design, this essay thus proposes edifying changes to higher education.

Teaching and Interrogating at a Distance

There is perhaps no more mentally distressing situation than cultural or ideological alienation from one's subject of study. Shakespeare's

---

[8] Hostos Community College, "Our Mission," https://hostos.cuny.edu/About-Hostos/Our-Mission (accessed October 20, 2022).
[9] Lara-Bonilla, "Crafting," 3.
[10] The college began under a dual-language transitional curricular model. Today, classes are taught in English, but lingual Hispanidad pervades college life.
[11] Castro, "Addressing," 6.

language is especially alienating for students who have not been acquainted with his works or who have otherwise rejected prior impositions of his presumed universality. When that general alienation is further aggravated by forces of social and economic oppression, the challenge of reading Shakespeare can be so personally devastating as to provoke feelings of inadequacy. Systemic factors stemming from an elitist academic monoculture reinforce the idea that Shakespeare is not meant for minoritized students—that college itself is not meant for them. This messaging evinces what Paolo Freire describes in *Pedagogy of the Oppressed* (1968) as the "myth of the industriousness of the oppressors and the laziness and dishonesty of the oppressed."[12] Higher education already holds students to inherently racist assessment standards.[13] Shakespeare's dominance in the curriculum further reinforces that prejudicial standard by suggesting that implements of academic expression and analysis, which are predicated on content mastery, are only available to the elites.

This is precisely what happens in Shakespeare classrooms where minoritized students are expected to demonstrate mastery of literary content that has historically excluded them and, furthermore, are judged when they fail to meet prejudicial norms. Castro describes this phenomenon as "educational deficit thinking," which occurs when "institutions, through their policies, practices, language, and thinking, blame individual students for what they perceivably lack."[14] Orator and writing center pedagogue Neisha-Anne Green offers one remedy for educational deficit thinking in her recollection of an incident from her early days as a tutor working with students at Bronx-based Lehman College, CUNY:

> And one day, this student walks in. [. . .] I look at the text the student was reading, and honest to God, I don't remember what the text was, but I do remember her and the braids she wore, I remember her complexion, and I do remember what I said to her. So, I looked at the text and I asked her to read this paragraph and to "tell me about it in your own words, what you think the author is saying?" and again she's got nothing. [. . .] I said, "Now look, when this stuff was written, as is most stuff, we weren't ever in the intended audience, especially this piece. [. . .] We were never expected to learn how to

---

[12] Paolo Freire, *Pedagogy of the Oppressed*, trans. Myra Bergman Ramos (New York: Bloomsbury, 2018), 140.

[13] See Alexandra L. Milsom, "Assessing and Transgressing: On the Racist Origins of Academic Standardization," *Nineteenth-Century Gender Studies* 17, no. 1 (2021): n.p., http://ncgsjournal.com/issue171/milsom.html.

[14] Castro, "Addressing," 9.

read, much less go to college, but you're here. And so even though shit isn't written for you, what you need to do is to take what you know, take what makes you you, take all that stuff and apply it to this work and make it yours."[15]

Imagine for a moment that Green's student were reading Shakespeare. How might this student feel if, instead of learning that this standard college reading material was never meant for her, she were told that her struggles resulted from a personal deficit in her college preparation? Might she subsequently conclude that students like her weren't meant for college?

What does it mean for teacher-scholars of Shakespeare that some students must reckon with the fact that this material wasn't written for them, and that, even still, they must struggle to understand it? This is a question that Shakespeare practitioners must themselves reckon with in the classroom, where the goal of all activities and assessments should be to give students equitable footing for success. In order to combat educational deficit thinking, instructors must first acknowledge that minoritized students' struggles with Shakespeare result not from a personal deficit in their preparation, but from the fact that this "shit [wasn't] written" for them, and then to advocate, as Green does, for students to find an entry point to the material in their own experiences. Instructors must meet these students where they are, at an ideological distance from the material, and then structure activities and assessments accordingly.

In my own research, I have personally grappled with Shakespeare's serviceability to myths of British imperial exceptionalism and white saviorism.[16] Trailblazing work by scholars of early modern race such as Kim F. Hall, Ania Loomba, Jonathan Burton, Peter Erickson, Imtiaz Habib, Urvashi Chakravarty, Ayanna Thompson, and Margo Hendricks, representing decades of archival and public-facing scholarship, has uncovered Shakespeare studies' complicity in that racial-imperial project.[17] Such scholars as David Sterling Brown

---

[15] Neisha-Anne Green, "Moving beyond Alright: And the Emotional Toll of This, My Life Matters Too, in the Writing Center Work," *The Writing Center Journal* 37, no. 1 (2018): 21–22.

[16] See Victoria M. Muñoz, *Spanish Romance in the Battle for Global Supremacy: Tudor and Stuart Black Legends*, Anthem World Epic and Romance (London: Anthem, 2021), esp. 191–201.

[17] Kim Hall, *Things of Darkness: Economies of Race and Gender in Early Modern England* (Ithaca: Cornell University Press, 1995); Ania Loomba and Jonathan Burton, eds., *Race in Early Modern England: A Documentary Companion* (London: Palgrave Macmillan, 2007); Peter Erickson and Kim F. Hall, "'A New Scholarly Song': Rereading Early Modern Race," *Shakespeare Quarterly* 67 (2016): 1–13; Imtiaz

and Arthur L. Little, Jr. have also brought conversations about (early) modern race to bear on Shakespeare's contemporary public standing.[18] In light of this pivotal work, I cannot divorce my own sense of Shakespeare as an adopted idol of Britain's colonial empire from my personal instruction to students who have been directly and indirectly impacted by colonialism's exploitative legacies. Atrocities past and present compel me to reject claims to Shakespeare's universality, a term that has often implied Shakespeare's presumed civilizing effect on students.

In this vein, one of the first issues students and I tackle is the proverbial inescapability of Shakespeare as an uncanny spirit of British imperialism haunting the literary and cultural present. Perhaps no play better encompasses this phenomenon than *Hamlet*. (*"Enter ghost."*[19]) *Hamlet*'s outsized influence as an imperial monument erected worldwide reinforces the idea that the professor acquainting students with the play is depositing civilization in them. This phenomenon evinces what Freire describes as the "banking concept of education, which serves the interests of oppression."[20] Freire advocates replacing this concept with a collaborative and dialogic one, in which students become knowledge co-creators, critiquing culture through collective discourse taking place against the ideological center. As collaborative dialogists, my students model Green's dictum to take what makes them them—their personal responses to the content—and use that as their entry point to grappling with Shakespeare.[21]

Habib, *Black Lives in the English Archives, 1500–1677: Imprints of the Invisible*, 2nd ed. (Abingdon: Routledge, 2016); Urvashi Chakravarty, "The Renaissance of Race and the Future of Early Modern Race Studies," *English Literary Renaissance* 50, no. 1 (2020): 17–24; Ayanna Thompson, *Passing Strange: Shakespeare, Race, and Contemporary America* (Oxford: Oxford University Press, 2011); Ayanna Thompson, ed., *The Cambridge Companion to Shakespeare and Race* (Cambridge: Cambridge University Press, 2021); Margo Hendricks, "Coloring the Past, Considerations on Our Future: RaceB4Race," *New Literary History* 52, no. 3/4 (2021): 365–84.

[18] David Sterling Brown and Arthur L. Little, Jr., "'To Teach Shakespeare for Survival: Talking with David Sterling Brown and Arthur L. Little Jr.,'" *Public Books*, November 5, 2021, https://www.publicbooks.org/to-teach-shakespeare-for-survival-talking-with-david-sterling-brown-and-arthur-l-little-jr/; Arthur L. Little, Jr., *Shakespeare Jungle Fever: National-Imperial Re-Visions of Race, Rape, and Sacrifice* (Stanford: Stanford University Press, 2000).

[19] All quotations from Shakespeare derive from the Folger Digital Texts edition. Barbara Mowat et al., *Shakespeare's Plays, Sonnets and Poems* (Washington, DC: Folger Shakespeare Library, n.d.), https://shakespeare.folger.edu (accessed October 25, 2022).

[20] Freire, *Pedagogy*, 77.

[21] Their assessed work comprises low-stakes, participatory, and drafted writing using a process- and growth-based course design.

Students also collaboratively dialogue with other first-person voices that model this kind of resistant interpretation of Shakespeare. One of these is Eugenio María de Hostos, who regarded *Hamlet* not as an episteme of imperial culture, but as an allegory for the anticolonial revolutionary's journey of conscience:

> Hamlet [. . .] ponders, in the most profound soliloquy ["To be or not to be—"] [. . .] the tremendous social and moral advantages enjoyed by him who lives in an unquestioning reality and, submitting himself to it, submits himself to the current of life, meeting obstacles perhaps, but undeterred by any of them. He will be shattered when he winds up his dizzy career, but he will have lived, because to live, in the social sense of the word, is to move, to act, to fulfill oneself, diffuse oneself in the common destiny of the current generation.[22]

In unpacking Hostos's argument, students discuss how and why Hamlet's journey represents an internal birth of consciousness that turns to revolution. They further consider what it means to devote one's life to righting an "oppressor's wrong" (3.1.79). Nevertheless, some students do not altogether buy Hostos's regard for "irresolute Hamlet"[23] as a model social dissenter. They often cite the stronger model in Fortinbras, who eagerly takes action to avenge his father's death and recover his stolen land, utterly steadfast in the righteousness of his cause. Yet, as we note, Hamlet's journey is perhaps more relatable. His diffident spirit, like the current generation's, is terrified to face the social and personal consequences of confronting injustice, but still he, and we, must act.[24]

My goal with this exercise is not only to acquaint students with the progressive ideology advocated by the celebrated Puerto Rican activist and intellectual after whom our college is named, but also to demonstrate to them how reading Shakespeare through the lens of one's personal experience, as Hostos does, can yield radically transgressive understanding of his works. As Ayanna Thompson and Laura Turchi observe, far short of universality, Shakespeare's plays

---

[22] Eugenio María de Hostos, "An Essay on 'Hamlet,'" trans. Mariesta Dodge Howland, in *Eugenio María de Hostos, Promotor of Pan Americanism*, ed. Eugenio Carlos de Hostos (Madrid: Juan Bravo, 1953), 263.

[23] Hostos, "Essay on 'Hamlet,'" 268.

[24] "There is in every revolution just such a moment," Hostos remarked. "When the unhappy peoples of Spanish America broke forever the chain which for three centuries had impeded their progress, they were launched against a void, and they were startled; they were confronted by anarchy and they were terrified. [. . .] For the peoples of Spanish America, there was a light—that of progress. They drew from it faith in their destiny, and triumphed." "Essay on 'Hamlet,'" 256.

nonetheless "offer moments of historical transcendence alongside moments of maddeningly mundane expressions of racism, sexism, anti-Semitism, etc." that gear classroom conversations toward larger questions in our social and public orbit.[25] Such moments do not establish that Shakespeare must be taught as part of a general education that all undergraduates must master. They nevertheless give cause and occasion for how Shakespeare should be taught in the service of social justice.

In my classroom, promoting social justice through thoughtful critique of Shakespeare means addressing how inequities shape students' experience of the modern world, a world that was formed in relief of Shakespeare's own. This work usually involves analytical comparison of the written text to real performance excerpts. My students have referred to performance as a "living museum" that exhibits Shakespeare to a new audience and brings timely questions about (in)justice and (in)humanity to the fore. For instance, in one activity, students must analyze Makram J. Khoury's performance of Shylock's "Hath not / a Jew eyes?" speech from the 2015 Royal Shakespeare Company production of *The Merchant of Venice* (Polly Findlay, dir.),[26] in which he rejects his mistreatment by the Christian Antonio, proclaiming:

> He hath disgraced me and
> hindered me half a million, laughed at my losses,
> mocked at my gains, scorned my nation, thwarted
> my bargains, cooled my friends, heated mine enemies—
> and what's his reason? I am a Jew. (3.1.53–57)

Students compare this emotionally charged performance to the "stranger's case" speech that Shakespeare is believed to have contributed to the play *Sir Thomas More*. In it, More condemns the "mountainish inhumanity" (6.156) of a mob of Londoners committing violence against the immigrant population.[27] I ask students, "Is Antonio guilty of 'mountainish inhumanity' in his treatment of Shylock?" "Yes!" they usually answer, elaborating their responses with references to modern-day border disputes, violence against

---

[25] Ayanna Thompson and Laura Turchi, *Teaching Shakespeare with Purpose: A Student-Centred Approach* (London: Bloomsbury, 2016), 7.

[26] Royal Shakespeare Company, *The Merchant of Venice*. Polly Findlay 2015 Production, https://www.rsc.org.uk/the-merchant-of-venice/past-productions/polly-findlay-2015-production (accessed October 26, 2022).

[27] John Jowett, ed., *Sir Thomas More*, Arden Shakespeare (London: Bloomsbury, 2011).

Latinx/e immigrants, and the Muslim ban.[28] Students typically empathize with Shylock, who has been marginalized and dehumanized, proclaimed an enemy and outsider, and yet forced to bear the brunt of his society's economic needs. They observe that Shylock's Venice seems a lot like modern-day New York City, a metropolis built by banking and corrupt money, even down to the maintenance of a ghetto for a despised underclass. Hence, to the question, "With whom would you like to share Shylock's speech?" a student once replied, "With everyone who hates us, and doesn't understand the struggle."

Understanding—At a Cost

One of the most distressing struggles that minoritized students confront in the classroom is economic insecurity. I observed this firsthand on my first day teaching at Hostos, which is situated within New York's fifteenth congressional district, the poorest in the country.[29] At the end of my first class, a student approached me to discuss the textbook selection.

"We are using [X] anthology this term," I related. "It costs twenty dollars new and fifteen dollars used. The second and third editions cost five to ten dollars."

"What if," he said slowly, "all I can afford is zero dollars?"

My face flushed with mortification. When my mother had arrived in this country as a teenager, she could not afford to buy books for school, and she had relied on the New York Public Library, along with her Spanish-English dictionary, to resource her education, including a bachelor's and two master's degrees from CUNY. She often relates how free access to books made the difference for her to ultimately climb out of poverty. I therefore should have anticipated that some students would not be able to buy the textbook. I had failed to recognize their struggle in my course design by placing the burden of access on them rather than on me.[30]

---

[28] They read Ruben Espinosa's essay, "Shakespeare and Your Mountainish Inhumanity," *The Sundial*, August 20, 2019, https://medium.com/the-sundial-acmrs/shakespeare-and-your-mountainish-inhumanity-d255474027de.

[29] The poorest congressional district since 2010, NY 15 was fused with wealthier Riverdale starting in 2023.

[30] Textbook costs can impose serious hardship on families in the South Bronx; even five dollars will cost some students their next meal.

This initial pedagogical misstep not only inspired me to craft courses with zero textbook costs, and to adopt Open Educational Resources (OER), but also implanted in me a firm awareness of how higher education's traditional structures create and sustain inequities that reinforce a culture of elitism. For years on the academic job market, I fielded the question, "Which Shakespeare textbook do you assign?" as if my answer would demonstrate my belonging to a prestigious inner circle of teacher-scholars of Shakespeare. As a doctoral candidate, I typically assigned the Norton or Bedford editions because these were assigned to me as an undergraduate. But when I shared a dissertation chapter draft with a mentor, this person bristled at my citation from Bedford, writing in a marginal note, "serious scholars cite the Oxford or Cambridge editions." Who makes these rules, anyway?

In my courses, I am free to assign Oxford, Cambridge, Norton, Bedford, or any other Shakespeare edition, but all these editions carry costs. Granted, earlier and used editions of these books are ubiquitous in public and university libraries, but these are bound to library operating hours and course reserve time limits. And why should the under-resourced student have to struggle to access the textbook while the fully resourced student can simply buy the new, full-priced copy from Amazon.com™ with two-day shipping?

These days, I typically assign the Folger Digital Texts edition of Shakespeare's plays. I applaud Folger for offering free versions of its printed plays, along with audio versions and other articles and resources. It is one of the best free editions for undergraduates anywhere. I do wish, however, that Folger Digital Texts could freely offer the notes and glosses that appear in the print and e-book copies. As with virtually any publisher, such tried-and-true tools for comprehension are provided only through the mechanism of purchase, with the material protected under copyright. Timothy Lee Wherry explains that by issuing a new edition of a creative work out of copyright, such as a Shakespeare play, a publisher claims copyright of "the reedited or changed book [. . .] with all the contents, including the text that was in the original publication, protected by a new copyright."[31] Ample labor by academic publishers, in concert with

---

[31] Wherry, *The Librarian's Guide to Intellectual Property in the Digital Age: Copyrights, Patents, and Trademarks* (Chicago: American Library Association, 2002), 23. As Wherry explains, in educational settings, distribution of creative works is subject to "fair use" guidelines, which consider the use's purpose and character, whether for commercial or nonprofit educational purposes; the nature of the copyrighted work; the proportion used; and the effect of use on potential market or value of copyrighted work (18–20).

leading scholars of Shakespeare—many of them insufficiently compensated for their efforts—and investments by funding institutions, frequently goes into the production of new editions of Shakespeare. These factors together determine the cost. Nevertheless, given that notes and glosses significantly aid students' understanding, doesn't this also mean that understanding itself is predicated on cost? For students receiving financial aid, which typically doesn't cover "variable costs" like textbooks, cost and copyright barriers not only imperil their chances of success but also further underscore the idea that, all claims to Shakespeare's universality notwithstanding, this material is emphatically not meant for them.

How can an elite literature be universal? And if a literature is truly universal, why isn't it free? When it comes to the Shakespeare textbook industry, the tacit buy-in of faculty, in conjunction with academic institutions and publishers who collectively produce and promote these editions, places minoritized students at odds with the privileged practices informing not only the traditional Shakespeare classroom, but also the college experience itself. There is already a growing movement for open access scholarly books like this volume, *Situating Shakespeare Pedagogy in US Higher Education*. There are moreover several free online editions of Shakespeare's works, though generally suited for more advanced readers.[32] What Shakespeare studies needs, therefore, is more widely available, open access editions of these and other works specifically targeted for undergraduates. Higher education and funding-granting institutions, in cooperation with academic publishers, need to recruit and adequately compensate faculty for producing OER editions of Shakespeare's works. And faculty at two- and four-year colleges, public and private, must embrace zero-cost materials. Until these measures are implemented, the unspoken divide in the college experience will remain firmly rooted, perceptible especially to those students experiencing the material plight of academic precarity.

---

[32] For example, Internet Shakespeare Editions (ISE) offers contextual essays and annotations, but these are generally too complex for beginning study; the line glosses are helpful. University of Victoria, *Internet Shakespeare Editions*, https://internetshakespeare.uvic.ca/. Open Source Shakespeare of George Mason University does not offer notes and glosses: https://www.opensourceshakespeare.org/. The MT Shakespeare and 1914 Oxford Edition do not offer line numbers, word glosses, or footnotes: Jeremy Hylton and MIT, *The Complete Works of William Shakespeare*, http://shakespeare.mit.edu/; W. J. Craig, ed. *The Complete Works of William Shakespeare* (London: Oxford University Press: 1914; Bartleby.com, 2000), www.bartleby.com/70/ (all accessed May 31, 2022).

Organize to Revolutionize

Not all students identify with what their peers call "the struggle," but economic need cuts deeply across CUNY. One moral imperative that must be heeded by the current generation is to confront this historic struggle that minoritized students have had to endure to access a quality education. Students in lower-income communities may lack necessary financial resources to attend college, but they may also lack other pivotal resources like time and attention to devote to their studies. For these students, online learning has been an especially vital, life-changing opportunity that allows them to better balance college with uncompromising work schedules and significant personal and family obligations. And yet, in spite of the equity gains made by this movement in recent years, especially during the COVID-19 pandemic, online education is still widely regarded as an albatross to a traditional liberal arts education—the kind where students sit in a circle to discuss a text. Some faculty remain deeply skeptical of remote learning, which ostensibly depersonalizes the learning experience, especially in asynchronous courses.[33] This has not been my personal experience of online education, where asynchronous instruction has promoted sustained student engagement rather than impeded it.[34]

When CUNY transitioned online in spring 2020, I had originally planned to teach my classes synchronously; it was only when I realized how utterly students' lives were being shuttered by the pandemic that I shifted modalities. While the bulk of New York's white-collar workforce was safely isolating at home, many of my students were working full time at the frontlines. A good number did not have personal computers or high-speed Wi-Fi connections. Others were sharing bandwidth with members of their households. Parenting students were educating their children at home while attempting to keep up with their own studies. In light of all this, I determined to teach my courses in an asynchronous and mobile phone-friendly format. Students would be able to access the material on their own time, whenever and wherever their temporal, technical, and

---

[33] Remote learning technologies are not unproblematic, however. For instance, many learning management systems employ in-built automatic grading programs like SafeAssign™ and Turnitin™, which have drawn criticism for archiving students' intellectual property to police for plagiarism.

[34] Nevertheless, online learning obviously does not suit everyone. Designing curricula to offer a mix of modalities will go a long way to meeting each student where they are.

emotional bandwidth was strongest. This equitable course design did not ultimately eradicate the additional cognitive load students were carrying, but it did work to ensure that they were not immediately disadvantaged by an uncompromising course design.

Given the knottiness of Shakespeare, however, my asynchronous course required ample planning and preparation to keep students informed and engaged through their self-paced work; much of my preparation time involved collating and producing materials. To serve the diverse student body, which also includes many English language learners, I practice differentiated instruction. This means meeting students exactly where they are with appropriate resources, whether they're grappling with vocabulary and plot, looking to visually process the drama, or seeking more advanced theoretical engagement with the material. During the pandemic, I differentiated my instruction to students by augmenting my personally recorded, closed captioned mini-topics lectures[35] and other resources with freely available, high-quality learning supplements produced by such venues as the Globe Theatre, Royal Shakespeare Company, Folger Shakespeare Library, British Library, Bodleian Library, National Archives, Library of Congress, National Library of Spain, National Library of Mexico, and PBS Learning. Fortuitously, following CUNY's return to mostly in-person instruction in the 2022 spring, I have been able to adapt this asynchronous sequence for my in-person classes. All the collected lectures, resources, and activities now essentially serve as my Shakespeare course's in-built zero-cost textbook. This positive result indicates one way that the COVID-19 pandemic, during which institutions like mine were training and supporting faculty to implement OER materials and asynchronous instruction, could be leveraged to elicit equitable changes in higher education.

As a result of measures I gradually implemented throughout the pandemic, my Shakespeare course is now more equitable. The work involved has been extensive, but one of the benefits of my working for a teaching-centered institution within the larger research network of CUNY is that pedagogical development has never been undervalued or regarded as some kind of soft academic labor. I have been supported, in the form of reappointment and positive evaluations by my department chair, senior colleagues, and higher administrators, in all the educational initiatives I have undertaken to serve students. Still, I could not have accomplished so much if my work had not also

---

[35] A best practice is to parcel online asynchronous lectures into focused, mini lectures of less than ten minutes.

been compensated and/or counted for tenure. Hence, by far the most extensive support that I have had to innovate my teaching has been my representation by the Professional Staff Congress (PSC), CUNY's employee union. PSC has secured tangible safeguards for faculty like compensated pedagogical development/training and grants for conference travel/research, along with credit load reductions (from 27 to 24 annual credit hours for community college faculty) and course releases for research (24 pre-tenure hours). PSC has also produced invaluable symbolic safeguards in promoting a culture of institutional accountability that affords me considerable security to be able to innovate and experiment in my teaching, even as an untenured professor.

Yet a majority of institutions lack employee unions or other bodies empowered to hold administrations accountable; some institutions altogether bar formal unionization. This can and should change to truly remedy deep-seated inequities in higher education affecting workers and students. As Andy Crow, who participated in the graduate students' unionizing effort at Columbia University, puts it, "unions are democratic in character, [. . .] they are a means to real power, and [. . .] they enable you to turn ideals of justice and equity into material improvements in people's daily lives."[36] Our community never forgets that Hostos was once nearly closed by a city that deemed it unworthy of educational investment. But the community organized to protect students and workers, and won. This story, among many across CUNY, animates the union's continued struggle to improve conditions for all.[37] Such examples may also spur faculty nationwide to organize to revolutionize the curriculum, beginning with tackling the unspoken inequities built into their own courses.

As proposed in this essay, equity-building has the potential to reform not only the elite discipline of Shakespeare studies, but also the institutional assumptions that structure academic life and praxis. But in order for faculty to be able to meet minoritized students where they are, institutions must also meet faculty where they are. They must come to regard pedagogical development as hard academic labor worthy of investment in the manner Hostos fought for. Likewise, for faculty to teach Shakespeare against his imperialist

---

[36] Andy Crow, "How to Win Your Grad Union," *Politics/Letters Quarterly*, February 27, 2017, http://quarterly.politicsslashletters.org/how-to-win-your-grad-union/ (accessed June 19, 2022).

[37] This legacy informs the currently proposed "New Deal for CUNY." See PSC CUNY, "Fight for Full State Funding of CUNY FY 2023," https://psc-cuny.org/issues/state budgetcampaign2022/.

legacies, they require access to resources that disclose his "living museum" to students' remaking. And for the Shakespeare curriculum to become more equitable, it must first address the unique situations of minoritized struggle. Then the heavy work of grappling with Shakespeare can begin.

Chapter 4

Teaching Shakespeare as a Killjoy Practice in a White Dominant Institution
Mary Janell Metzger

What does it require to teach Shakespeare's representation of tragic action, race, and adaptation in a school founded on unceded native land by a white female settler whose aim was to proliferate a "civilizing curriculum" lacking in the "wilderness" with which she identified her Indigenous hosts and neighbors? This is an abiding question of my work teaching Shakespeare in the far northwest corner of the United States. The ontological expansiveness of my white students, who have grown up in overwhelmingly if not exclusively white and persistently segregated communities, means that studying the production of whiteness in Shakespeare is often a destabilizing experience at odds with their expectations of our work together.[1] Attending to the poetic and rhetorical force of Shakespeare's work, his representation of racialized hierarchy, and the antiracist critical response to his work by scholars and artists in the US is difficult. But understanding the racial history of our settler colonial community and institution helps explode the invisibility of

---

[1] By "whiteness" here and throughout this essay, I refer to the "recurring patterns of behavior that systemically benefit White people" (Jennifer L. S. Chandler and Erica Wiborg, "Whiteness Norms," in Zachary A. Case, ed., *Encyclopedia of Critical White Studies in Education* [Leiden: Brill, 2021], 714–21). These behaviors may differ depending on their location and social context, and are enacted by all people, not just people who identify as white. Because whiteness is a set of social practices, education is a crucial location for its reproduction. Ontological expansiveness, conceptualized by Shannon Sullivan, describes the relationship between racialization, whiteness, and space, "such that space is raced and that bodies become raced through their lived spatiality" (*Revealing Whiteness: The Unconscious Habits of Racial Privilege* [Bloomington: Indiana University Press, 2006], 143). As Sullivan points out and illustrates in detail, colonialism as the drive for absolute mastery epitomizes white expansiveness, chattel slavery, and their persistent legacies. These forms she explores as the "possessive geographies" of whiteness (Sullivan, *Revealing*, 121). See also Elizabeth A. Collins, Devon Thomas, Chris Corces-Zimmerman, and Nolan Cabrera, "Ontological Expansiveness," in Case, *Encyclopedia*, 432–38.

whiteness—and thus the ahistorical universality of Shakespeare—as a means of its reproduction.

Founded in 1893, Western Washington University in Bellingham, Washington, has roots in settler colonial expectations. These roots are visible in its start in 1886 as Northwest Normal School. Established overwhelmingly in the American South and west of the Mississippi, "normal schools" focused on teacher training in elementary education.[2] The county's first normal school, like most normal schools, advanced the social and educational norms and nationalist narratives of settler colonial culture through the formation of white Christian teachers and their students—norms and narratives reinforced by the ideology of Manifest Destiny established almost fifty years before with the Mexican-American War.[3] Indeed, the realization in 1895 of "New Whatcom Normal School" in the newly minted state of Washington was an effect of the militant white settler presence made possible by the British ceding of the Oregon Territory as a consequence of their alignment with Mexico in that war. The founder of the earlier Northwest Normal School, white Canadian American settler Phoebe Judson, justified her dispossession of and attempts to Christianize the native Coast Salish L'Aqhtemish (Lummi) and Noxws'áʔaq (Nooksack) people through the Doctrine of Discovery established by Pope Nicholas V in 1455, which authorized the conquest, dispossession, and enslavement of all non-Christians.[4] Four hundred years later, Judson, like earlier white Christian colonizers, saw in her "ideal home" an aesthetic space within which she would establish her place in the world, geographically and spiritually.[5]

---

[2] Wendy Patterson, "From 1871–2021: A Short History of Education in the United States," Buffalo State, The State University of New York, 2021, https://suny.buffalostate.edu/news/1871-2021-short-history-education-united-states.

[3] Notably, the first Indian Boarding School in the US was established in Washington state on Yakima land in 1860, the aim of which was to assimilate students to an "American way of life," including the importance of private property, material wealth, and gender hierarchy in communal and family formation, depriving Indigenous people of their language, culture, and relations in the process. Anne Bond and Joshua F. Inwood, "Beyond White Privilege: Geographies of White Supremacy and Settler Colonialism," *Progress in Human Geography* (2015): 1–19; and National Native American Boarding School Healing Coalition, https://boardingschoolhealing.org/.

[4] Nicholas V, "The Bull Romanus Pontifex (Nicholas V), January 8, 1455," *Papal Encyclicals Online*, https://www.papalencyclicals.net/nichol05/romanus-pontifex.htm. The Coast Salish people were dispossessed of their land, placed on reservations, and prevented from entering Bellingham except by permission in 1855 exactly 400 years later ("Bellingham Racial History Timeline," https://wp.wwu.edu/timeline/).

[5] In her 1925 memoir *A Pioneer's Search for an Ideal Home*, Judson wrote explicitly of her family's motive "to obtain from the government of the United States a grant of land that 'Uncle Sam' had promised to give to the head of each family who settled in

Though eventually state funding of New Whatcom Normal School helped the struggling Western Washington College open its doors in 1899, and put an end to Judson's school, the curriculum and white immigrant teachers and students remained the same. Judson's legacy lives on in the demographics of our city, which is over 80 percent white, and my university's students, 70 percent of whom are white, 10 percent Latinx, 2.6 percent Black, and less than 1 percent Indigenous. The representation of nonwhites in the faculty is far worse.[6]

Such "Critical Geography" as pedagogical orientation "is based upon the principle that questions about spatial relations … are important because political behaviour is embedded in socio-political structures based on ideas about space." Understanding how "scholarship and political behaviour are ingrained in socio-political structures" illuminates how seemingly objective analysis relies on the "impossibility" of other perspectives and experiences.[7]

The institutional resonance for my students of examining our history can be found in the shared values of settler colonialism and academic policies, practices, and behaviors. As Patrick Wolfe explains, "Settlers generally have a lot to say about work, sacrifice, and earning things the hard way."[8] Like ambitious academics, settlers' emphasis on "industry" as establishing rights "bespeaks a primal anxiety" about belonging for which their labors are

---

this new country." She recalls, "The many air castles that I built concerning my 'ideal home' while the preparations for our long journey were being made, are still fresh in my memory. It should be built by a mountain stream that flowed to the Pacific, or by some lake, or bay, and *nothing should obstruct our view* of the beautiful snow-capped mountains" (Phoebe Goodell Judson, *A Pioneer's Search for an Ideal Home: A Book of Personal Memoirs* [Bellingham: Union Printing, Binding and Stationary Co., 1925], 8 (emphasis mine), https://www.sos.wa.gov/legacy/publicationsviewer/?title=Pioneer%27s%20search%20for%20an%20ideal%20home&ID=21). Nowhere in her vision does she account for the native inhabitants, or later Chinese and Sikh immigrants employed in the industry created by colonizers' clear-cut logging and unrestricted fishing, all violently expelled from their homes and land not long before she recorded these memories. Notably, Bellingham, the county seat and home of Western Washington University, maintained a sundown law until the 1970s; consult "Bellingham."

[6] Raine Dozier, "Experiences of Faculty of Color at Western Washington University: For the President's Taskforce on Equity, Inclusion, and Diversity," 2019, https://crtc.wwu.edu/files/2019-11/ExperiencesofFacultyOfColorAtWWU.pdf.

[7] Irena Leisbet Ceridwen Connon and Archie W. Simpson, "Critical Geography: An Introduction," in *International Relations Theory*, ed. Stephen McGlinchey, Rosie Walters and Christian Scheinpflug (E-International Relations Publishing, 2018), https://www.e-ir.info/2018/01/21/critical-geography-an-introduction/.

[8] Patrick Wolfe, "The Settler Colonial Complex: An Introduction," *American Indian Culture and Research Journal* 37, no. 2 (2013): 1.

"always exculpatory." Wolfe's insight illuminates the emphasis on the authorized forms of exculpatory industry at white dominant institutions like mine. Principal among them is the authorizing and alienating power of Shakespeare within higher education as a form of whiteness. Having made it to college as the descendants of native or enslaved people, settlers, or immigrants seeking meaningful work and a better life for their families, my students know that assimilating to the norms of cultural whiteness in higher education offers them relative measures of institutional belonging and educational and thus socioeconomic achievement. They also know that Shakespeare has long been a means of demonstrating just such qualifications.

Teaching Shakespeare with commitments to critical geography, and dialogical community-building foundational to a socially just pedagogy, has helped me recognize and respond to how our school's origin as a normal school shows up in my students' expectations of their learning and sense of belonging in my Shakespeare course, the racial myths that shape these expectations, and their sense of agency and vulnerability in reckoning with tragedy as a literary form. I am committed to teaching students that where we learn informs how we do so, and thus shapes our sense of what we study. Though my nonwhite students are usually keenly aware of where we are when we study Shakespeare and tragedy, given the whiteness of our university, town, county, and state, many of my white students have yet to question their relation to racialization and communal belonging in these settings. For example, because the promise of assimilation available to those students of European descent often obscures their families' dispossession of their historical and cultural origins, their reinvention as normative Americans, let alone its literal foundation on unceded native land, are rarely seen as tragic losses. Yet such erasure, like Shakespeare's transformation into a tool of cultural homogeneity by those seeking to reproduce colonial social hierarchies, is crucial to engaging the violence in Shakespeare's tragedies. Recognition of Shakespeare's tragic representation of the violence of absolute social hierarchy and models of resistance to such violence by antiracist artists, invites students to "restory" his work in terms of their embodied interdependent lives.[9] In anagnorisis/recognition and

---

[9] I am deeply indebted to the generous collaboration and brilliant work of Penelope Geng and Elisa Oh included in this volume. Geng's essay introduced me to Ebony Elizabeth Thomas's coining of "restorying" to describe "the complex ways that contemporary young people narrate the word and the world, analyze their lived experiences, and then synthesize and recontextualize a multiplicity of stories ... reimagining time, place, identity, perspective, mode, and metanarratives through retold stories" (Thomas, *The*

adaptation of our own and Shakespeare's "difficult histories" lies the pleasures of the Shakespearean killjoy.

For all these reasons, building classroom community is especially crucial. In a white dominant settler community like ours, in a course on a cultural icon of whiteness like Shakespeare, with a teacher committed to exploring the nature of white supremacy in our community and Shakespeare's works, I create the means for collaboration by being transparent about my expectations of and for community-building. As Katherine Gillen and Lisa Jennings argue, while decolonizing our teaching of Shakespeare answers our students' need to understand the connection of such work to their lives, how we do so depends on our "particular contexts."[10] Acknowledging our presence on the unceded native land of our Lummi and Nooksack neighbors and our focus on Shakespeare's tragic representation of racialization, what such work requires of us, the practices that will support our collaborations, and the risks we take together, I cultivate an environment that lessens student anxiety and cultivates student engagement.

I begin such work on day one by making critical space for my students' expectations and lived experience. Doing so is a means of welcoming their unpartitioned selves via interest in their fears and desires about studying Shakespeare and race. Both terms are haunted by the unspoken expectations of our university: Shakespeare is a figure of cultural and institutional power and has been a historical tool of racial exclusion in the advancement of white dominance in our region since the mid-nineteenth century.[11] Defying such silences on day one, I ask students to anonymously complete the following sentences on index cards: "In this class I hope . . ." and "In this class I fear . . . ." I am always moved by the honesty of my students' fears of "inadequacy" to Shakespeare and hopes for "mastering" his work.

On day two I share their hopes and fears as a means of demonstrating that they are not alone, whatever their fears or hopes. Doing

---

Dark Fantastic: Race and the Imagination from Harry Potter to the Hunger Games [New York: New York University Press, 2019], 159). Oh's essay illuminates the distinct challenges and opportunities of racial homogeneity in a HBCU classroom, especially one led by a teacher who does not share their students' ancestry.

[10] Katherine Gillen and Lisa Jennings, "Decolonizing Shakespeare? Toward an Antiracist, Culturally Sustaining Practice," *The Sundial*, November 26, 2019, https://medium.com/the-sundial-acmrs/decolonizing-shakespeare-toward-an-antiracist-culturally-sustaining-praxis-904cb9ff8a96.

[11] My position as "the Shakespearean" at my hiring in 1995 was the sole department tenure line requiring expertise in a single author.

so also allows me to connect their experience with the colonizing history of Shakespeare's institutionalization. Inadequate to whom? Mastery of what? In such conversations I briefly share the gap between Shakespeare's origins and centuries-long home in public theater and diverse theatrical societies, on the one hand, and his politicized use by British colonizers and American white supremacists, on the other. I tell them about Joseph Quincy Adams, for example, for whom Shakespeare "preserv[ed] in America a homogeneity of English culture" in the face of immigrants who threatened Anglo-Saxon culture with "a babel of tongues and cultures."[12] I set that depiction against Amiri Baraka's claim that, "[i]f the people that rule [the US] thought that you could understand what Shakespeare's really saying, they would remove him from us [because] ... Shakespeare is a revolutionary."[13] These conversations invoke questions about the relation not only between these figures' views of Shakespeare and my students' own hopes and fears, but also between their study of Shakespeare and the possibility of refusing a racialized Shakespeare in favor of forging our own experience.

Given the ways in which racialized normativity functions through silencing, judgment, and exclusion, students' resistance to critical pedagogies such as mine can understandably stem from discomfort with the absence of "right" answers and fear of being "wrong," especially out loud.

Yet the possibility of joy in the analysis of Shakespeare's work and productions that speak to our lives as vulnerable racialized beings is rooted in our recognition of shared experience with others. As scholar-activist Adrienne Maree Brown explains, "interdependence requires being seen, as much as possible, as your true self," "accepting our inner multitudes," recognizing "that where you are wrong might be the most fertile ground" for connection, and learning how to "ask for and receive what you need."[14] Creating such

---

[12] Joseph Quincy Adams, "Shakespeare and American Culture," in *Shakespeare in America*, ed. James Shapiro (New York: The Library of America, 2014), 431.

[13] This claim appears in Baraka's 1984 speech at Rutgers University, a clip of which may be heard on Michael Witmore, host, "Freedom, Heyday! Heyday, Freedom!" *Shakespeare Unlimited* (podcast), episode 20, Folger Shakespeare Library, February 11, 2015, https://www.folger.edu/shakespeare-unlimited/african-americans-shakespeare.

[14] Adrienne Maree Brown, *Emergent Strategy: Shaping Chance, Changing Worlds* (Chico, CA: A. K. Worlds Press, 2017), 93–94. Brown is an Afro-futurist who combines science and science fiction to advocate for forms of activism that transform our relations to the planet and each other. Offering an "adaptive and relational leadership model," she demonstrates how such an approach can grow "plans of action, personal practices and collective organizing tools that account for constant change and rely on the strength of relationships for adaptation" (Brown, *Emergent*, 23).

collaborative interdependence in a white dominant institutional setting dependent on hierarchy and competitive performance is never easy. Listening actively to others, for example, without immediately reaching for response or judgment takes time. But it cultivates connection and feeds our sense of possibility. As Brown reminds us, "being interdependent is a series of small repetitive motions."[15] The following practices, to which we all commit, nurture such collaboration.

1. **Be accountable.** Show up. Commit to the work.
2. **Stay Engaged.** Avoid checking out or changing the topic to make yourself feel more comfortable.
3. **Be an Active Listener.** Listen for understanding, not response. Think about what you want to say before speaking and consider how it will move us toward greater understanding.
4. **Avoid comparing your experience or ideas with those of another person.** Avoid rationalizing your comments or personalizing those of others. Individual actions matter, but injustice is overwhelmingly structurally enforced, so consider how those structures impact your perspective and practices.
5. **If you regret what you've said, apologize without justification.** Reckon with impact, not intent.
6. **Speak your truth.** Speak only from your own experience and avoid generalizations about other people. Instead, help us understand you by owning your ideas and feelings.
7. **Observe the "lean in and lean back" rule:** If you've spoken a lot, try to lean back and make space for others—even if that means some silence. If you've rarely or never spoken, lean in; aim to contribute regularly—whether that's once a class or once a week. Note that simply saying, "I'm really interested in what you just said. Can you tell me more?" acknowledges the testimony of another, its value to you, and builds community.
8. **Expect and accept non-closure.** In classrooms, we often assess what we've learned. And there will be some of that here as you rally your experience and learning in a variety of activities and assignments that will receive specific feedback from your peers and me. But there may be times when you feel a lack of closure in your grasp of the material or your understanding of or relation to another person in the class. Trust the process. Take risks. Stay curious.
9. **Use your resources.** Come to see me in office hours if you want to

---

[15] Brown, *Emergent*, 93.

talk about something that there isn't time or space for in class. Look things up. Research answers to basic questions outside of class. Step up to the challenges and own your education.[16]

Admittedly, these behaviors are hard to sustain, especially in an institution such as ours. But, as I tell my students, every day provides a new opportunity to show up willing to engage each other and the material thoughtfully and with care. Doing so develops a community that empowers us all.

Holding ourselves accountable to these commitments is crucial, especially in the early days as we prepare to read Shakespeare's tragic representation of race by reading works other than Shakespeare: Ijeoma Oluo's "What is racism?" and "What if I talk about race wrong?" model interracial dialogue from a Black perspective. Nell Irvin Painter's "White Slavery" demystifies the history of slavery, documents the medieval and early modern production of whiteness, and opens conversations about what we learn about "race" and how. And Isabel Wilkerson's "The Eight Pillars of Caste" provides students with a language useful in analyzing the recurrent means of establishing and enforcing racialized hierarchies.

During these early discussions, I model the vulnerability that sharing our experience of racialization requires. In tracing medieval white slavery Painter reveals that "Dublin was Europe's largest slave market during the eleventh century" and Ireland's patron saint its "most famous British slave of the period." Welsh and Celts, we learn, were stereotyped as "weak, sexually aggressive, dark skinned and haired, dirty, ugly, quarrelsome, lazy, and ignorant."[17] As I am the descendant of Irish grandparents on both sides, these are my people, I tell my students. I was taught to be proud of being Irish, I admit, but my understanding of my ethnic culture was defined by anti-English sentiment vaguely connected to the Great Famine (a.k.a., Irish Potato Famine), familiarity with the traditional food and drink of St. Patrick's Day, and an occasionally devotional but mostly social Irish Catholicism. I knew nothing of the centuries-long racialization of the Irish by the Vikings and later the Anglo-Saxons. Neither did I

---

[16] I am indebted to Patrice Hollins and Ilsa Govan, *Diversity, Equity, and Inclusion: Strategies for Facilitating Conversations on Race* (Guilford, CT: Rowman and Littlefield Press, 2013), which allows so many to pursue bell hooks's vision of "education as the practice of freedom" (hooks, *Teaching to Transgress: Education as the Practice of Freedom* [New York: Routledge, 1994], 21).

[17] Nell Irvin Painter, *The History of White People* (New York: W. W. Norton, 2010), 34–35.

know how the Irish immigrants who fled the English penal colonies and potato famine to the United States in the mid-nineteenth century quickly supported the slavery and political violence they and their ancestors had suffered as a means of gaining status as "white" Americans, with its attendant access to work, housing, and political power denied their free Black neighbors.[18] My Irish ancestors' pursuit of status as white Americans depended on the subjugation of Black Americans. Tragically, they did so at the cost of their own history as dehumanized Celts and their potential solidarity with African Americans against those who defined them as but "probationa[lly] white."[19] As Wolfe recognizes in his reading of settler colonials, the precarity of whiteness breeds insecurity fed by ignorance, as the weak sense of cultural heritage my parents offered attests.

Along with Oluo's narratives of her experience growing up Black in an interracial family in white dominant Seattle, Painter's expansive history of slavery, Wilkerson's account of the features of racialized dehumanization, and the example of my immigrant family's racial bargains, my students develop a sense that our *capacity* for racial discourse is a *process*, not an event. Following small group discussion of these works as students share out, I model the commitment to active listening in checking my understanding of my students' words. I offer heartfelt gratitude for meaningful contributions, risk-taking, curiosity, generosity, and attentive recognition of the work of others. Modeling the interest demonstrated by the simple request to "Tell me more," suggested above, illuminates the power of questions over rhetorical assertions. Invariably, students find a way to speak in less reactive or rehearsed terms and demonstrate the unexpected possibilities created by our curiosity. Even when the request gives someone pause, these moments of recognition fuel their courage and grow our collective capacity for dialogical relationships, leading students to follow up on such invitations later.

Such understanding is crucial for our study of Shakespeare, race, and adaptation and requires clarity about our learning objectives.[20]

---

[18] Noel Ignatiev, *How the Irish Became White* (New York: Routledge, 2009).

[19] "The definition of whiteness framed politics and policy in early America. In 1859, the terms 'Anglo-Saxon race,' and, 'English race,' were added to the lexicon. And after a naturalization law that granted Europeans open, absolute immigration ... 'white' was broken down into different white groups .... Distinctions continued to be made between the various European immigrants. These stereotypes were pervasive, impacting institutions, politics and cultural practices. In particular, the Irish were under constant verbal attack—they were consistently and publicly dehumanized" (Annie Jaffee, "Probationary Whiteness," in Case, *Encyclopedia*, 506–7).

[20] Such transparency is a crucial feature of "backward design"—a pedagogy in which

These include: familiarity with the tragic action and poetic language of Shakespeare's plays and their representation of racialized difference within a historical and comparative analysis that sets his age against our own; understanding the dynamic between inherited forms of belief and the action and speech of Shakespeare's drama, and thus the power of revision and adaptation; developing our abilities to actively listen and read for understanding; engaging with a diverse set of human experiences and contexts; and speaking and writing with clarity and purpose about Shakespeare's work and others' views and adaptations of it. Not least, we reflect on the ethical dimensions of our work.

I use two classical texts to help my students grapple with these concerns via the long history and literary and aesthetic effects of European hierarchies of value that inform Shakespeare's work and the white settler colonial spaces we occupy: Aristotle's account of tragic performance in his *Poetics*' anatomy of literary kinds and his *Politics*' description of the natural order of being. In *Poetics*, Aristotle's emphasis on human action and vulnerability to error as essential to the affective power of tragic drama challenges students to explore questions of human agency and vulnerability; how action contends with speech in our judgment of culpability; and the force of recognition of harm and reparation.[21] In these conversations, students verbalize their own cultural and communal notions of what our relation to others illuminates and demands and how the performance of tragic action shapes our view of social norms. By grappling with Aristotle's insistence on action as the heart of tragedy and the human vulnerability of tragic figures—rejecting both devils and saints—students grapple with the danger of "fate" as an ethical and thus interpretive dead end. Aristotle's sense of tragedy as inciting viewers' pity and fear requires recognition of the human capacity for blindness and insight about their ethical relation to others. Shakespeare's texts, his characters and plots, their speech and action, in this way come alive in the context of students' experiences and beliefs about how they have been taught to live, choose to

---

student learning objectives are established before choosing instructional tools, methods and forms of assessment, thus prioritizing student learning and instructional transparency. Consult Grant Wiggins and Jay McTighue, *Understanding by Design* (Alexandria, VA: Association for Supervision and Curriculum Development, 2005).

[21] Aristotle, *Poetics*, in *Aristotle in 23 Volumes*, vol. 21, trans. H. Rackham (Cambridge, MA: Harvard University Press; London: William Heinemann Ltd., 1944), 1453A-B. *Perseus Digital Library*, http://www.perseus.tufts.edu/hopper/text.jsp?doc=Perseus:text:1999.01.0056.

live, and the consequences of doing harm, no matter their intentions. As J. M. Bernstein explains, the ritual of tragedy is a "form of attention that brings into view the limiting condition of cultural life," the inescapable nature of our vulnerability to loss, suffering, and death, and the significance of our choices in the face of such contingency.[22]

Turning from the Aristotelian ground of Shakespeare's representation of tragic action, I offer students his absolutist description of "the natural order" of the world in his *Politics*. Rooted in his platonic disdain for the body's transiency and therefore untrustworthiness, Aristotle asserts a hierarchy of existence where the soul "must" rule over the body, the mind over emotion, "men" over "other animals," domesticated creatures are "better" than wild, and men necessarily "superior and ruler" over women. Noting Aristotle's use of "must" and the "chaos" he argues would result from resistance to this "natural" order, students recognize the troubling logic of his appeal to natural law *and* social efficiency. Doing so illuminates the violence of his categorical limits in claiming that "wherever" the distance between human beings mirrors the "wide discrepancy" between soul and body or "man and beast" then such beings are reduced to "slaves by nature," being but tools valuable for "the use of their bodies and nothing better."[23]

Aristotle's refusal of absolutism in his account of tragic human error in *Poetics* paired with the rigid absolutism and violent demonization of the body in his *Politics* exposes the weak foundations of othering in Anglo-European sociopolitical theory, practice, and art. How can Aristotle insist on the complex force of human beings as cognitive and affective creatures in tragic drama *and* use that very human complexity to denigrate human beings by virtue of their embodiment? Why is the body—without which no life exists—set up so absolutely against the soul and the mind? Why does he distrust the natural world, upon which he nevertheless relies as an argument for human *qua* male superiority and dominion? And how do these ideas continue to shape our relation to each other and the natural world upon which we also rely?

I nurture these questions relative to Shakespeare's age via the work of early modern scholars who dispel erroneous preconceptions

---

[22] J. M. Bernstein, "Tragedy," in *Oxford Encyclopedia of Philosophy and Literature*, ed. Richard Eldridge (Oxford: Oxford University Press, 2009), 73.

[23] Aristotle, *Politics*, in *Aristotle in 23 Volumes*, vol. 23, trans. W. H. Fyfe (Cambridge, MA: Harvard University Press; London: William Heinemann Ltd., 1932), 1.4.1254b. *Perseus Digital Library*, http://www.perseus.tufts.edu/hopper/text?doc=Perseus:text:1999.01.0058.

of Shakespeare's work or who it belongs to, and the white Christian homogeneity of Shakespeare's London given the global contexts and discourses of "others" upon which Shakespeare draws.[24] In this way, our attention to the representation of whiteness as forms of social power and its violent enforcement in specific plays (*King Lear*, *Titus Andronicus*, *Coriolanus*, *Othello*, *Romeo and Juliet*, and *The Merchant of Venice*) invites conversation about how racialization is, as Ann Stoler argues, not subsequent to social order but constitutive of it.[25] Because white characters of many kinds in these plays naturalize and reinforce an absolute racial hierarchy, even in the absence of nonwhite others, the nature of racialization's effects becomes clearer, both in our own communities and in Shakespeare's work. Attention to whiteness as a desire for "mastery" in Shakespeare thus becomes a killjoy means of acknowledging the fiction of race as essence *and* its material power as a form of social belief. Our study of Shakespeare's tragedies thus affirms our capacity for solidarity in the shared struggle against such a harmful ideology.

Acknowledging Shakespeare's representation of the violence of white supremacy is not difficult. Of course, it is explicit in *The Merchant of Venice* when the "fair Portia" dismisses the socially superior Prince of Morocco to bachelorhood with a racist jibe and then deploys antisemitic Venetian law to condemn Shylock to conversion to Christianity on pain of death. Comparison of Aaron the Moor's choice to risk his life for his son and Titus the Roman's instinctive brutal murders of his children for betraying his sense of honor illuminates the power of whiteness as absolutism on behalf of power in *Titus Andronicus*. Once familiar with racialization in Shakespeare as a discourse rooted in racial tropes of black and white, students begin to see the hierarchies of value that support such tropes where no bodies of color appear, such as *The Rape of Lucrece* and *Coriolanus*. Ultimately, students possess the knowledge and skills necessary to explore what resistance to such myths and the

---

[24] Among others, Patricia Akhimie, *Shakespeare and the Cultivation of Difference: Race and Conduct in the Early Modern World* (Oxfordshire: Routledge, 2018); David Sterling Brown, "'Is Black so Base a Hue?': Black Life Matters in Shakespeare's *Titus Andronicus*," in *Early Modern Black Diaspora Studies: A Critical Anthology*, ed. Cassander L. Smith, Nicholas R. Jones, and Miles P. Grier (New York: Palgrave Macmillan, 2017), 137–55; Imtiaz Habib, *Black Lives in the English Archives, 1500–1677: Imprints of the Invisible* (New York: Routledge, 2008; rpt. 2020); and Kim F. Hall, *Things of Darkness: Economies of Race and Gender in Early Modern England* (Ithaca: Cornell University Press, 1995).

[25] Ann Stoler, *Carnal Knowledge and Imperial Power: Race and the Intimate in Colonial Rule* (Berkeley: University of California Press, 1995; 2010).

violent erasures they entail looks like, and thus what Shakespeare's work can mean to us. Such is the work of becoming a Shakespearean killjoy. As Sara Ahmed puts it, we become killjoys "when we refuse to *be* the master's tools."[26] In the study of Shakespeare, this refusal involves an unwillingness to reproduce the "violence of an order" to "justify social norms as social goods," like Shakespeare as a tool of white supremacy.[27]

Respect for each other's testimony throughout, as the communal commitments require, is an essential means of transforming our relation to Shakespeare's work and each other as members of the classroom, university, and larger regional community. As Ahmed—drawing on Audre Lorde—explains, "The killjoy is testimony . . . because she speaks about damage."[28] *Testimony* in this sense draws on both early modern and contemporary meanings of the term as attestation, witnessing, professing, and protest and speech acts in which perceptual knowledge is shared.[29] Significantly, creating the space and support for my students' testimony counters the colonizing testimony white settlers used to dispossess Indigenous and non-white members of our community and institution.[30] Rather than testimony authorized by church, government, or educational authorities to secure power—power marked by the exclusion, silencing, and repression of others—we use testimony to create solidarity and community by welcoming, listening to, and learning from one another. We honor each other's capacity to provide the lived, textual, and communal experiences which shape our beliefs about and readings of Shakespeare and the worlds in which his work appears, not least our own.

Still, committing to a student-centered practice and refusing the cultural sacralization of Shakespeare's text when its depiction of white-

---

[26] Sara Ahmed, *Living a Feminist Life* (Durham: Duke University Press, 2017), 256, emphasis mine.
[27] Ahmed, *Living*, 251, 254.
[28] Ahmed, *Living*, 260. See Audre Lorde, "The Transformation of Silence into Language and Action," in *Sister Outsider* (Berkeley: Crossing Press, 1984), 40–44.
[29] "testimony, n.," OED Online, December 2022 (Oxford University Press); Miranda Fricker, *Epistemic Injustice: Power and the Ethics of Knowing* (Oxford: Oxford University Press, 2007), 69.
[30] Our institution's history of white supremacy was recently revisited in the dedication of a new dorm named for Alma Glass, the first Black student at WWU, who left after two quarters in the spring of 1906 after facing racist rejection by "the young white women" at the college, to which the president of the school responded that "the school knew neither race nor color." Alisha Dixon, "Western's First Black Student, Alma Clark," *The Western Front*, February 21, 2019. https://cpb-us-e1.wpmucdn.com/wp.wwu.edu/dist/0/3143/files/2019/11/Alma-Clark.pdf.

ness on which our own communities are centered requires more than respect for and faith in students' capacity for solidarity. Asking my students to see the violence of racialization as cruelty and dehumanization in Shakespeare means observing when and how Shakespeare relies not only on an authorizing whiteness but on the spectacle of the suffering of Blacks, Jews, and Muslims.[31] In doing so we slowly develop a more just and potent sense of Shakespeare's tragic import.

Listening to my students debate the troubled and troubling intersection of racial myths in which Shakespeare's work is implicated, I observe their initial anxiety become willful refusal as they find in reading and revisioning Shakespeare's tragic representation the ability "to widen the scripts available for what counts" as meaningful suffering.[32] They begin to celebrate willful refusal as just action in worlds or "organizations predicated on violence" and resist the "narrow scripts of happiness" that define their own and others' lives.[33] What Ahmed describes as the "appeal" of the killjoy emerges particularly in my students' weekly care in attending to the strengths of each other's writing about the violence of racialization and the power of reading for resistance in Shakespeare. But the most potent realization of this joy appears in their reading and viewing of Keith Hamilton Cobb's *American Moor*. The crucial role embodied life and performance plays in understanding both the power of Shakespeare and the power of whiteness in predominantly white spaces—not least those of higher education—is made palpable for them in Cobb's love of Shakespeare and the pain of his experience as a Black Shakespearean actor in a white dominant theater. Focusing on Cobb's exploration of the violence of whiteness in his dialogue with an offstage "unseasoned, white director,"[34] students encounter his profound pleasure in the "**RHY**thms **OF** art**TI**cu**LA**ted **JOY**" and "The **FREE**dom **OF** e**MO**tio**NAL** release" of Shakespeare's language, and the depth of his feeling for Othello as a "self-possess[ed]" Black man with "knowledge of [his] own worth" in a white dominant society.[35] This adaptation fires my students' sense of what a historically, aesthetically, and racially aware connection to Shakespeare

---

[31] See David Sterling Brown, "The 'Sonic Color Line': Shakespeare and the Canonization of Sexual Violence against Black Men," *The Sundial*, August 16, 2019, https://medium.com/the-sundial-acmrs/the-sonic-color-line-shakespeare-and-the-canonization-of-sexual-violence-against-black-men-cb166dca9af8.
[32] Ahmed, *Living*, 264.
[33] Ahmed, *Living*, 264–65.
[34] Kim F. Hall, "Introduction" to Keith Hamilton Cobb, *American Moor* (London: Methuen, 2020), 1.
[35] Keith Hamilton Cobb, *American Moor* (London: Methuen, 2020), 8, 19.

might entail.

This awareness of connectivity shows up as recognition of racist erasure on the one hand and racial empowerment on the other. White students often shamefacedly admit after reading *Othello* and *American Moor* that they did not feel Othello's power or pain until they witnessed Cobb's performance, and consequently question their affiliation with the racist white director. A white student wrote of Cobb's performance, "While reading the play, I thought the actor came off as a bit abrasive toward the director, but when viewing it, the [director's] racist micro-aggression, it stands out so much more when [I] s[aw] the face reacting to them." Students of color find in Cobb's text and performance an affirmation. "What Cobb sought to explore is a lot bigger than any of us imagine," one student of color wrote, "and his bravery allows a thorough dissection of deep-rooted norms than can't be ignored any longer." Another student noted that the Director's rejection of Cobb's invitation to talk in the final moment of the play—to "have the dauntless courage to challenge [Cobb] with [the director's] beliefs, but also the valor to have those beliefs challenged"—calls out white refusal, white silence in the face of antiblackness.[36] This student suggested that the white director's refusal of Cobb's challenge with a dismissive "Thanks for coming in"[37] echoes Iago's final line, "Demand me nothing. What you know you know."[38] "And he's not speaking to Black folk either," the student added.

I am moved by my students' testimony, their increasing sense of educational agency, and their growing solidarity in Fred Moten and Stefano Harney's sense of the *undercommons* as "dislocation" as "relation" among us all as students of ourselves, our communities, and the university—not the university as ideal or marketplace but as "a nonplace of abolition" in "the founding of a new society."[39] They teach me about the possible. But I also continually see the ways in which teaching the whiteness of Shakespeare as a white woman in a space imbued with the traumatic violence of settler colonialism illuminates the difficulty of this work. Because talking about the nature of whiteness in Shakespeare has its ghostly effects. It haunts white people by way of its insistence on primacy, its assumption of power,

---

[36] Cobb, *American Moor*, 41.
[37] Cobb, *American Moor*, 42.
[38] William Shakespeare, *Othello*, in *Norton Shakespeare: Tragedies*, 3rd ed., ed. Stephen Greenblatt et al. (New York: Norton, 2015), 5.2.296.
[39] Fred Moten and Stefano Harney, *The Undercommons: Fugitive Planning and Black Study* (Brooklyn: Minor Compositions, 2013), 149.

its demand for complicity, its silencing and violent effects in exchange for inclusion and illusions of safety. In a university, department, and classroom that are predominantly white, as mine are, the haunting is pervasive and, once acknowledged, palpable despite any initial relief in naming racialized constructs and their very real effects.

The discussion of the meaning of whiteness as settler ideology in my classes—and analysis of the variations and effects of whiteness in Shakespeare, many other texts, and our own lives—is hard. To an extent, failure is inevitable. White students, fearful or tired of the burdens of the work, can fall back into formulaic readings to recoup a reassuring practice and the sense of authority they experience in deploying it, apart from the erasures such readings entail. Others see this newly complicated Shakespeare as affirming their experience of the world, its injustices, its forms of communal identification and violent exclusion, but lose their ability to see its moments of compassion or resistance. Students who aspire to become teachers are especially at risk of insecurity and exhaustion. They worry about their capacity to teach the functions of whiteness in Shakespeare's texts, asking: What use is Shakespeare when they could be teaching texts that more directly challenge white supremacy? Would they, could they, do this work as high school teachers without being branded political, risking their new, hard-won livelihood? These are not trivial experiences or questions. Recognizing the humanity of such fears—of exclusion, violence, and suffering as grief and rage—is antiracist practice as recognition of our shared human yet distinctly racialized vulnerabilities.

Like Cobb, I relish the pleasures of Shakespeare's language and value his representation of human violence, suffering, and loss. I also believe, like Cobb, such pleasures are most profound when rooted in a complex and historically grounded understanding of his work in relation to the lives and legacies that shape our own existence, communities, and institutions—from ancient Greece, through early modern England, to the modern-day United States, including our own state and university. The teaching of Shakespeare has long been a means of obscuring and denying that history. The students' collaborative and sometimes combative reckoning with the power and tragic effects of whiteness in Shakespeare's work, and the painful history of their own instruction in its defining significance and violent enforcement, make my classes a rich and often fraught experience. Sometimes I trust that experience; sometimes I worry about it.

Yet I celebrate the work we do to become killjoy Shakespeareans, reckoning with Shakespeare's language, his capacity to give vivid life to embodied suffering and acts of resistance to the hierarchies of power he represents. Doing so means trusting my students' unsettled but larger and more intimate understanding of a Shakespeare tied to their past, present, and potential futures. Focusing on the tragedy of racialization and the production of whiteness in Shakespeare and our worlds is unsettling and affirming. Situating ourselves on and in Indigenous land allows us to see the problem of racialization as one rooted in the hierarchies of settler ideology that shapes our institution and thus the forms of connection that empower our resistance to its reproduction, girding us against the ever-resurgent idea of Shakespeare's work as uniform in meaning and value, as residing in the histories, lives, and practices of people whose claimed whiteness and its cost remain unacknowledged.

More than twenty-five years ago, Kim F. Hall concluded *Things of Darkness* with a challenge to "acknowledge the ongoing legacy of 'this thing of darkness' and use that knowledge to create new ways of thinking about difference."[40] Many scholars of color, and some white ones, have taken up this challenge. Yet so much work remains, especially for white teachers in predominantly white classrooms, institutions, and communities like mine.[41]

---

[40] Hall, *Things of Darkness*, 268.
[41] As I was finalizing edits of this essay, Jamie Paris published "On Teaching *The Tempest* in the Shadow of Unmarked Indian Residential School Graves," *The Sundial*, November 15, 2022, https://medium.com/the-sundial-acmrs/on-teaching-the-tempest-in-the-shadow-of-unmarked-indian-residential-school-graves-f6803fecbdda. Paris offers all teachers committed to culturally responsive teaching rooted in critical geography a potent example of "intergenerational trauma-informed teaching" that accounts for the role of early modern literature in advancing "settler supremacy."

Chapter 5

Shakespeare and Environmental Justice: Collaborative Eco-Theater in Yosemite National Park and the San Joaquin Valley

Katherine Steele Brokaw

Climate change, pollution, and biodiversity loss disproportionately affect the people who are least responsible for creating these ecological catastrophes. Where I teach, at the University of California Merced, such environmental injustice is keenly felt. Our campus is in California's San Joaquin Valley, plagued by the worst air quality and extreme heat in the United States, but within a two-hour drive of Yosemite National Park, a beloved protected wilderness that's repeatedly shut down due to fire and flood. As a scholar, teacher, and theater artist embedded in a public institution in this context, I have increasingly focused my scholarly and pedagogical work on the question of how adaptations of Shakespeare might address issues of environmental justice. In 2017, I co-founded Shakespeare in Yosemite with Paul Prescott: it is a student-centered performing arts initiative funded by a small grant from UC Merced's Office of the Chancellor and done in collaboration with the National Park Service (NPS). Along with our students, we create shows to be performed in Yosemite each April for Earth Day and Shakespeare's birthday, presenting productions that are site-specific and ecologically inflected.[1] Ecological catastrophes demand nothing less than full, active engagement in all arenas, even the Shakespeare classroom. In my institutional context, I have found that engaging students in theater-making and practice-based research is one of the highest-impact ways in which I as an academy-based Shakespearean can practice socially and environmentally engaged pedagogy. As such, work on Shakespeare in Yosemite shows is now incorporated into my classroom teaching.

---

[1] For information about past and future shows, see the *Shakespeare in Yosemite* website: yosemiteshakes.ucmerced.edu.

In what follows, I describe the institutional contexts in which Shakespeare in Yosemite is produced, explain the methods that inform our practice, and detail student work on *Imogen in the Wild*, our 2021 90-minute film adaptation of *Cymbeline*. While Shakespeare in Yosemite and its institutional contexts are unique, this work leads me to propose the following principles, to which I will refer throughout the essay and return in the final section. I hope some of them are relevant to readers interested in doing similar student projects:

- Performance projects let students engage in practice-based research, which often plays to students' skillsets better than traditional forms of research and allows them a more relevant engagement with Shakespeare.
- If we want institutions to be more inclusive and equitable, we need to remove barriers and amplify the creativity and insight of those students traditionally marginalized from these spaces.
- If, as Ayanna Thompson asserts, "Shakespeare needs social justice pedagogies as much as social justice pedagogies benefit from Shakespeare," this is also true when it comes to engaging with pedagogies of environmental justice.[2]
- Creative collaboration and community-building have always been important to the mental health of college students and have become more vital in the post-COVID era.

Institutional Contexts: Academic, Theatrical, and Environmental

Shakespeare in Yosemite brings together three institutional contexts—academia, the Shakespearean stage, and American National Parks—each of which has a history of excluding BIPOC, female and nonbinary, LGBTQ+, disabled, and neurodivergent people. When welcoming our students into these spaces, I must center traditionally marginalized voices and de-center my own, break down barriers to access, and challenge the traditionally white, privileged, male, and heteronormative power structures and narratives that have long been dominant in universities, theater companies, and America's wildernesses.

---

[2] Ayanna Thompson, "An Afterword about Self/Communal Care," in *Teaching Social Justice Through Shakespeare: Why Renaissance Literature Matters Now*, ed. Hillary Eklund and Wendy Beth Hyman (Edinburgh: Edinburgh University Press, 2019), 236.

Serving traditionally marginalized students is central to UC Merced's mission. It opened its doors in 2005 as the tenth campus of the University of California, and its current student body (of just over 9,000 students in 2022) demographically reflects the state's future: students are 90 percent people of color, 54 percent of them identify as Latine, 70 percent are the first in their families to attend college. Our campus was intentionally placed in the underserved San Joaquin Valley, between the Sierra Nevada mountains (in which Yosemite is located) to the east and the coastal mountains to the west. This polluted agricultural area has low rates of educational attainment. Wildfire smoke sometimes makes it difficult to walk outside. Summers are unbearably hot and lasting longer each year. The citizenship status of many of our students is uncertain—and many more have family members living precariously. Our students feel the sharp edges of environmental and social injustices keenly, and crave engagement with the forces that affect their families, communities, and futures.

As for the Shakespearean stage, readers of this volume will likely be familiar with long histories of that space being dominated by white, male, Anglo-American voices. I won't elaborate at length except to say that I hope this essay demonstrates the way our collaborative project differs from many theatrical institutions, which tend to prioritize the authorities of "the text" and the director, rather than engagement with our world.

The final institution relevant to this work is Yosemite National Park, which is increasingly threatened not only by fires and droughts but also by a federal government that tends to prioritize resource extraction over preservation of America's wildernesses (trends which historically accelerate during Republican administrations). When we began our work in the park in 2017, many NPS climate policies were being rescinded, and park rangers were forbidden from discussing human-made climate change with visitors.[3] Yosemite is located on land with a violent colonial history of displacing the Indigenous tribes who for 8,000 years maintained the land's ecosystem, though recently the park has begun to collaborate with local Southern Sierra Miwuk members on the reconstruction of a roundhouse and sweat lodge in Yosemite.[4]

---

[3] This article by former NPS director Jonathan Jarvis and career parks advocate Destry Jarvis is particularly salient: "The Great Dismantling of America's National Parks is Under Way," *Guardian*, January 10, 2020, https://www.theguardian.com/environment/2020/jan/10/us-national-parks-dismantling-under-way.

[4] See for example Kurtis Alexander, "How the Miwuk Tribe is Reclaiming Part of Yosemite Valley," *San Francisco Chronicle*, April 26, 2018, https://www.sfgate.com/science/article/How-the-Miwuk-tribe-is-reclaiming-part-of-12866845.php.

In 2016, with the support of then-Chancellor Dorothy Leland, Shakespeare in Yosemite was founded with the blessing and assistance of park officials.[5] We perform one public show on campus before spending Earth Day weekend performing in the park. We have brought in buses of UC Merced and high school students to some shows, but most spectators are Yosemite visitors who see our posters or stumble upon free Shakespeare while hiking. Our proof-of-concept production, in spring 2017, was a collage show that spliced several Shakespeare scenes with the writings of John Muir (1838–1914), the Scottish naturalist and writer credited with inspiring the National Parks movement.[6] Our 2018 site-specific *Midsummer Night's Dream* focused on consumerism and trash.[7] In 2019, we staged *As You Like It* to explore how forested Ardens are not only places of social renewal, but also carbon sinks that mitigate the warming of our planet and harbor the ecosystems that keep Earth's creatures fed and alive.[8] After a COVID hiatus in 2020, we safely filmed *Imogen in the Wild* in 2021, and returned to live performance with our *Love's Labor's Lost*, originally slated for 2020, in 2022. That adaptation, a film of which is available on YouTube, was set in 1969 and reworks Shakespeare's comedy to imagine two bands on songwriting retreat in Yosemite. It refers to and honors the many movements of 1969–70: the first Earth Day, Stonewall, and fights for equity for women, people of color, and farmworkers. After an open mic night is interrupted by the news that Princess's brother has been killed in Vietnam, the departing "Sierra Girls" (their band name) tell their suitors to spend a year doing some good for the environment. The production's finale stages a sort of *Love's Labor's Won*, with the bands reassembling in 1970 to report on the first Earth Day, the establishment of the Environmental Protection Agency, and other landmark action on the environment from the early '70s.

---

[5] I am particularly grateful to Rangers Scott Gediman, Jamie Richards, Shelton Johnson, and Sabrina Diaz for their support of the project.
[6] This initial production is described in Brokaw and Paul Prescott, "Applied Shakespeare in Yosemite National Park," *Critical Survey* 31, no. 4 (Winter 2019): 15–28, and in Brokaw, "Shakespeare as Community Practice," *Shakespeare Bulletin* 35, no. 3 (Fall 2017): 445–61.
[7] Described in Brokaw and Paul Prescott, "Reduce, Rewrite, Recycle: Adapting Shakespeare for the Environment," in *The Arden Research Companion to Shakespeare and Adaptation*, ed. Diana Henderson and Stephen O'Neill (London: Bloomsbury, 2022), 303–22, and on the *Shakespeare in Yosemite* website.
[8] Described in Brokaw, "Text-Based/Concept-Driven," in *Shakespeare/Text: Arden Critical Intersections*, ed. Claire Bourne (London: Bloomsbury, 2021), 245–63.

Figure 5.1 The stage at Curry Village on which Shakespeare in Yosemite performs, with Half Dome in the background. Photo: Shawn Overton.

While students have always been central to our projects, these last two projects—*Imogen in the Wild* and *Love's Labor's Lost*—were thoroughly integrated into my teaching, creating a model from which I continue to work.

Methods

Shakespeare in Yosemite's collaborative process synthesizes several methods: Practice as Research (PaR; sometimes "Performance as Research" in the US), Community Engaged Scholarship (CES), and ecodramaturgy. PaR refers to "the uses of practical creativity as reflexive enquiry into significant research concerns."[9] Crucial to PaR is the recognition that performance is best understood when the researcher is an active co-maker rather than observer. Our student

---

[9] Baz Kershaw, "Performance Practice as Research: Perspectives from a Small Island," in *Mapping Landscapes for Performance as Research: Scholarly Acts and Creative Cartographies*, ed. Shannon Rose Riley and Lynette Hunter (London: Palgrave Macmillan, 2009), 4.

participants are creators of both theater and knowledge when producing Shakespeare in Yosemite shows, and many of them have done small to lengthy research projects based on their practical work.

The creation of socially engaged scholarship is increasingly recognized as fundamental to a university's mission. The weight given to "impact" case studies in the UK's Research Excellence Framework (REF) indicates the rising value of such work in that country. In the US, the Carnegie Foundation for the Advancement of Teaching introduced the "community engaged" classification in 2006. Shakespeare in Yosemite collaborates with community members in the Merced, Yosemite/Sierra, and foothill regions, and invites members of these communities, as well as the international park-going public, to attend and offer feedback. The films are made available for free to anyone who can access YouTube. Hillary Eklund has well explained how, in the Shakespeare classroom, community engagement has the potential to free us from "the burden of proving the relevance of Shakespeare in our world," instead prioritizing students' "encounters with texts and with the community, which heighten both the intellectual and civic stakes of our teaching."[10]

Finally, we practice what Theresa J. May calls "ecodramaturgy," which is theater-making that puts ecological reciprocity and community at the center of its theatrical and thematic intent.[11] As Paul Prescott and I have argued elsewhere,[12] Shakespeare is a renewable cultural resource: we can plunder and adapt his texts for new purposes without diminishing them for future generations. But many of Earth's pillaged resources will never come back, and their destruction is wiping out species and threatening human health and safety. We agree with Randall Martin and Evelyn O'Malley's claim that, "far from shying away from Shakespeare's canonicity, it seems worth trying to exploit it for whatever (limited) potential it may contain."[13] Indeed, perhaps the greatest advantages of this long dead, European

---

[10] Hillary Eklund, "Shakespeare, Service Learning, and the Embattled Humanities," in Eklund and Hyman, *Teaching Social Justice*, 188. See also Jan Cohen-Cruz's discussion of higher education as a site of engaged art pedagogy in *Engaging Performance: Theatre as Call and Response* (London: Routledge, 2010), 177–91.

[11] May defines 'ecodramaturgy' in "*Tú eres mi otro yo*—Staying with the Trouble: Ecodramaturgy and the AnthropoScene," *Journal of American Drama and Theatre* 29, no. 2 (2017): 1–18.

[12] Brokaw and Paul Prescott, "Saving the Earth Needs All Hands on Deck, Including Shakespeare's," *Modesto Bee* and *Merced Sun-Star*, April 11, 2018, https://www.modbee.com/opinion/article208648584.html.

[13] Randall Martin and Evelyn O'Malley, "Eco-Shakespeare in Performance: Introduction," *Shakespeare Bulletin* 36, no. 3 (Fall 2018): 386.

playwright are that his out-of-copyright plays are malleable enough to be adaptable for a variety of purposes, and continue to appeal across political divides. We found this to be the case when adapting *Cymbeline* for our 2021 film.

Imogen in the Wild (2021)

Imogen in the Wild addresses local ecological challenges, a brief given to our company when we joined the global Cymbeline in the Anthropocene project, which brought together ten theaters from around the world to create eco-adaptations of the play.[14] Our 90-minute movie was safely filmed in March 2021 on the empty campus of UC Merced and in Yosemite, and released on our YouTube channel in fall 2021.[15]

After a January 2020 retreat of the Cymbeline in the Anthropocene group (and the sudden onset of a global pandemic), work on *Imogen* began in earnest in fall 2020, when I was teaching an online seminar on Shakespeare and Ecology. Sensing the importance of community-building work for these physically disconnected students, I introduced a collaborative creative project to the class, asking student groups to adapt *Cymbeline* for ecological purposes. Their ideas informed the draft screenplay that I co-adapted with Paul Prescott and then UC Merced lecturer Billy Wolfgang in winter 2020–21. In spring 2021, my online Advanced Shakespeare class was also required to do a collaborative creative project. I gave them the option of working on *Imogen in the Wild*, and about half of the class signed on as actors, songwriters, film editors, and prop and costume designers. The cast featured seven UC Merced students, five professional or semi-professional actors, and six Yosemite rangers (including one current and another former UC Merced student). Given the community from which we draw and the intentionality of our auditions and practices, our cast was predominantly female or nonbinary, and predominantly people of color, as is always the case for Shakespeare in Yosemite.

Imogen in the Wild is particularly focused on issues of environmental justice and the links between land abuse and misogyny.

---

[14] The project website can be viewed at https://www.cymbeline-anthropocene.com.
[15] William Shakespeare and Katherine Steele Brokaw, Paul Prescott, and Billy Wolfgang, *Imogen in the Wild*, dir. Katherine Steele Brokaw (Merced: Shakespeare in Yosemite, 2021). Available on YouTube and at https://yosemiteshakes.ucmerced.edu/films/imogen-wild-film-2021.

Figure 5.2 Lee Stetson, Sofia Andom, and Ángel Nuñez on set in Yosemite. Photo: Katherine Steele Brokaw.

The opening scenes show that Mayor Cymbeline (Dennis Brown) is being urged by his wife Queenie (Connie Stetson) and her son Cloten (Chase Brantley) to sign a deal that will damage "the wild" that borders his town. Queenie's business partner and secret lover Iachimo (Lisa Wolpe, playing the role as a man)[16] is a major investor in the deal, and has an interest in stopping those who protest it. Cymbeline's son-in-law Leo (Tonatiuh Newbold, a former UC Merced student who now works in Yosemite) is one of many people objecting to the destructive project, and thus must be banished and estranged from the mayor's daughter Imogen (then student Sofia Andom). Another campaigner is Belarius, played by Lee Stetson; Guiderius and Arviragus were played by then students Amber Loper and Ángel Nuñez. Ranger Lucía, a radically reimagined Lucius played by UC Merced alumna and then Yosemite ranger Jess Rivas, meets with Cymbeline several times to urge him to protect the wild, and later confers with her colleagues, all played by real Yosemite rangers.

---

[16] Lisa Wolpe is an LA-based equity actor who has played more male Shakespearean roles professionally than any other living woman.

Figure 5.3 Cat Flores singing in *Love's Labor's Lost*. Photo: Darah Carrillo Vargas.

Belarius's efforts to interrupt the destruction are picked up by youth protesters who create a viral eco-anthem, based on Titania's "climate change speech" in *A Midsummer Night's Dream*, written by then student Cat Flores. These joint efforts to protect the wild climax with a protest that replaces the battles of *Cymbeline*. All the show's many songs—from Leo's gorgeous love ballad about Imogen's "manacle of love" to a stunning, environmentally aware recasting of "Fear No More the Heat of the Sun" by Rena Johnson—were written and performed by students.

The film highlights how capitalism and political greed have long combined with misogyny and racism to destroy lands, plants, animals, and human lives. One of the rangers in the film, Emily Dayhoff, is a member of the Southern Sierra Miwuk tribe. She speaks extra-Shakespearean lines about the histories of "those who have been here the longest meeting those who would use their land for their own dark purposes." The film concludes with Ranger Shelton Johnson, a Black and Cherokee man, joining Sofia Andom (Imogen) to acknowledge the local tribes who have stewarded "what flows beneath our feet, the plants, the wildlife, and everything that is

Figure 5.4 Tonatiuh Newbold (Leo) and Dennis Brown (Cymbeline) embrace. Still from *Imogen in the Wild*.

around us for thousands of years, and [who] continue to do so." Of that experience, Andom wrote,

> one moment I will carry with me was when Ranger Shelton Johnson and I acknowledged the Indigenous tribes who were the original caretakers of Yosemite. It was visually and spiritually powerful to have two Black people doing that in Yosemite, a space that is not usually inviting to people of color, and voicing that these lands do not belong to us, and thank you for letting us be in this space.[17]

Andom highlights how the project thought about intersecting questions of who owns and who feels welcome in America's wildernesses.

Indeed, conversations about belonging, colonialism, and environmental justice were central to the adaptative and production process, and to discussions about the film with my 2021 Advanced Shakespeare class (of which Andom was a part). The entire class viewed and responded to early cuts, which at the time were being edited by three of their classmates.[18] Having read *Cymbeline* in class, they were ready to understand how *Imogen* connected misogynistic and environmental violence. Student Remy Sunada-Tate wrote that "*Imogen*, like *Cymbeline*, aligns its villains with the threat to both Imogen's physical body and to the land itself. The harm men threaten

---

[17] Sofia Andom, "Reflection on *Imogen in the Wild*" (unpublished essay, May 8, 2021), Microsoft Word file.

[18] UC Merced students Brandon Cooper, Will Darpinian, and Rilee Hoch put in countless hours on the film, working with our paid Director of Photography, Shawn Overton.

to inflict upon her physical body is representative of the harm done to the land."[19] Other students related parts of the film to their own experiences. Responding to her classmate's rendition of "Fear No More," Arlyne Gonzalez reflected that

> the line "chimney smoke fills our skies" stuck out to me as I remember the skies from the 2017 Thomas fire in Southern California. I want to always see clear blue skies and breathe in clean air and this production showed me how planet Earth is supposed to look, with clear skies. We made a mistake these last generations, and now it is time to unite and help save our one Earth.[20]

Imogen in the Wild has been viewed nearly a thousand times on YouTube, and I hope that it can continue to live on as a way for students beyond UC Merced to engage with issues of environmental justice through Shakespeare.

When we returned to live performance in 2022, I was teaching a Theatre and Ecology class (of which Shakespeare was just one part). I gave students the option of working on a real-life collaborative project: about half the class worked on *Love's Labor's Lost*; a few worked on the EarthShakes Alliance, an initiative to connect Shakespeare theaters and scholars around the world who are interested in environmental issues;[21] and two co-organized UC Merced's Earth Day climate rally for a Green New Deal in the University of California system. My reflections below draw from student experiences with both *Imogen in the Wild* and *Love's Labor's Lost*.

Practice-Based Research, Collaboration, and Mental Health

Students who worked on *Imogen in the Wild* and *Love's Labor's Lost* wrote reflections about their experiences and understood that they were engaging in Practice as Research. I assigned student interviewers to both projects, who conducted on set (for *Imogen*) and on site (for *LLL*) interviews, deepening the reflective experience and helping to build a Shakespeare in Yosemite archive.

---

[19] Remy Sunada-Tate, "Reflection on *Imogen in the Wild*" (unpublished essay, May 2, 2021), Microsoft Word file.
[20] Arlyne Gonzalez, "Reflection on *Imogen in the Wild*" (unpublished essay, May 1, 2021), Microsoft Word file.
[21] The project website is earthshakes.ucmerced.edu.

Working on Shakespeare in Yosemite has led several students to pursue related projects and careers. After then student Ángel Nuñez helped to make our *As You Like It* more accessible to Spanish speakers, in 2020 he began working with Billy Wolfgang and two other then student members of that cast, Maria Nguyen-Cruz and Cat Flores, on a new bilingual adaptation of *Richard II* (*Ricardo el Segundo*), which was filmed in summer 2020 by Merced Shakespearefest, a community company. The careers of these three students post-graduation is a testament to the impact that involvement in this type of work can have on students: Ángel is artistic director of a Pennsylvania-based theater company where he continues to create bilingual theater; Maria integrates environmental activism into their middle-school English classroom; and after completing a research honors project on Shakespeare, bilingualism, and music, Cat began a PhD in English to continue her research and creative work at UC Davis. Several more Shakespeare in Yosemite alums are pursuing careers in academia and education, the arts, and the NPS and environmental justice organizations.

Shakespeare in Yosemite gives students opportunities that help open doors to the worlds of academia, theater, and environmental protection. But regardless of what they do post-graduation, the experience of working creatively in spaces with which most of them are not familiar can, after initial challenges, allow for what several of them have referred to as an expansion of the self. Will Darpinian, who worked as film editor and sound director on *Imogen* and sound director on *Love's Labor's Lost*, wrote that

> working on *Imogen in the Wild* reminded me of how malleable identity is, if people are willing to acknowledge you could be something outside the frame of your current existence. The film editing experience I gained is professionally valuable, but the true relevance to me was tuning the instrument of myself to play the song of *Imogen in the Wild*. When I had to see the whole pattern of the film, I stepped outside of myself and saw not only other people and their labor of passion, but also a more hopeful version of myself ... the reminder that it's possible to be more than the person I was yesterday has been profound to me.[22]

Will's reflections on a renewed sense of self were echoed by Sofia Andom (Imogen) in conversation with myself and Debra Ann Byrd,

---

[22] Will Darpinian, "Reflection on *Imogen in the Wild*" (unpublished essay, May 1, 2021), Microsoft Word file.

founder of Harlem Shakespeare Festival, whom I brought to my online Advanced Shakespeare class while *Imogen* was in rehearsals. Byrd spoke of her work as a queer Afro-Latina woman who was told from a young age what she could and couldn't be, and explained how her work in theater allowed her eventually to become the self that many couldn't see. Andom then addressed both me and Byrd, who responded to her:

> Andom: Casting people, they see you in a certain way. I understand. With my hair, I'm 5'10", I'm a plus-size woman. People want to make you the mother, or a dominating figure. But my personality is so . . . opposite that. So when you cast me as Imogen, Katie, it flipped my world around. Because I never saw myself as that. And hearing you speak about that experience, Debra Ann, made me realize that I'm not alone.

> Byrd: When we get to see ourselves as something different, and then there comes that one person—it only takes the one—that person who says "I see you. And not only do I see you, but I see you and I celebrate you, and I know that in you is the ability to make this happen." Then something magical happens in that person.[23]

It was an extraordinary moment for me as a teacher. Inasmuch as I have a teaching philosophy, it is most crucially to see and celebrate each of my students, to help them discover and become their own best and truest selves—and when it comes to Shakespeare, to bring that whole, true self to the text. Sofia and Debra Ann articulated that these discoveries are possible, and life altering.

Bringing students to Shakespeare is not without challenges, and we must never forget the ways in which Shakespeare has long been used to intimidate, assimilate, and exclude. Students need space to reflect on that. Sofia spoke frequently of her impostor syndrome in both playing the ingenue in a Shakespearean play, and entering the space of the Yosemite wilderness. After filming *Imogen*, Cymbeline in the Anthropocene project convener Randall Martin and his research assistant Rebecca Salazar interviewed Sofia about what it means to approach the traditionally white, elite spaces of Shakespearean performance and the outdoors as a woman of color and daughter of immigrants:

---

[23] Sofia Andom and Debra Ann Byrd, conversation in recorded Zoom class, March 4, 2021.

My dad is Black man, he's from Eritrea, and my mom is Filipino. They are both immigrants and they see Shakespeare as something for white people. And when I told them I'd be in Yosemite, and sleep in a cabin and everything, they said "really?" While they respect the work, they wondered "why would you do that?" My parents, they come from third world countries, so it's like "why would you want to sleep outside when you have a house, indoors, air conditioning? We escaped from that!" I know it mentally, that it's a great thing to be in nature. But as a person of color and as a daughter whose parents stepped away from what in their mind is poor, well, they want me to take advantage of the technology, of the bed that we paid for, that we struggled for; it's challenging.[24]

Sofia's articulations are profound, and I have long thought that the insights of my student collaborators are as valuable as anyone's when it comes to professional conversations about access and equity in Shakespearean performance, academia, and protected wildernesses.

In April 2021, I invited Sofia, Ángel, and Cat to co-present on Yosemite Shakes for Globe4Globe: Shakespeare and the Climate Emergency, an online conference co-sponsored by the Globe Theatre in London and UC Merced that was the first known conference to explicitly focus on Shakespeare and ecological issues.[25] They were the only undergraduate presenters at the conference (which brought together academics, theater artists, and activists), and their impact was profound. It made me wonder, not for the first time, what is lost by the gatekeeping of traditional academic conferences.

One of many things my students and I have come to understand is the role that art—Shakespearean or otherwise—can play in the battle to save a habitable planet. Speaking with student interviewer Isaac Gállegos-Rodriguez during the *Love's Labor's Lost* weekend, Sofia reflected that

> there's a lot of people who may be introduced to the issues of climate change or the disaster of the environment through ways that *aren't* creative. And it could sound a lot more complex when it's not communicated well. I was reading one of the surveys that somebody left today about our show and they said it was so easy to understand.

---

[24] Interview with Sofia Andom conducted by Randall Martin and Rebecca Salazar, May 30, 2021, https://www.cymbeline-anthropocene.com/article/17972-imogen-in-the-wild-interview-with-sofia-andom.

[25] Videos of all presentations are available at The EarthShakes Alliance: earthshakes.ucmerced.edu/globe4globe-videos.

Figure 5.5 Andrew Hardy, Tonatiuh Newbold, Sofia Andom, Cat Flores, Bella Camfield, and Bethy Harmelin in *Love's Labor's Lost*. Photo: Grace Garnica.

> And that's what we're trying to do, to make climate change easy to understand for everyone of all ages.[26]

Her words echoed those of Jess Rivas in 2018, who then was working in Yosemite and played Snout the Wilderness Ranger and the fairy Orange Poppy in *Dream*:

> This adaptation is very inclusive. People in the audience feel connected to the show; they are a part of this experience instead of just observing. And that's really important when you are addressing issues like climate change, and some of these very hard to accept and maybe even uncomfortable conversations—it's really important that we are all included, because otherwise, if we are not connected to that, we are also not connected to the solution.[27]

---

[26] Interview with Sofia Andom by Isaac Gállegos-Rodriguez, April 23, 2022.
[27] Author interview with Jessica Rivas, April 22, 2018.

Jess—at the time a ranger censored from directly discussing anthropogenic climate change—went on to describe how historical, seemingly apolitical Shakespeare provided a way into a topic in which others might not engage:

> I can't bring up climate change right now—I'm not allowed. I *do* get to say "Shakespeare's fairies, you know, they are explaining that the weather is changing. Titania talks about how the humans lost their winter cheer." And we can talk about how we feel bad we can't enjoy winter, we feel bad that it's hot in the middle of January. So the play opens up conversations we aren't allowed to bring up directly.[28]

While Jess reflected on how the show's eco-messages could connect to audiences, others discussed their personal connections.

Many students, like their Generation Z peers, expressed keenly a feeling of eco-grief.[29] Student turned alumnus Andrew Hardy (Orlando in *As You Like It*, Cloten's Lord in *Imogen*, Dumaine in *Love's Labor's Lost*) reflected on how Dumaine's lobbying for the Clean Water Act resonated for him, because

> there's lots of water issues in the Central Valley, whether it's irrigation or it's contamination of groundwater because of fracking and agriculture. There's lots of crazy stuff that just keeps happening, fifty years after the Clean Water Act. In Merced County, you're not supposed to even drink the tap water without extra filtration.[30]

Student interviewer Isaac was particularly interested in how collaborative art might be one balm for this anxiety, and he asked team members about it. Many echoed Darah Carrillo Vargas, the show's student graphic designer and photographer, who said:

> I feel that theater and art have a big role to play in getting us together, getting us united behind these problems. And the biggest cause of all this destruction is our disconnection from each other. So events like this: we are actually *doing* something. I'm not putting out any fires, but just being together and just spreading this message does quite a bit. It's very sad to see our Earth dying and it's so easy to fall

---

[28] Author interview with Jessica Rivas, April 22, 2018.
[29] See, for example, Matthew Taylor and Jessica Murray, "'Overwhelming and terrifying': The Rise of Climate Anxiety," *Guardian*, February 10, 2020, https://www.theguardian.com/environment/2020/feb/10/overwhelming-and-terrifying-impact-of-climate-crisis-on-mental-health.
[30] Interview with Andrew Hardy by Isaac Gállegos-Rodriguez, April 24, 2022.

into depression, but events like this make you see in different light, and give us hope.³¹

Darah articulates two points that are crucial to this work: it gives students agency, the feeling of *doing* something rather than just reading or writing about it; and they are doing that something together. Mahea LaRosa, one of the prop and costume designers for *Love's Labor's Lost*, reflected on the efficacy of the project, and how it changed her perspective:

> Enjoying the theatre and engaging with the ideas presented showed me how theatre allows people to connect with a more empathetic view regarding ecological problem-solving. It also taught me that I need to be less critical of myself and others when it comes to doing *enough*, because introducing people to the idea that they are connected to the natural world around them and trying to bridge the gap between generations, it is completely *enough*. With this production, and with my assistance, we were able to impact people emotionally, make them think about their own place in the world, and I am so lucky to have been a part of this.³²

Bringing students together in such an empowering way provided social and emotional balm for them at a particularly difficult time. In both 2021 and 2022, nearly every student involved spoke about the boon the project was to their mental health: helping them overcome academic, personal, and ecological anxiety; making them feel a sense of community during remote instruction; giving them a sense of purpose. As the 2020s wear on and mental health becomes an increasingly urgent issue on college campuses, it becomes ever more imperative that our Shakespearean classrooms inspire confidence, spark creativity, and facilitate connection, rather than—as is too often the case—incite feelings of inadequacy. While Shakespeare in Yosemite is a unique project, at its heart it is a simple, transferable approach: it connects Shakespeare to the issues that affect our students the most, and gives them collaborative and creative opportunities to do something tangible in a world that desperately needs their voices and creativity.

---

[31] Interview with Darah Carrillo Vargas by Isaac Gállegos-Rodriguez, April 23, 2022.
[32] Mahea LaRosa, "Reflection on *Love's Labor's Lost*" (unpublished essay, May 8, 2022), Microsoft Word file.

Chapter 6

Where Curriculum Meets Community: Teaching Borderlands Shakespeare in San Antonio
Katherine Gillen and Kathryn Vomero Santos

The conflict between colonial power and decolonial resistance is not unique to San Antonio, Texas, but it is especially palpable in this predominantly Mexican American city whose hybrid culture has been shaped by layers of colonization. First known as the Yanaguana, so named by the original inhabitants for its life-giving waters, San Antonio was and continues to be home to the Payaya, Coahuilteca, Lipan Apache, and Comanche, as well as other diasporic peoples from across the Americas. As a city in the Texas–Mexico Borderlands, San Antonio is home to what Gloria E. Anzaldúa describes as a "border culture" that has emerged through centuries of "possession and ill-use" by multiple colonial powers, including "Spain, Mexico, the Republic of Texas, the US, the Confederacy, and the US again."[1] The inhumane treatment of migrants at the increasingly militarized border reflects the ongoing nature of this coloniality in our current moment.

These histories and present realities permeate educational spaces, which have long been sites of conflict. Most recently, the Texas state legislature passed laws prohibiting educators in public schools from teaching the full history of systemic racism and its social impacts. Such laws attempt to undo decades of work by educators and activists to include ethnic studies in curricula, while also seeking to impose a colonial, white supremacist fantasy of the founding and expansion of the United States. Though initially targeted at primary and secondary education, such attacks are also beginning to affect the climate at institutions of higher education. Faculty who teach about race have been reported by students and put on conservative watch lists, and in February 2022 Lieutenant Governor Dan Patrick

---

[1] Gloria E. Anzaldúa, *Borderlands/La Frontera: The New Mestiza*, 5th ed. (San Francisco: Aunt Lute Press, 2022), 94.

suggested that faculty at public institutions who teach critical race theory should have their tenure revoked. Laws that restrict reproductive rights, LGBTQIA2+ rights, and the rights of undocumented immigrants, moreover, have a direct impact on many students' ability to access education in Texas.

This is the context in which we—white settlers who moved to Texas for our academic jobs—teach Shakespeare, an author whose work has played an outsized role in British and US colonial projects. Although we are both located in San Antonio, we teach at very different institutions, each with its own particular history, demographics, and mission. Kathryn teaches at Trinity University, a small private, residential, predominantly white liberal arts university that aspires to become a Hispanic-Serving Institution (HSI). Katherine teaches at Texas A&M University–San Antonio (A&M–SA), a recently established comprehensive state university and HSI located on the primarily Mexican American and historically underserved Southside of San Antonio. The differences in our institutional contexts reflect the long legacies of colonialism and the current racial and economic forms of segregation that result from them. Our Shakespeare pedagogy, therefore, has been shaped by our different institutional contexts, developed with and in relation to our colleagues and students. Our approaches, however, are joined by shared attention to the colonial and Indigenous histories of the region and by our common efforts to destabilize disciplinary boundaries as well as the boundaries between educational institutions and the communities they purport to serve.

Broadly, we have been influenced by work in critical race pedagogy, culturally sustaining pedagogy, and decolonial pedagogy. Theorists from these pedagogical traditions suggest that our courses and curricula can potentially serve as sites of resistance to the practices and epistemologies of higher education that often reinforce colonial structures and enact racist violence. Such resistance involves centering local conditions and Indigenous histories and inviting diverse ways of knowing into the classroom. We have sought, therefore, to ground our pedagogy in our communities and to validate students' knowledges—especially those cultural, racial, and linguistic knowledges that have been suppressed by forces of coloniality, white supremacy, and heteropatriarchy.[2] As George

---

[2] For a discussion of the vital funds of knowledge that students bring to the classroom, see Django Paris, "Culturally Sustaining Pedagogy: A Needed Change in Stance, Terminology, and Practice," *Educational Researcher* 41, no. 3 (2012): 93–97.

J. Sefa Dei and Meredith Lordan suggest, decolonial pedagogical praxis involves a "counter-visioning" that "offers the intellectual space for Indigeneity to emerge as a site of authentic knowledge production and protection."[3] Such an educational approach, they argue, "needs to be posited to help foster a strong sense of identity, self and collective agency and empowerment to communities."[4] To enact our antiracist and decolonial commitments, our teaching must challenge the coloniality of our disciplines, their curricula, their methodologies, and their canons. This is especially imperative for teaching Shakespeare, the canonical author par excellence.

This essay focuses on the pedagogical potential of engaging with Shakespeare through the lens of Borderlands theories, histories, and cultural production. In particular, we will discuss the value of teaching works of adaptation, translation, and appropriation that fall under the category of what we call Borderlands Shakespeare. These works, predominantly by Chicanx and Indigenous playwrights, reimagine Shakespeare's plays through Borderlands frameworks to reflect local communities and concerns. Borderlands Shakespeare plays, we contend, give students the tools to interrogate Shakespeare's place in the region and to interpret his works in conversation with their lived experiences and cultural traditions. We thus join Ruben Espinosa in his desire to encourage student readers to see that Shakespeare "is not the incontestable focal point, but rather an element to which we, on the temporal and physical borderlands, can add nuance and layer with manifold meanings."[5] Our work teaching Shakespeare and Shakespeare appropriations in the Borderlands, moreover, has revealed the importance of undertaking curricular revisions and of collaborating with communities outside our academic institutions.

Teaching Borderlands Shakespeare

While teaching Shakespeare's plays can often lead to a recapitulation of white, colonial ways of knowing, we have found that Borderlands Shakespeare plays provide valuable models for forms

---

[3] George J. Sefa Dei and Meredith Lordan, "Introduction: Envisioning New Meanings, Memories and Actions for Anti-Colonial Theory and Decolonial Praxis," in *Anti-Colonial Theory and Decolonial Praxis*, ed. Sefa Dei and Lordan (New York: Peter Lang Publishing, 2016), xii.
[4] Sefa Dei and Lordan, "Introduction," xii.
[5] Ruben Espinosa, "Traversing the Temporal Borderlands of Shakespeare," *New Literary History* 52, no. 3/4 (2021): 605–23, esp. 606.

of interpretation that not only bring Borderlands epistemologies to bear on early modern English texts but also use the resonances and dissonances between them to create new works of art that tell stories of and for La Frontera. Borderlands Shakespeare plays such as Edit Villarreal's *The Language of Flowers*, James Lujan's *Kino and Teresa*, Herbert Siguenza's *El Henry*, Seres Jaime Magaña's *The Tragic Corrido of Romeo and Lupe*, Josh Inocéncio's *Ofélio*, and José Cruz González's *Invierno* are rooted in the communities to which many of our students belong, and they prioritize place-based Indigenous and Chicanx epistemologies, languages, and practices. Borderlands Shakespeare reflects the vibrancy of Mexican American theater, which has its roots in El Teatro Campesino, an activist theater that arose as part of the farm workers' movement in the 1960s. These plays actively confront colonial power, engaging with the most prominent author in the white English canon to craft decolonial counternarratives.

Both *El Henry* and *The Tragic Corrido of Romeo and Lupe*, for instance, invoke the geographical and political imaginary of Atzlán, thus signaling their engagement with the politics of El Movimiento, the Chicano civil rights movement, and their continuing interest in engendering a liberated future for Chicanxs. *The Language of Flowers* sets *Romeo and Juliet* during Día de los Muertos to emphasize the enduring power of Mexica spiritual beliefs to heal the wounds of Chicanxs whose lives have been destroyed by colonial violence. Like many Borderlands plays, *The Language of Flowers* questions the power of love to solve deep conflicts in the region. *Invierno* reimagines the famous "gap of time" in *The Winter's Tale* through Indigenous temporalities in order to create spaces for healing. The play's Paulina character, who is a Chumash healer woman, articulates the possibilities opened up by Borderlands Shakespeare when she says, "Sometimes there are tiny cracks, small openings, allowing the past to live differently in the present and the present to become truthful because of the past, joining us together in ways we never thought possible."[6] Rather than treating Shakespeare as sacrosanct, Borderlands Shakespeare plays take what is of use in Shakespeare and repurpose it to meet the needs of their communities and to imagine new futures. Reading Borderlands Shakespeare

---

[6] José Cruz González, *Invierno*, in *The Bard in the Borderlands: An Anthology of Shakespeare Appropriations en La Frontera*, vol. 2, ed. Katherine Gillen, Adrianna M. Santos, and Kathryn Vomero Santos (Tempe: ACMRS Press, forthcoming 2024), Prelude.

empowers students to do the same and to bring their own cultural, racial, and linguistic knowledges to bear on material often considered elite white property.[7]

Our experiences teaching Magaña's *The Tragic Corrido* in particular offer illustrative examples of the kinds of learning that these plays can facilitate. Set in the agricultural communities of the Rio Grande Valley, *The Tragic Corrido* appropriates *Romeo and Juliet* to engage with questions of land dispossession, water rights, agricultural labor, language politics, and the reclamation of Indigenous culture by Mexican Americans. Examining Magaña's presentation of these issues provides students with an opportunity not only to study dynamics of adaptation, appropriation, and translation, but also to learn about the history, politics, and geography of the Valley. Students benefit from comparing *Romeo and Juliet* and *The Tragic Corrido* in detail, looking, for example, at how the so-called ancient grudge in Shakespeare's play acquires new meanings in the context of the feud between landowners and the laborers who work in their fields. Students examine Magaña's depiction of regional politics and discuss the ways in which banishment from Verona is refracted as deportation to Mexico and compelled military service. Furthermore, students study Magaña's mixture of Spanish and English, noting, for example, how he transforms Romeo and Juliet's shared sonnet into an occasion to create poetry across languages.

To decenter Shakespeare in these classroom discussions, we emphasize the various sources and intertexts that shape *The Tragic Corrido*. We listen to corridos—Mexican ballads that often tell stories of tragic lovers and border-crossers—and we analyze the significance of Magaña's use of the form in his play as well as his decision to use a corrido singer as a choric figure. Further, we examine Magaña's use of both Christian and Indigenous spiritual figures. We consider the importance of la Virgen de Guadalupe, for whom Lupe is named, and the ways in which she embodies the syncretism of Indigenous and colonial religions. We pay particular attention to Magaña's engagement with Mexica mythology, especially his brief reference to the legend of Popocatépetl, a Chichimeca warrior, and Iztaccíhuatl, a Tlaxcala princess, who are often referred to as the Mexican Romeo and Juliet because their love story is similarly tragic. Magaña's invocation of this story, which predates Shakespeare's play, disrupts

---

[7] For a discussion of Shakespeare as white property, see Arthur L. Little, Jr., "Re-Historicizing Race, White Melancholia, and the Shakespearean Property," *Shakespeare Quarterly* 67, no. 1 (2016): 84–103, esp. 88.

colonial timelines as well as Shakespeare's perceived supremacy as a "universal" storyteller. Thinking with our students about how the myth of Popocatépetl and Iztaccíhuatl has been reframed as a *Romeo and Juliet* analogue reveals the harmful effects of bardolatry in the Borderlands: even in a reclamation of an Indigenous myth, the white racial frame of Shakespeare and his supposed universality is still invoked to understand it. Attending to the many contexts and intertexts of Borderlands Shakespeare demonstrates that Chicanx theater is as complex as Shakespeare's and therefore deserves and rewards careful attention.

Teaching Borderlands Shakespeare plays provides an opportunity—at both Trinity and A&M–SA—to decenter and disrupt the white epistemologies that often pervade English literature classrooms. Such epistemologies are perhaps more prevalent at Trinity, but they are also present at A&M–SA, as it is part of the Texas A&M University system and is infused with the ideologies that dominate higher education in the United States.[8] Analyzing these plays privileges the knowledges and skills of Mexican American and Indigenous students, which are often elided or denigrated in universities. For example, close reading bilingual scenes from *The Tragic Corrido* engages the linguistic skills of Spanish-speaking students. At both Trinity and A&M–SA, some students in any given class may have connections to the Valley and are thus able to share their own knowledge with the class. Such discussions also serve white students as they develop racial literacy and become aware of bodies of knowledge that they do not—and may not ever—fully have access to.

For students who often enter a Shakespeare class with assumptions about Shakespeare's difficulty, inaccessibility, and irrelevance to their lives, reading Borderlands Shakespeare helps them to see the value of the perspectives they bring to these texts. Analyzing appropriations created by Borderlands artists hones students' skills as readers of Shakespeare, encouraging them to rethink central themes such as family dynamics, political power, death, healing practices, and warfare and to understand characters as border-crossers, code-switchers, and figures of resistance. In addition, these plays model modes of negotiating and resisting the ways in which, as Madeline Sayet argues, Shakespeare's work "has been used historically as a weapon to remove other people's cultures and teach them that one

---

[8] For the ongoing impacts of colonialism at HSIs, see Gina Ann García, "Decolonizing Hispanic-Serving Institutions: A Framework for Organizing," *Journal of Hispanic Higher Education* 17, no. 2 (2018): 132–47.

British playwright is superior to all other writers."⁹ Once this violence is acknowledged and countered, students are freer to draw on their own perspectives in essays, performances, and other creative and intellectual productions.

Co-creating Borderlands Shakespeare

When we started integrating Borderlands Shakespeare plays into our classes, we were working from the unpublished typescripts that playwrights had generously shared with us. Through conversations with students and fellow teachers, we realized the necessity of making these texts more accessible and of offering a critical apparatus that situates them within the longer tradition of teatro and Borderlands art. To meet this need, we have been working with our colleague Adrianna M. Santos on a three-volume anthology called *The Bard in the Borderlands: An Anthology of Shakespeare Appropriations en La Frontera*, which is forthcoming with ACMRS Press. We strive to align this work with what Alexis Pauline Gumbs calls "community accountable scholarship," an approach which demands that our work benefits and is responsive to artists, scholars, teachers, and students working and living in the Borderlands.¹⁰ We see this anthology—and ACMRS's open access publishing model—as a crucial tool for forging ethical and reciprocal relationships with the communities we seek to serve.

In keeping with the pedagogical origins of our anthology, we have created opportunities to involve our students in the editorial and knowledge production process. In Kathryn's classes, students began the work of crowdsourcing annotations by identifying aspects of the plays that might require translation or explication for readers. When they read James Lujan's *Kino and Teresa*, for example, students not only commented on the play's engagement with *Romeo and Juliet* but also researched its references to Pueblo spiritual practices. And when they read Herbert Siguenza's *El Henry*, an appropriation of *Henry IV, Part I*, students looked up Caló words and details about Chicanx political movements. Under her mentorship, four Trinity students have worked as Summer Undergraduate Research Fellows

---

⁹ Madeline Sayet, "Interrogating the Shakespeare System," *HowlRound*, August 31, 2020, https://howlround.com/interrogating-shakespeare-system.

¹⁰ Alexis Pauline Gumbs, "Daily Bread: Nourishing Sustainable Practices for Community Accountable Scholars," *Brilliance Remastered*, July 31, 2012.

in a Mellon-funded program that allowed them to gain firsthand research experience by generating annotations for historical and cultural references, creating glossary entries, gathering information about performance histories, interviewing the playwrights, and developing resources for teaching the plays. This experiential learning has been transformative for these fellows, most of whom have personal connections to the Borderlands region, and it has helped to prepare them for their future educational and professional endeavors in creative writing, library and information science, and immigration law. Our anthology, in turn, reflects the collective insights of students, shared in class discussions and through these research experiences.

Student performances of these texts have proven similarly fruitful. For example, Katherine's students worked toward a performance of Josh Inocéncio's *Ofélio*, a short play that draws on Shakespeare's Ophelia in its rendering of a queer Latino survivor of sexual assault. After studying and writing about the play, students created their own performance, in which they interspliced scenes from *Ofélio* with scenes from *Hamlet* that depict Ophelia's distress in response to abuse. They later performed *Ofélio* with the playwright in the audience as part of a symposium on Latinx Shakespeare and Borderlands drama hosted by A&M–SA in 2018. Students had the chance to engage in conversation with Inocéncio during a creative writing workshop that he led at that event. They were thus able to bring together playwriting, theater-making, and textual analysis and were invited to see themselves as part of a community of Borderlands artists.

Engaging with the Borderlands appropriations included in our anthology has also empowered our students to create their own. A successful example of such work is a short multilingual film that A&M–SA students produced as part of the Qualities of Mercy Project. Coordinated by Jonathan Burton, who teaches at Whittier College, this project asked classes from around the country to create locally resonant productions of scenes from *The Merchant of Venice*.[11] The A&M–SA students produced a film that spoke to issues of immigration, colorism, linguistic diversity, and identity on the Southside of San Antonio. In their appropriation of Act 1, Scene 3,

---

[11] Katherine Gillen has also written about this production in "Language, Race, and Shakespeare Appropriation on San Antonio's Southside: A Qualities of Mercy Dispatch," *The Sundial*, August 19, 2020, https://medium.com/the-sundial-acmrs/language-race-and-shakespeare-appropriation-on-san-antonios-southside-a-qualities-of-mercy-9baed8e93599.

Shylock, an undocumented Mexican immigrant with a payday loan business, threatens to cut out the tongue of Antonio, who is himself Mexican American but prejudiced against undocumented people.

Drawing on Gloria Anzaldúa's meditations on the relationship between identity and language in her essay "How to Tame a Wild Tongue," the students transformed *Merchant*'s famous pound of flesh into *una lengua*, a tongue. Their video thus highlights the oppression faced by Spanish-speaking Mexican immigrants, particularly those who are undocumented, and it celebrates the vibrancy of Borderlands languages, which are often derided as improper, incorrect, or impure. Shylock's ability to translanguage is emphasized throughout, as exemplified in his threat to Antonio: "If I don't get my money back within three months, te corto la lengua." Without his tongue, Shylock asserts, Antonio will "never speak badly about our people again." This appropriation of *The Merchant of Venice* insists that the A&M–SA students' Borderlands perspectives have a place in the Shakespeare classroom.

Decolonial praxis necessitates that we see creative and experiential projects as central to knowledge production. Doing this work gives students confidence that their perspectives matter not only in classroom assignments but in other professional, artistic, and community contexts as well. When given the space and freedom to remake Shakespeare in their own vision, students feel less pressure to subordinate themselves to the authority of white Eurocentric worldviews. The impact of their creations is not limited just to these students' lives. Their innovative interventions into conversations about Shakespeare's canonical body of work have the potential to influence artistic and intellectual spheres within their communities and beyond. Indeed, the A&M–SA students' *Merchant of Venice* production has itself helped to identify new and exciting paths forward for Shakespeare studies. As Espinosa writes,

> The students in this project put forward an antiracist message anchored in the legacies of colonialism and imperialism. And yet, like Shylock speaking to audiences who might not care, they speak in a language that is poignant and necessary. This type of engagement with Shakespeare, I firmly believe, points to the future of our field—a future so many postcolonial critics of Shakespeare have helped to shape.[12]

---

[12] Ruben Espinosa, "Postcolonial Studies," in *The Arden Handbook of Contemporary Shakespeare Criticism*, ed. Evelyn Gajowski (London: Bloomsbury Arden, 2020), 170.

Through their critical and creative engagement, students at both A&M–SA and Trinity contribute to scholarly conversations and to vibrant bodies of art. They thus join the ongoing Borderlands tradition of reading and remaking Shakespeare as practiced by playwrights such as Magaña, Villarreal, Lujan, Siguenza, González, and Inocéncio.

Rethinking Shakespeare's Place in the Curriculum

The activities and opportunities we have outlined above illustrate the importance of expanding the Shakespeare classroom to include knowledges and histories that have traditionally been regarded as marginal to the study of early modern drama and its afterlives. Because this work is by nature interdisciplinary, it has also opened up new avenues and occasions to break the boundaries of our discipline and to forge alliances with colleagues in other fields and departments across our campuses. By building these partnerships, we have worked to decenter Shakespeare in our curricula and to mobilize Shakespeare's institutional capital to align our work with ongoing efforts to create opportunities that sustain the histories and cultures of our students in San Antonio and the Borderlands more broadly.

We have both used our universities' curricular revision and approval processes to integrate culturally sustaining approaches to Shakespeare within programs of study. This not only serves to make the work visible in catalogues and on transcripts but also ensures the sustainability of our pedagogical interventions. Kathryn has sought to formalize her teaching of Borderlands Shakespeare plays by creating a separate Decolonial Shakespeares course dedicated to the topic. This flexible framework will allow for her and other faculty members to teach different iterations of the course, some of which will be dedicated exclusively to Borderlands Shakespeare while others will put these plays into conversation with decolonial traditions of Shakespeare appropriation throughout the Americas and the global South. Similarly, Katherine and her colleague Lisa Jennings revised A&M–SA's English program's introductory Shakespeare course, which is now called Intersectional Shakespeare in the course catalogue.[13] In addition to drawing on Kimberlé Crenshaw's theory

---

[13] Gillen and Jennings write about this course and their approaches in Katherine Gillen and Lisa Jennings, "Decolonizing Shakespeare? Toward an Antiracist, Culturally Sustaining Praxis," *The Sundial*, November 6, 2019, https://medium.com/the-sundial-acmrs/decolonizing-shakespeare-toward-an-antiracist-culturally-sustaining-praxis-904cb9ff8a96.

of intersectionality to examine questions of identity and power in Shakespeare's period and our own, this course privileges critical and creative responses to Shakespeare by a diverse array of BIPOC authors, including those writing in the US–Mexico Borderlands. As such, Intersectional Shakespeare explicitly interrogates Shakespeare's colonial legacies, and it provides space for students to examine the ways in which whiteness has been produced and sustained through Shakespeare studies and, by extension, literary studies as a field. While it is valuable for individual instructors to integrate diverse texts and decolonial, antiracist, and community-based practices into their own classes, work at the curricular level is also important because it validates these approaches and values by making them legible to prospective students, to communities, and to administrators who may be evaluating faculty performance or programmatic effectiveness.

These new courses, moreover, are part of larger curricular shifts within and among departments. Katherine's co-created Intersectional Shakespeare course aligns with the broader efforts of A&M–SA's English program to integrate decolonial and antiracist approaches throughout their curriculum.[14] To best serve A&M–SA's student body, curricular revisions in the English program have sought to center Indigenous, Mexican American, and Black intellectual and creative traditions, both within degree plans and in individual courses, including those traditionally taught from Eurocentric perspectives. Within such a curriculum, Borderlands Shakespeare plays such as Magaña's, Villarreal's, Lujan's, Siguenza's, González's, and Inocéncio's become just as important as Shakespeare's plays, reflecting Mexican American and Indigenous traditions as well as decolonial responses to Shakespeare's canonicity.

One potential response to Shakespeare's persistent and sometimes harmful canonicity is to stop engaging with his works altogether. While we recognize the power of such an approach, the playwrights collected in our anthology demonstrate the value of engaging with Shakespeare, both to claim ownership of canonical literature and to negotiate or resist white, colonial power more generally. To teach these works is to teach literature by artists from the Borderlands region while also helping students to satisfy degree requirements

---

[14] For more on this curricular revision, see Jackson Ayres, Katherine Bridgman, Scott Gage, Katherine Gillen, and Lizbett Tinoco, "Toward Decolonization: Integrating the English Studies Curriculum at Texas A&M University–San Antonio," forthcoming in the *ADE Bulletin*.

and, in some cases, prepare for careers in teaching high school. Our hope is that changing how Shakespeare is taught at the university level will inspire new approaches to engaging with the canon and will create space for other traditions to flourish in classrooms.

Courses such as Decolonial Shakespeares and Intersectional Shakespeare also offer models for thinking across traditions, geographies, and temporalities. For this reason, they can join and inspire larger interdisciplinary projects on campus. One driving factor for the creation of Kathryn's Decolonial Shakespeares course, for example, was the formal creation of a Global Latinx Studies major by Trinity's Mexico, the Americas, and Spain (MAS) Program. When taught primarily as a Borderlands or Latinx Shakespeare course, Decolonial Shakespeares will count toward this major and contribute to related efforts to make Trinity an HSI whose offerings are responsive to its student population and location. Katherine's Intersectional Shakespeare course, similarly, creates connections with other programs that are vital to an HSI, including Spanish, Creative Arts and Performance Studies, and Mexican American, Latinx, and Borderlands Studies.

Doing such culturally sustaining work with care is especially important at HSIs and aspiring HSIs, which in many cases benefit from federal funding while continuing to inflict colonial violence on Latinx communities. In addition, interdisciplinary projects have the potential to destabilize academic disciplines that have sought to fragment, commodify, and devalue holistic Indigenous knowledge systems.[15] As Linda Tuhiwai Smith explains, "Reclaiming a voice in this context has been about reclaiming, reconnecting and reordering those ways of knowing which were submerged, hidden or driven underground."[16] This work, as Christina Sharpe suggests from a Black feminist perspective, may require a kind of "undisciplining" that rejects white dominance and that creates space to recover oppressed methodologies and to create new ones.[17]

---

[15] For discussions of Indigenous worldviews and their relationship to academic frameworks, see Margaret Kovach, "Epistemology and Research: Centring Tribal Knowledge," in *Indigenous Methodologies: Characteristics, Conversations, and Contexts*, ed. Kovach (Toronto: University of Toronto Press, 2010), 55–74, and Linda Tuhiwai Smith, *Decolonizing Methodologies: Research and Indigenous Peoples*, 2nd ed. (London: Zed Books, 2012).

[16] Smith, *Decolonizing Methodologies*, 72.

[17] Christina Sharpe, *In the Wake: On Blackness and Being* (Durham: Duke University Press, 2016), 13.

Collectivity and Community

To extend our scholarly and pedagogical work and to root it in our community, we co-founded the Borderlands Shakespeare Colectiva with our colleague Adrianna M. Santos. The Colectiva works to create a community of praxis in which students, teachers, scholars, activists, and theater practitioners generate ideas about how we might approach works of Borderlands art, especially pieces that engage with canonical European traditions. In doing so, we create reciprocal relationships that destabilize artificial boundaries that often separate universities, community colleges, high schools, and community arts organizations, opening space for dialogue and shared learning. Our current and former students are an integral part of this community, as many go on to be teachers, artists, and activists themselves.

The Borderlands Shakespeare Colectiva has found opportunities to create and to participate in public-facing events that engage communities beyond academic institutions. We collaborate across disciplines to organize programming that is inclusive, accessible, and innovative in its blending of traditional academic approaches with creative and embodied expression. The 2018 symposium held at A&M–SA, for example, invited community members to attend, offered local teachers professional development credit, and included interactive workshops on creative writing, acting, and dance led by artists from the region. As with this symposium, the virtual roundtable that we hosted in collaboration with the Arizona Center for Medieval and Renaissance Studies in 2021 was designed to invite a wide-ranging audience from the Borderlands and beyond into dialogue with the speakers. The teaching-focused questions we heard from the audience indicated a growing desire among fellow teachers to incorporate Borderlands adaptations and approaches into their classrooms.

For this reason, much of our outreach has focused on teachers. In collaboration with Humanities Texas and the Folger Shakespeare Library, we have presented on the pedagogical potential of Borderlands Shakespeare. In these workshops, we focus on strategies for teaching Shakespeare in the culturally sustaining ways we have described above. Our anthology, *The Bard in the Borderlands*, is poised to become a crucial tool for fostering this kind of work, but we recognize that it cannot do so on its own without structures of support and opportunities for meaningful engagement. We therefore plan to continue offering workshops and will develop supplementary pedagogical materials in collaboration with our own students and with local teachers.

These materials will be available on a companion website for the anthology, where users will also be able to access a digital archive and database of Borderlands Shakespeare productions and related media in the form of an interactive and searchable map. Our mapping practice is aligned with several public-facing and community-based digital humanities projects in the field of Mexican American and Borderlands Studies. These projects include *Mapping the Movimiento*, a story map of key locations in the history of the Chicano Movement in San Antonio, created by UTSA Libraries and the Institute of Texan Cultures, and *Mapping Violence*, an archival map project spearheaded by Monica Muñoz Martinez that documents the history of anti-Mexican violence in the Borderlands during the early twentieth century. Our database and archive will become a living, place-based record of the many ways in which communities in this culturally diverse region have used Shakespeare's oeuvre to grapple with the cultural, linguistic, racial, and political issues of both the past and the present. As Kathryn demonstrates in her essay "¿Shakespeare para todos?," works of Borderlands Shakespeare have not been well documented or preserved by mainstream humanities libraries and institutions.[18] It is therefore necessary to archive them with care and to make this work available to teachers, scholars, and artists. Coupled with the anthology, our website will become an important site for housing, sharing, and generating knowledge about works of Borderlands Shakespeare, thus helping us build the Borderlands Shakespeare Colectiva into a true community of praxis.

Teaching in San Antonio, and teaching together in San Antonio, has shown us the importance of rooting our work within our community and negotiating the particular institutional contexts that affect how students see themselves in relation to the city and the Borderlands more broadly. Whereas A&M–SA is situated within the community it was founded to serve, Trinity is a residential campus in which the majority of students come from elsewhere. For different reasons, both of these institutional realities point to the need to ground our pedagogy in place. While students at A&M–SA often feel as though they are being asked to leave their cultures and languages at the door when they enter the classroom, Trinity students tend

---

[18] See Kathryn Vomero Santos "¿Shakespeare para todos?" *Shakespeare Quarterly* 73, no. 1 (2022): 49–75.

to struggle to find opportunities to learn about and connect to the city while pursuing their degrees. In both contexts, grounding their learning in the region and its histories helps students develop racial literacy and validates the identities and knowledges of local students. Our collaborations with Borderlands artists and activists, moreover, have affirmed the importance of working outside our institutions, in community with a range of learners and knowledge creators throughout the Borderlands. We therefore see our projects not as attempts to reaffirm the value of Shakespeare but as part of a shared effort to create opportunities for liberatory learning, creativity, and social justice.

Chapter 7

Dressing to Transgress: Aesthetic Matching, Historical Costumers of Color, and the Restorying of Institutional Spaces
Penelope Geng

I begin with a personal story. At my first campus interview for a Shakespeare and early modern literature job, a member of the search committee asked me in front of the entire committee, "How would you teach Asian American literature?" I wish I had replied, "I wouldn't, for I'll be teaching Shakespeare."[1] But inexperience and surprise prompted me to speculate how I would, indeed, teach Jhumpa Lahiri and David Henry Hwang. I learned that day that my Asian features dictated my subject-area and research expertise in the minds of some faculty.[2] This experience highlights a stealthy form of institutional investment in whiteness—what I term "aesthetic matching" or the compulsion to match a scholar's race with their chosen subject of study. In progressive and polite spaces such as the interview room, the classroom, and the academic conference, aesthetic matching exists as an unspoken question: "why are you (a person of color) studying this (white) subject?" The profession of literary criticism is predominantly white. This is especially true in

---

[1] This essay would not exist but for Shasta Schatz's generosity as a correspondent and interviewee and the input of the students who have taken my ENGL200 Major British Authors class at Macalester College. I am grateful to Marissa Greenberg and Elizabeth Williamson for the invitation to contribute to the collection and for their immensely helpful editorial interventions. The anonymous readers for the press sharpened the focus of my argument: thank you. My understanding of restorying was deepened by conversations with Jonathan Hsy, Jennie Row, Lydia Garver, the attendees of the UMN CPS Regional Conference and the spring 2022 Uncommon Bodies reading group. Fellow contributors Elisa Oh and Mary Janell Metzger asked clarifying questions. Will Fisher, Simone Chess, Colby Gordon, Michael Prior, Cody Klippenstein, Satoko Suzuki, Kadin Henningsen, and Alice Asch shared invaluable advice and encouragement during the writing process. This essay is dedicated to Will Fisher, who insisted that I write it.

[2] This question was posed to me by a faculty of color.

the fields of medieval and early modern studies.³ Racist stereotypes shape perceptions of who can and cannot competently interpret the works of Chaucer, Shakespeare, Virginia Woolf, and other white writers of the western canon. In the humanities and fine arts, interpretations of art created by white people are thought to come more naturally and spontaneously to white audiences and critics on account of their ancestry. It is in these fields that one encounters talk about the soul of classical music, the powerful feeling of lyric poetry, and the universal humanism of Shakespeare. These numinous experiences are imagined as the birthright of white audiences and readers.

Aesthetic matching is so widespread that it recently surfaced as a joke in Netflix's series *The Chair*. In the first episode, Ji-Yoon Kim, the newly appointed chair of English at a predominantly white university, wryly discloses to her pre-tenure Black colleague Yasmin McKay: "When I started, it was like, 'Why's some Asian lady teaching Emily Dickinson?'"⁴ There is a lot to say about Kim's inept attempt at striking solidarity with McKay in this scene. For now, I simply want to note that this scene sparked recognition among Asian viewers. In her *LA Times* OpEd, sociologist Nancy Wang Yuen writes:

> Ji-Yoon names a bias Asian Americans face in the humanities . . . As a former English major, I've had strangers question why I majored in English and not math. By casting [Sandra] Oh as an English professor and Mallory Low as an English doctoral student, the show helps dispel the racist idea that English professors or students cannot be Asian.⁵

I agree with Yuen and would add that the comedic punch of the line lies in the fact that Kim's presence in the department contests not only the notion that she cannot be a professor of English, but that she could not possibly be a scholar of Emily Dickinson. The assumption is that had she entered the ranks as a professor of Asian or Asian American literature, she would not have encountered the same degree of hostile incredulity.

---

³ See the articles and essays listed on the "Inclusive Pedagogy" page of the Shakespeare Association of America website: https://shakespeareassociation.org/resources/inclusive-pedagogy/ (accessed on November 12, 2022).
⁴ *The Chair*, episode 1, "Brilliant Mistake" (Netflix, 2021).
⁵ Nancy Wang Yuen, "'The Chair' Is a Surprisingly Accurate—If Farcical—Reflection of Issues Facing Women, People of Color in Academia," *LA Times*, August 23, 2021, E6. I thank Larry Allen for sending me the clipping.

Historically, the university was an elite space reserved for white, Protestant, able-bodied men to build intellectual and political community—and that legacy remains palpable. "Space invaders" is the term that Nirmal Puwar uses to describe minoritized subjects who experience surveillance and hostility on entering a space previously designated the domain of members of the white, usually male, ruling class. In these spaces, the white male body is unmarked and is imagined as the norm, the default, and the neutral form of embodiment.[6] As Sara Ahmed has documented, minorized subjects who seek redress for gender- and race-based discrimination from institutional offices face an uphill battle. The very offices that investigate harassment in the workplace often adopt a corporate logic of liability instead of justice, subjecting victims of harassment to gaslighting and hostility. By naming the problem, the victim becomes the problem: "if we talk about how racism affects us, then we are getting in the way of reconciliation, as if our talk is what prevents us all from 'just' getting along."[7] Such is the reality at many institutions. College campuses are not exempt. Thus, I hear a joke within the joke: Kim thinks that aesthetic gatekeeping is a thing of the past (its pastness signaled by her phrasing "when I started . . ."), but viewers know that her white male colleagues feel so threatened and emasculated by McKay that they are willing to tear apart their department to secure their place in the racial hierarchy.

I connect the phenomenon of aesthetic matching to the institutional investment in "whiteness as property." In her 1993 article, Cheryl I. Harris unpacks "property interest in whiteness" through two landmark Supreme Court rulings: *Plessy v. Ferguson*, 163 US 537 (1896), a precedent-setting case that affirmed the legality of racial segregation, and *Brown v. Board of Education*, 347 US 483 (1954), which ostensibly ended race-based segregation. Harris points out that the latter case may have ended "de jure [legal] segregation" but, like the ghost that refuses to be exorcised, the "separate but equal" clause enabling racial segregation lingered in the "cultural practices of whites."[8] The Supreme Court had "dismantled an old form of whiteness as property while simultaneously permitting its

---

[6] Nirmal Puwar, *Space Invaders: Race, Gender, and Bodies Out of Place* (Oxford: Berg [Bloomsbury], 2004), 8.

[7] Sara Ahmed, *On Being Included: Racism and Diversity in Institutional Life* (Durham: Duke University Press, 2012), 161.

[8] Cheryl I. Harris, "Whiteness as Property," *Harvard Law Review* 610, no. 8 (1993): 1721.

reemergence in a more subtle form."[9] What counts as the "more subtle form" of whiteness as property has been analyzed by humanities scholars including Loren Kajikawa and Arthur L. Little, Jr.[10] My discussion of aesthetic matching extends their analysis and participates in the ongoing effort in Shakespeare and premodern English literary studies to identify, theorize, illustrate, and resist institutional and personal possessive investment in whiteness.

The case study for my analysis is the British literature survey. How does one prevent it from becoming the site of the reproduction of whiteness? By virtue of its subject, this course can too easily reinforce structures of white feeling and epistemology.[11] I know this because, when I first started teaching my version of this course, I did little to problematize the nationalist, racist, and imperialist ideologies that shaped the creation and reception of these canonical texts. I failed to critique racist constructions in texts which did not explicitly mention race. The majority of students who take this class are white. As of the time of publication, domestic students of color make up 32 percent of all students at Macalester College, but in my classes, including my Brit lit survey, that number tends to be significantly lower.[12] Thus, I was rarely challenged on my presentation of the material. Understanding how I could teach the survey differently has been an ongoing journey involving reading, reflection, writing, research, attending online and in-person antiracist pedagogy workshops, and having candid conversations with colleagues, administrators, and most of all my students. Like many educators, I had to rethink my teaching after the murder of George Floyd by Minneapolis police officers on May 25, 2020. Floyd died not twenty minutes from Macalester, which is located in St. Paul on the eastern bank of the Mississippi River. The river divides the neighborhood of Mac-Groveland from Powderhorn, the Minneapolis neighborhood at the center of America's racial justice protests following Floyd's

---

[9] Harris, "Whiteness," 1753.

[10] Loren Kajikawa, "The Possessive Investment in Classical Music: Confronting Legacies of White Supremacy in US Schools and Departments of Music," in *Seeing Race Again: Countering Colorblindness across the Disciplines*, ed. Kimberlé Williams Crenshaw et al. (Oakland: University of California Press, 2019), 307–26; Arthur L. Little, Jr., "Re-Historicizing Race, White Melancholia, and the Shakespearean Property," *Shakespeare Quarterly* 67, no. 1 (2016): 84–103.

[11] On epistemology and systemic whiteness, see Ian Smith, *Black Shakespeare: Reading and Misreading Race* (Cambridge: Cambridge University Press, 2022).

[12] "Quick Facts about Macalester Students: Fall 2022 Census Data," Macalester College, https://www.macalester.edu/ir/wp-content/uploads/sites/156/Quick-Facts-Fall-2022.pdf, accessed on November 2, 2022.

murder. When I returned to teaching in fall 2020, I revised my Brit lit survey to emphasize not only the global histories that shaped the formation of this body of literature, but also the ability of marginalized writers today to restory canonical texts. Adaptation and translation became more central to the course than before. Additionally, I began to approach the Brit lit survey class in light of the political resistance pioneered by fans of color. The practice of costumers of color who combine research, crafting, and theatrical performance inspired me. Dressing to transgress, costumers of color fundamentally challenge the logic of aesthetic matching.[13]

Restorying as Resistance

Long before I was a scholar, I was a fan. My first conference was an anime convention, and participating in fandom was equal parts consolation and distraction from the alienation that I experienced as a commuter student and one of the very few nonwhite students in my English program. It was perhaps inevitable that I found myself drawn to Shasta Schatz's Carracci project.

Schatz is an American Black hobby historical costumer and cosplayer who posts under the username @scificheergirl on Instagram. Costumers have specialties, and Schatz is known for historical and comic-book mashups like her "Batgirl, 1567" and "Regency Sailor Mercury." In 2020, during pandemic lockdowns and protests for racial justice following the murders of Breonna Taylor, George Floyd, and other Black Americans, she embarked on an ambitious new project: a recreation of the *Portrait of an African Woman Holding a Clock* (c. 1583–5), which is attributed to the Italian artist Annibale Carracci (Figure 7.1).[14] Despite her experience, the scale of the work, coupled with the demands of working a full-time job and pandemic parenting, presented challenges.[15] Many hours were needed for sewing the full-length gown, recreating details like the sitter's *saccoccia* (pocket), partlet, girdle, coral necklace, and golden

---

[13] Readers will recognize that the title of my essay pays tribute to bell hooks's *Teaching to Transgress: Education as the Practice of Freedom* (New York: Routledge, 1994), which I discuss in the next section.

[14] The painting was acquired by Tomasso Brothers Fine Art gallery (based in Leeds) in auction in 2005. It was loaned by the gallery to the Walters Art Museum in Baltimore for their pathbreaking exhibit, *Revealing the African Presence in European Art* (2013), where it was used in all the promotional materials for the exhibit; see Joaneath Spicer, ed., *Revealing the African Presence in Renaissance Art* (Baltimore: Walters, 2012).

[15] Shasta Schatz, "Interview," conducted by Penelope Geng, August 12, 2021.

clock. When she finished, she shared pictures of herself in the gown on her social media accounts (Figure 7.2).

Schatz's Carracci project is a fascinating example of what education studies scholar Ebony Elizabeth Thomas calls "restorying":

> Restorying describes the complex ways that contemporary young people narrate the word and the world, analyze their lived experiences, and then synthesize and recontextualize a multiplicity of stories in forming new narratives. In other words, as young readers imagine themselves into stories, they *reimagine the very stories themselves*. Now more than ever before, people of all ages are collectively reimagining time, place, identity, perspective, mode, and metanarratives through retold stories.[16]

Thomas notes that restorying so practiced is an extension of "critical race counterstorytelling" and that the "racebending" works of fans of color expand on a "rich restorying tradition" established by nineteenth- and twentieth-century Black American writers.[17]

Restorying affirms a reader's questions about whose stories have been written out and marginalized, and how that erasure enacts a kind of racial segregation and reproduction of whiteness. The academic study of restorying reinforces the efforts of fans of color to reimagine the text through their own embodied experiences of race. Corporate media environments center white characters, storylines, and feelings; restorying empowers fans of color to use their creative skills—as costumers and storytellers—to resist institutional whitewashing and homogenization. When fans of color living in a culturally white space share and circulate their restoried fanworks (cosplay, fan art, fan videos, and fanfiction), they unsettle the presumption that franchises like *Harry Potter* and *Star Wars* are meant for the exclusive enrichment and enjoyment of white fans. Building on Thomas's analysis, Jonathan Hsy has drawn attention to Asian American writers' use of restorying (of medieval literature) to critique structural violence in the United States. In the works of Sui Sin Far (born Edith Maude Eaton), a writer of English and Chinese

---

[16] Ebony Elizabeth Thomas, *The Dark Fantastic: Race and the Imagination from Harry Potter to the Hunger Games* (New York: New York University Press, 2019), 159. For another understanding of restorying, see Jonathan Hsy, *Antiracist Medievalisms: From "Yellow Peril" to Black Lives Matter* (Amsterdam: ARC, 2021), 5–7.

[17] Thomas, *The Dark Fantastic*, 162. "Racebending" refers to "fanworks" that alter the "racial or ethnic makeup" of "popular, usually White, characters" (Thomas, *The Dark Fantastic*, 162). On fiction as a document for truth-finding, see Toni Morrison, "The Site of Memory," in *Inventing the Truth: The Art and Craft of Memoir*, ed. William Zinsser (Boston: Houghton, 1995), 83–102.

Figure 7.1 *Portrait of an African Woman holding a Clock*, c. 1583–5. Annibale Carracci (attributed), oil on canvas, 23¾ × 15½ inches. © Department of Culture and Tourism, Abu Dhabi. Photo by Ismail Noor, Seeing Things. Reproduced with permission.

Figure 7.2 *The Carracci Project*, 2021. Shasta Schatz, digital photography. © Shasta Schatz. Reproduced with permission.

descent writing in North America in the 1890s, restorying takes the form of "cripping" the sentimentalism of medieval romances.[18]

Schatz's Carracci project exemplifies the political potential of restorying. Like almost all early modern European art depicting

---

[18] Hsy, *Antiracist Medievalisms*, 56–57.

nonwhite subjects, Carracci's painting unconditionally reproduces the white gaze of the artist and with it an objectification of the sitter. Schatz's project challenges the original painting's racial logic. The spirit of her project vividly exemplifies bell hooks's concept of the "oppositional gaze," which is one of the "gestures of defiance" available to Black viewers in an age of white-dominated media.[19] hooks writes:

> All attempts to repress our/black people's right to gaze had produced in us an overwhelming longing to look, a rebellious desire, an oppositional gaze.... Even in the worst circumstances of domination, the ability to manipulate one's gaze in the face of structures of domination that would contain it, opens up the possibility of agency.[20]

When Schatz presents herself as both artist and sitter, she turns the painting's inherent logic of domination on its head. In hooks's analysis, the oppositional gaze is furtive—an act of defiance that operates under the radar of the white establishment. Schatz's gaze is not furtive, but direct. Schatz's performance recalls fans of colors' "raceplay" (i.e., when a BIPOC fan cosplays as a famous white superhero), which joan miller relates to Jacques Rancière's theory of "dissensus" and José Esteban Muñoz's concept of "disidentification."[21] (Many of Schatz's costuming projects can be read as raceplay.) In today's social media environment, self-produced content can successfully compete with images made by big studios. Because her portrait is a digital artifact, the project is accessible to anyone with an internet connection. Schatz's project is not, then, a solo performance enacted to please herself but, like race-bending fanfiction or a cosplayer's raceplay, a display that invites everyone, everywhere, to look. The unique power of her project lies in the tension between the digital and the material life of the gown. Schatz's creation is a testament to the hours she spent on research, fitting, and sewing. Because of its material form—one that radiates expert craftsmanship and aesthetic taste—her gown beckons

---

[19] bell hooks, *Black Looks: Race and Representation* (Boston: South End, 1992), 4. I am grateful to Alice Asch for making this connection.

[20] hooks, *Black Looks*, 116.

[21] joan miller, "Raceplay: Whiteness and Erasure in Cross-Racial Cosplay," in *Fandom, Now in Color: A Collection of Voices*, ed. Rukmini Pande (Iowa City: University of Iowa Press, 2020), 65–78. See Jacques Rancière, *Dissensus: On Politics and Aesthetics*, trans. Steven Corcoran (New York: Continuum, 2010); José Esteban Muñoz, *Disidentifications: Queers of Color and the Performance of Politics* (Minneapolis: University of Minnesota Press, 1999).

viewers with an "aura" which Walter Benjamin ascribes to original art produced in the age of mechanical reproduction.[22]

Schatz's self-identification as a hobby costumer raises a question about the division between professional and amateur knowledge production. In my initial explanation of aesthetic matching, I located the phenomenon in the elite spaces of institutions like universities and colleges. These are spaces with some of the strictest forms of epistemological policing. As I have said, this policing purports to be objective, but in reality, it stems from and perpetuates a possessive investment in whiteness. Schatz and other hobbyists challenge the academy at large to consider the urgent question of audience. The fan community is more diverse than the professional one with respect to race, class, and age. Like the professional critic, fans study history, literature, and art with unflagging passion. As for impact, I would suggest that hobbyists are better poised to reach a public audience than academics. As a Black American fan who engages with a large online community, Schatz is able to connect with a youthful demographic engaged with social justice issues.[23] Citing a 2015 Pew research survey listing "African-American teens [as] the most likely of any group of teens to have a smartphone," Thomas argues that "Black youth and young adults [are] driving the tenor of the conversations on social media" as witnessed by Black fans' use of "social media to ... advocat[e] for more and better representations."[24] If some of the most energized and diverse communities that share the scholar's habits of research and storytelling operate outside the academy, what is preventing scholars from collaborating with them?

In the spring of 2021, I invited Schatz to Zoom with the students of my Brit lit survey class.[25] On that day, my students mirrored back her enthusiasm for what she called "nerd" culture. They asked her questions about her completed and ongoing projects. She pulled the Carracci dress out of the closet for the occasion and answered questions about its construction. The conversation, however, was not limited to that gown. As part of their preparation for the meeting, students were tasked with exploring her website and social media

---

[22] Walter Benjamin, "The Work of Art in the Age of Mechanical Reproduction," in *Illuminations*, trans. Harry Zohn (New York: Schocken, 1969), 217–51.

[23] On students' protests of the canon in the wake of George Floyd's death, see Elisa Oh's essay in this volume.

[24] Thomas, *The Dark Fantastic*, 128.

[25] Before the class visit, Schatz and I chatted for nearly an hour, going over logistical details and, importantly, connecting with each other as fans who came of age when only the English dubbed version of *Sailor Moon* was available and *Buffy the Vampire Slayer* was must-see TV.

accounts, and they asked questions about her past and current costuming projects. Suffice it to say, my students and I cherished the time with Schatz and that feeling was reciprocated. Later, on her blog, Schatz reflected on this experience: "I love talking 'at' students in the Zoom format, giving visuals that were not possible in a Career Day setting and answering questions without the kids feeling the burden of peer pressure or embarrassment."[26]

By bringing Schatz into my class, I wanted to demonstrate that a deep study of Renaissance art and literature was happening in non-institutional spaces. I wanted to show how academics and non-academics could champion each other's work. I wanted to challenge the professional's dismissal of fan labor and to suggest that those who disagreed with this devaluation did not have to abide by the old rules. I knew from personal experience that talking about one's fan pursuits was not always well received in academic spaces. That was why, on that day, I wanted to affirm my students' inner fan. According to a recent departmental alumni survey, the majority of Macalester's English majors pursue careers in creative writing, K–12 teaching, communications, journalism, and law. Yet their curiosity about history, art, and literature never leaves them. Doing historical research does not, or should not, depend on one's proximity to campus.

In summer 2021, a couple of months after her class visit, I reached out to Schatz for an interview, hoping to learn more about her journey as a costumer. She was busy with work, childcare, and many costuming projects, so we communicated by email. Reflecting on my question, "Can you talk about how the choice to major in English shaped your journey as a costumer?", Schatz commented that it was in English classes that she "felt empowered to enjoy any and all literature regardless of what was 'meant' for me. I look at costuming in exactly the same way." Specifically, "for costuming, I know where to look for historical research, I can follow the breadcrumbs to interpret sources for my projects rather than taking them at their written word, and I can see the value in looking at multiple points of view."[27] Studying the literature and art of historical periods is a lifelong passion for Schatz. If aesthetic matching polices intellectual curiosity, and if it zealously guards boundaries, not only those surrounding traditionally white spaces, but also the boundaries

---

[26] Shasta Schatz, "I'll Make This Brief," *Green Linen Shirt* (blog), April 19, 2021, https://greenlinenshirt.com/2021/04/29/ill-make-this-brief/#more-3490.
[27] Schatz, "Interview."

separating professional and lay knowledge, then hobby costumers specializing in historical European fashion challenge that norming impulse.

I asked Schatz how she saw her hobby intersecting with political activism: "Historical costuming seems to be so much about the pleasure of entering history through clothes. How do you reconcile that pleasure with a desire to use historical costuming as a vehicle for social justice or political activism?" I quote her response in full:

> For most of my life, I dismissed the racism in fandom and costuming circles as "just" gatekeeping, seeing the latter as a nuance reserved for hobbies and specializations. As a female fan of comic books and other geeky interests, I was also dealing with a hefty amount of sexism, so I felt the need to "pick a struggle" and shouting "Girl Power" was easier than (anachronistically, the equivalent of) "Black Lives Matter" at the time [original parentheses]. When I had negative interactions, I either brushed them off as unimportant or made myself scarce to avoid those people and situations in the future. It wasn't until the last few years of attending public events that were created as safe spaces (like the black nerd convention, BlerDCon [in Washington, DC]) that I saw the opportunity to be open about the harm that had been done to me as a costumer of color in those perceived whites-only spaces—both by my friends & family and by strangers. Close to home (but not in my actual home, as my parents, sibling, spouse, and kids are all hugely supportive), I was told over and over again that what I was doing—watching anime, reading fantasy books, playing board games—was all "White People Stuff." I strive with every costume to show that whatever I'm doing is in fact "Black People Stuff" because I, a black person, am doing it.[28]

Schatz situates her activism in her decades-long experience navigating the "whites-only spaces" of the fan conventions. She emphasizes the gap between the utopian ideal of these spaces as being radically inclusive and the reality of racist microaggressions and gatekeeping.[29] In earlier times, Schatz had to ignore or minimize the negative experiences, practicing a stoic resolve that recalls Ji-Yoon Kim's desire to overcome the painful memory of being marked out as a space invader by minimalizing its impact on her happiness. Yet as Schatz observes, brushing off these encounters is not the solution. These incidents

---

[28] Schatz, "Interview."

[29] Digital fan spaces are rife with racism; Rukmini Pande observes that "many nonwhite fans (and allies) . . . point to an insidious pattern seen in fandom after fandom . . . [the] sidelining and erasing nonwhite characters." Rukmini Pande, *Squee from the Margins: Fandom and Race* (Iowa City: University of Iowa Press, 2018), 9.

need to be called out for what they are: racist gatekeeping of intellectual property. So, in Instagram posts, Schatz pushes back against naysayers who leave disparaging comments about her presence in the costuming world. On her blog, she reflects on the experience of being a Black woman living in the United States navigating public spaces that are not safe.[30] Schatz's activism helps to foster safer spaces (digital and physical) for other costumers of color. After attending conventions like BlerDCon (Black nerd convention), she learned to "be open about the harm that had been done to me." The creation of safe spaces, and the wider community's respect for those spaces, facilitate serendipitous encounters. Finding solidarity with others has given her a reason for "speaking out, because so many of us have been going at this alone."[31]

Schatz knows how it feels to be excluded in elite institutional spaces. After college, she briefly considered pursuing curatorial work, but was stymied by the hostility she experienced in the museum space:

> I was an educational assistant at a museum and every time a school group came through, the white teachers would look to the white education assistants on my team for confirmation that the information I was presenting was true—as in physically looking past my shoulder to whoever was assisting me to look for that imperceptible nod of agreement. It was disgusting.[32]

The rejection that Schatz faced may be traced to a number of factors. Historically in the west, museums were created as "temples" of art to reinforce European and American imperial and nationalist ambitions, its collections showcasing the economic wealth and military strength of select nation-states.[33] As curator Lisa G. Corrin explains, "museums are places where sacrosanct belief systems are confirmed on the basis of hierarchies valuing one culture over another."[34] This imperial and colonial legacy is hard to shake off. Furthermore, museums reproduce whiteness through its almost exclusively white curatorial staffing. An Andrew W. Mellon 2018 survey of museum

---

[30] Schatz, "I'll Make This Brief."
[31] Schatz, "I'll Make This Brief."
[32] Schatz, "Interview."
[33] Divya P. Tolia-Kelly, "Rancière and the Re-distribution of the Sensible: The Artist Rosanna Raymond, Dissensus and Postcolonial Sensibilities within the Spaces of the Museum," *Progress in Human Geography* 43, no. 1 (2019): 127.
[34] Lisa G. Corrin, ed., *Mining the Museum: An Installation by Fred Wilson* (New York: New Press, 1994), 1.

staffing revealed that only 4 percent of curators in American museums identified as Black.[35]

It is fair to say that through costuming, Schatz has used her past experience to fuel her intellectual passion for Renaissance objects, art, literature, and culture. As a hobbyist, she enjoys maximum creative control over her projects. Historical costuming takes a lot of time. Part of the pleasure of slowly completing the project is the opportunity to share updates with the community. At the end of the week, the costumer might post a picture of her progress on social media. These communal asides build a bond between the maker and her followers. This is an exercise of freedom from institutionally standard or normative time. It is also a subtle, but powerful, refusal of neoliberalism's demand for efficiency and productivity. Schatz is in charge of her own learning. She conducts research on her own terms, at her own pace, and in the safety of her own studio. Finally, with respect to personal safety, the home studio offers a refuge from the judgment, surveillance, and harassment that BIPOC patrons experience in white-dominated institutional spaces.

Many costumers of color use Instagram and other platforms to share self-portraits of themselves recreating notable European portraits as a way to resist the tendency in commercial media to whitewash the past. Costumers of color find each other on social media by using hashtags like #reenactorsofcolor, #costumersofcolor, #blackfaeday, and #enchantedasianday. They use social media to coordinate group outings, where—in full historical costume—they stroll through properties that formerly excluded people of color: palaces, estates, royal gardens, rare book libraries, art museums, ruined castles, and more. Their costuming projects challenge the optics of who gets to participate in medieval, Renaissance, and fantasy culture. Their practice is dynamic, intersectional, joyful, and, above all, communal.

Lessons

Although I have only had one occasion to bring Schatz to Zoom with my class, I have taken numerous lessons from talking to Schatz

---

[35] Association of Art Museum Directors, "Latest Art Museum Staff Demographic Survey Shows Number of African American Curators and Women in Leadership Roles Increased," Press Releases & Statements, January 28, 2019, https://aamd.org/for-the-media/press-release/latest-art-museum-staff-demographic-survey-shows-number-of-african.

and from immersing myself in the hobby costumer's world. For me, the most important takeaway is an understanding of restorying as a creative, communal, and performative act of political resistance. In my updated Brit lit survey, I incorporate assignments that give students the opportunity to practice transformative and resistant restorying. My favorite of these assignments is a curation exercise that takes advantage of Macalester's geographical proximity to the Minneapolis Institute of Art. Mia (as it is known) boasts an encyclopedic collection of 90,000 items spanning roughly five thousand years of world history.[36] I explain the curation assignment in week one so that students have plenty of time to think about their selection. The instructions are as follows:

1. Find one object (any object) using Mia's online catalogue that relates to the global Middle Ages or the Renaissance.
2. Design a Google slide containing a photo of that object and explain its significance as a cultural artifact, its material or artistic condition, and its usage or function.
3. Finally, share a personal takeaway: why are you drawn to *this* object? How did this object spark your curiosity?[37]

Their Google slides are due in week ten (classes run for fifteen weeks).

The curation exercise culminates in a group outing. On a Saturday morning, we meet at Mia, spending roughly three to five minutes talking about an item to accommodate all the objects people have chosen. Interstitial time is spent navigating the cavernous, multilevel, complex space of the galleries. This is not time wasted. It is in these moments that students get to talk to each other in a social setting. Liberated from classroom furniture, they are able to move with each other, to move with me, and we get to share in a common experience. Getting lost, retracing steps, breaking for refreshments—these are the moments that help us to bond as a group. Some want to wander away to objects that are not part of the tour; others find more enjoyment in each other's company than finding the next item on our list. Each person moves according to their unique rhythm. Navigating the museum on our own terms and in negotiation with

---

[36] "Collections," Minneapolis Institute of Art, https://collections.artsmia.org/ (accessed November 13, 2022). Admission to Mia is free.

[37] In the weeks leading up to the deadline, I practice finding items with students in class and we brainstorm the different ways one might want to curate an item.

the group recalls Schatz's practice of working in her home studio as a form of resistance to the academy's normative time.

Perhaps the most valuable aspect of the group outing is the embodied performance of knowledge, research, and storytelling done by students for each other. In *Teaching to Transgress*, bell hooks emphasizes that "Teaching is a performative act" and that the "work" of teachers is "meant to serve as a catalyst that calls everyone to become more and more engaged, to become active participants in learning."[38] The curation exercise challenges the ingrained habit of deference to professional knowledge and uncritical looking. It assumes that every viewer has the ability to do the necessary research and reflection to tell the story of the object. This is a chance for students who previously might have been reticent to be in the spotlight. The presenter stands in the docent's position and draws our attention to peculiar details. The group applauds the presenter for their research and insights. Thus, the curation exercise offers students a chance to restory a major civic institution like Mia. The exercise reimagines museum patronage: rather than passively receive information, students actively create it. It gives students an opportunity to publicly perform the role of the knowledgeable expert in an institutional space that has traditionally curtailed their participation and devalued their knowledge.

For students of color, the experience of speaking in this marbled neoclassical space—a space that announces its connection to elite, white culture—can be transformative. Historically, the museum did not welcome patrons of color, and to this day some of my students of color feel like space invaders when they enter the gallery. When I lead my students into these galleries, then allow them to lead me, trading the teacher-student roles, I affirm their competence as storytellers. The experience can leave a deep impression. For example, one of my students, the daughter of Hmong immigrants, told me that she was born and raised in the Twin Cities but had never set foot in Mia. It had never felt like a space that could be welcoming. The class outing made her feel more at ease crossing into this formerly forbidding space. When I checked in with her a year later, I learned that following our class, she had taken her young cousins to the museum, serving as their guide.

---

[38] hooks, *Teaching to Transgress*, 11.

Conclusion

What forms of freedom become possible when we encourage students to read, critique, and rewrite canonical literature with the passion of a fan? For students of color, the literature classroom can be what BlerDCon is to Schatz: a refuge where it is a given that there is no right or wrong way to use the property—be it the text, the criticism, the aesthetic—of white culture. Literary criticism and literary theory routinely trouble binary thinking, and teaching offers opportunities to engage students in discussions of how differences in nationality, race, gender, sexuality, class, and disability shape readerly identification and disidentification with the texts. Yet critique, always an important first step, cannot be the only outlet for students to express their critical imagination. It is not enough to verbally encourage students to forge their own paths into and out of the literature. It is important to create assignments that give students the opportunity to leave their lasting mark on a text.

To be clear, I believe in the value of traditional assignments (close reading analyses, research essays, etc.). I still think these are some of the most effective genres for developing students' critical vocabulary and imagination. But I also see students benefiting from assignments that tap their creative and performance skills. This is the lesson that Schatz and hobby costumers have taught me. Restorying texts is a slow, communally oriented practice where processes are shared with fellow fans. Restorying enables a public performance of expertise. The fan-creator does not regret the hours spent on such a project because, as all fans know, there is nothing more satisfying than transforming an original text in light of one's own hopes and desires. For the fan, pleasure is found in the freedom to make work that is not intended for monetization. There is the added pleasure of voluntarily entering a community of fellow fans.

Given my investments in fan culture, and my own experience of being interpolated within and by white-dominated institutions, a longer version of this essay would include a personal reflection on the distinction between restorying and assimilation. Despite my understanding of restorying as a form of protest, despite being inspired by the transformative work of amazing fans of color like Shasta Schatz, and despite all my thinking about aesthetic matching and whiteness as property, I feel a degree of ambivalence when I teach the Brit lit survey. How might a discussion of restorying be complicated by the theory of disidentification or critiques of multiculturalism and assimilation?[39] To put it another way, when might a nonwhite reader's restorying of white intellectual properties inadvertently reproduce whiteness? I hope to be able to consider these questions in the future, and I look forward to finding and creating spaces where I can learn from others who are grappling with similar questions.

I will end on a note of optimism. Restorying undermines the segregation impulses behind aesthetic matching. Restorying takes a collective effort. Fans write for other fans. As a collective, people have the power to shift the discourse about who gets to access white intellectual properties once and for all. Transforming any culturally white space, whether the academic institution, the fan convention, or the museum, is grinding, slow, iterative work. For the work to last, it has to involve the labor and insights of both professional and non-professional scholars, artists, and writers of all ages. The fabric of social justice is more consequential—not to mention more durable—when it is woven by many hands.

---

[39] On disidentification, see Muñoz, *Disidentifications*. On the politics of multiculturalism and its impact on Asian American assimilation, see James Kyung-Jin Lee, "Multiculturalism," in *Keywords for Asian American Studies*, ed. Cathy J. Schlund-Vials, K. Scott Wong, and Trinh Vo (New York: New York University Press, 2015), n.p., *Credo Reference*.

Chapter 8

Shakespeare in a Catholic University: (Re)creating Knowledge in a Divided Landscape
Kirsten N. Mendoza

The University of Dayton is a predominantly white Catholic Marianist institution with a mission and curriculum centered on education for the common good as a means to promote rights and the dignity of all people.[1] In this chapter, I reflect on my experiences teaching Shakespeare in a politically divided landscape, and I share my pedagogical approaches that center on modes of inquiry as part of my commitment to inspire liberatory action and social change. In *Teaching Social Justice Through Shakespeare,* Wendy Beth Hyman and Hillary Eklund remind teachers that "[l]iterary learning, specifically, ought not to be about the veneration of any particular text or object, but the cultivation of a way of looking at the world."[2] Shakespeare's privileged place in the English literary canon means that I have yet to encounter a student taking a Shakespeare seminar who does not have a very clear preconceived idea of Shakespeare. This, in turn, makes the Shakespeare classroom, in my experience, the most powerful and apt learning space (and, in that way, perhaps one of the most contested spaces as well) to have students think deeply about the politics of knowledge creation, especially as it relates to the religious "truths" we have come to accept, the norms we inhabit, and the assumptions we make, which are yoked to gendered and racialized violence.

---

[1] For example, the University of Dayton began the first undergraduate human rights studies program in the United States. Part of the Common Academic Program (CAP) that all undergraduate students must complete regardless of their major includes a Diversity and Social Justice component.

[2] Wendy Beth Hyman and Hillary Eklund, "Introduction," in *Teaching Social Justice Through Shakespeare: Why Renaissance Literature Matters Now* (Edinburgh: Edinburgh University Press, 2019), 6.

Shakespeare, Christianity, and Morality

In the spring semester of my first year at the University of Dayton (UD), I had a meet-and-greet conversation during the second week of classes with a student from my Shakespeare seminar. The student informed me that she may have to leave the course since she was concerned that the contents and discussions of the class would be in conflict with her spiritual development. She was "a woman of faith," she declared while clutching her cross-pendant necklace. The student was very eager to convey that she was learning in the course and that she liked me as an instructor. However, she was struggling due to the conflict she perceived between our work in the classroom and her Catholic values. She believed, in particular, that our discussions on *The Rape of Lucrece* were not "things she should be talking about" as a young Catholic woman.

What stays with me from that conversation is her affect, the intensity of her earnestness, and her commitment to a particular vision of Shakespeare that she had prior to coming to the course and that she anticipated the seminar would confirm. She shared that I should have had the class read works that were "more Shakespeare," which she equated with being "happier" and "less violent," like "*The Tempest*." Of course, there is violence in *The Tempest* and certainly scenes of domestic abuse. And I too find great value in discussing *The Tempest* with students, but in part because the play provides us with material to analyze critically dynamics of power and to question the narratives of violence that are effaced or justified. In our discussions of this dramatic work, learning communities can consider who deserves forgiveness and happiness, whose privilege is enabled through the oppression and dispossession of others. For the student, however, *The Tempest* was a "happy" play, which was far more fitting for a Catholic woman to study, analyze, and discuss. Within the student's response, one can see how an ethically oriented and politically responsive approach to education was perceived as being in conflict with her religious identity. Furthermore, the student believed that an education in line with Catholicism would also be pleasure-oriented, which was in keeping with her particular idea of Shakespeare. The student's experience of a specific affect while studying *The Tempest* led the student to assume that the play *is* happy. Was the student's view of this play an effect of the removal and censure of potential lines and phrases that could be perceived as improper for a Catholic high school student to contemplate?

Was Prospero's abusive behavior acknowledged but simply not interrogated critically, and, therefore, forgotten? Or did her previous class discuss Caliban's enslavement as a necessary corrective imposed by a benevolent and protective father?

In the week of our meet-and-greet, the class had been analyzing how chastity in *The Rape of Lucrece* is linked to Lucrece's status as property, as a movable good that can be expropriated and taken from her owner—how chastity and the violence Lucrece sustained were entwined.[3] Shakespeare's narrative poem illustrates the dangers of discourses that fetishize feminine sexual purity (religious and otherwise), discourses that excite violence against women and also add to the psychological duress experienced by survivors of rape. For example, rather than deter her rapist, discourses of chastity, which endow women with value and present them as prizes to be had and conquered by men, pique Tarquin's interest in the Roman matron: "Haply that name of chaste unhapp'ly set / This bateless edge on his keen appetite" (8–9).[4] Lucrece is figured as an "iuorie wall"—pure and unconquered—a worthy and tempting challenge for the martial Tarquin to besiege (464). And, as the oxymorons "O modest wantons, wanton modestie!" (401) convey, modesty itself can be made into its seeming opposite—seductive, provoking sexual immodesty.

Chastity discourse not only dangerously fetishizes sexual purity and arouses lust, but it can also negatively impact the way survivors of violence view themselves. Shakespeare's narrative poem dedicates approximately 835 lines to presenting Lucrece's internal turmoil as she attempts to make sense of the violence she sustained and how she should perceive herself in the aftermath of trauma. In doing so, Shakespeare's *Lucrece* refuses to let readers forget that the trauma Lucrece sustained was first and foremost hers, despite her status as the possession of men. The narrative poem offers readers one of the first extensive reckonings with the psychological trauma impacting survivors of sexual violence in English literature and challenges misogynist arguments that displace blame on the victim rather than her assailant.[5]

---

[3] Discussions of the commodification of chastity and its economic signification in the early modern period have also been very useful in helping students recognize that chastity was as much economic as it was religious and social. See Katherine Gillen's *Chaste Value: Economic Crisis, Female Chastity and the Production of Social Difference on Shakespeare's Stage* (Edinburgh: Edinburgh University Press, 2019).

[4] William Shakespeare, *The Rape of Lucrece*, *The Norton Shakespeare: Based on the Oxford Edition*, 2nd ed. (New York: W. W. Norton & Company, 2008), 663–710.

[5] For example, according to Galenic reproductive theories, conception proved that an alleged rape was actually consensual sex because conception required a

Misogynist arguments that turn survival of rape into incriminating evidence against the victim have a long history, which Catholic theologians, educators, and leaders had a significant role in perpetuating. For example, in his *Instruction of a Christen Woman*, which was dedicated to Catherine of Aragon and was popular among both Catholics and Protestants alike, Juan Luis Vives, a Valencian Renaissance humanist and educational theorist, espoused that virginity came with its own powers to protect women from the lusts of men. In fact, according to Vives, it is a virgin's praiseworthy armor of virtue that deters rapists. By locating the ability to deter rape onto the woman's virginity, Vives problematically contends that a survivor of sexual assault was simply not virtuous "enough" to prevent the attack. In his list of exemplars, virgins would rather die than experience rape or would kill themselves after procuring vengeance upon their attackers.[6]

Approximately eleven hundred years prior, St. Augustine of Hippo already attempted to argue against the communal pressures on rape survivors to commit suicide in his seminal work of Christian philosophy *The City of God*. Especially in a Catholic university, it is not uncommon for students to be aware of this work or, at the very least, to know Augustine's privileged place in the Catholic tradition. In making a case for why survivors of sexual assault should not follow Lucretia's example and take their lives, Augustine casts blame on Lucretia for being either an adulteress or a murderer. "*Si adulterate, cur laudata; si pudica, cur occisa?* If she was made an adulteress, why has she been praised; if she was chaste, why was she

---

woman's experience of pleasure, and pleasure was understood as a sign of consent. In Thomas Edgar's *Lawes Resolution of Women's Rights*, Galenic theories of reproduction were used to discredit a victim of rape who escaped from her kidnapper after having lived seven years with him and having borne his child. Parliament countered her suit and "demanded how she could now say that she neuer assented, hauing conceiued" (Thomas Edgar, *The Lawes Resolutions of Womens Rights* [London, 1632], 400). In the narrative poem, Tarquin's attack is depicted as unequivocally nonconsensual. Tarquin overpowered and violently silenced Lucrece, who was unable to voice her will (678). Rather than ignore the issue of pregnancy (which had been viewed by some early moderns as evidence of adultery and not rape), Shakespeare presents Lucrece's fears that the "bastard graft" will grow and that her husband will be ridiculed for being a "doting father" to Tarquin's child (1062, 1064). In this way, Shakespeare's poem disentangles conception from consent.

[6] Juan Luis Vives, *A Very frutefull and pleasant boke called the Instruction of a Christen Woman* (London, 1529). See also Kathryn Schwarz, "Chastity, Militant and Married: Cavendish's Romance, Milton's Masque," *PMLA* 118, no. 2 (2003): 270–85.

slain?"[7] For Augustine, Lucretia's self-harm—her chastisement of the body—would only make sense if she had committed the sin of adultery. Since Lucretia remains chaste and the sin of rape lies with Tarquin, then the punishment of her body serves to damn her soul, which, Augustine argues, is more egregious. This reputable Christian theologian, then, in his attempt to prevent victims of sexual assault from being coerced into self-harm, fails to consider the psychology of a woman in the aftermath of trauma. Shakespeare's narrative poem illustrates the potential anguish, confusion, guilt, and debilitating self-perception that survivors of sexual assault may navigate after the violation they had sustained. Although Shakespeare's Lucrece understands that suicide would lead to her "poor soul's pollution" (1157), she—as Katharine Eisaman Maus underscores—"thinks about her body in terms of metaphors: house, fortress, mansion, temple, tree bark . . . [and o]nce the house is sacked and battered, the inhabitant suffers, regardless of her guilt or innocence."[8] In the narrative poem, Lucrece cannot accept the Augustinian separation of soul and body, in which the soul takes primacy over the flesh. After all, as a Roman matron, she has been taught to understand her worth as the possession of her husband is entwined with the state of her body. She has learned to make sense of herself though metaphors—like the "iuorie wall" (464) whose primary purpose is to be impregnable. In Shakespeare's narrative poem, it is not guilt for having consented (that is, for having committed adultery) that leads to Lucrece's suicide, as Augustine suggests, but the debilitating discourses of chastity—the misogynist and objectifying lexicon available to women that presents them as bereft of value and dignity after suffering the trauma of rape.

Chastity and sexual purity are stressed within the Christian faith and are particularly demanded of women. It is understandable, then, that students may experience discomfort when being asked to consider critically the negative impact of discourses that they have been taught are integral to the salvation of their souls as well as to the protection of their bodies. Shakespeare's Lucrece enables readers to recognize that chastity does not prevent a woman from experiencing

---

[7] Augustine of Hippo, *The City of God*, trans. George E. McCracken, Loeb Classical Library (Cambridge, MA: Harvard University Press, 1957), Book I, 19. St. Augustine of Hippo, who was from Northern Africa, is an example of a Catholic saint and Church Father who has been and continues to be whitewashed in Christian iconography.

[8] Katharine Eisaman Maus, "Taking Tropes Seriously: Language and Violence in Shakespeare's *Rape of Lucrece*," *Shakespeare Quarterly* 37, no. 1 (1986): 70.

sexual violence; for this Roman matron, being "good" and performing duties of hospitality put her in harm's way. For some, although chastity cannot provide an armor of protection, it is at least the means by which the soul remains pure, regardless of the state of the body. While for Augustine this mind-body division is both liberating and easy to accept, Shakespeare points out that such a separation is not so simple for a person who has suffered sexual violence, especially if that person has been inured to understanding their self-worth through the state of their physical body. Shakespeare's *Lucrece* opens the possibility for teachers engaged in social justice pedagogy to help students think critically about the intersections of religious and sexist discourses that shape moral values and that locate dignity in feminine "bodily purity," discourses that continue to influence our perceptions of others and of ourselves. We can help students think about the potential negative effects of virtues many of us have been taught to extol and embody, and we can use Shakespeare's works to unsettle the religious or moral "truths" that had previously been unquestioned.

The goal of unsettling what students "know" is very much embraced by the University of Dayton, which prioritizes inquiry as an institutional learning goal. While the majority of students I have worked with view a social justice approach to Shakespeare to be in concert with the Marianist values of the university, I have had a few other students—not many—who have voiced at some point in the semester their concern that our discussions were not in keeping with Christian values. I had not experienced this until teaching at UD. At a religious institution, a claim that labels or describes a particular mode of inquiry in teaching as being at odds with the foundational faith of the university questions—to a certain extent—the belonging of that pedagogical approach (or even the educator) within a Catholic institution. What has remained with me from my conversation with the student who felt that our discussions of Shakespeare's *Lucrece* were not appropriate for a Catholic woman to ponder is not the student's discomfort and struggles, for such feelings can actually be generative when thinking about the long-term learning of the course. What sticks with me from that specific conversation is the yoking of discussions that are unchristian with being *un-Shakespearean*. Some of our students are likely drawn to Shakespeare because they anticipate that his works will confirm their niche idea of "proper" Christian morals.

I think about the student's alignment of Shakespeare with a particular kind of Americanized right-wing version of Christian faith, in which the pursuit of justice is all well and good until you begin questioning or lacking reverence for white patriarchal heterosexist Christian values. Students who are not pursuing a career in education (e.g., primary, secondary, and higher ed) and who elect to take this course often do so because they previously enjoyed classes on Shakespeare in high school. It is also clear to me that some students love Shakespeare not only because they are drawn to his works or to his centrality in the British literary canon but also because they have been taught to see him as "good for you"—intellectually and morally.[9] UD students are not unique in this regard, a reality driven home for me in 2014 when I joined a collective conversation in Nashville, TN, that was part of "Shakespeare on the Road."[10] The forum gathered practitioners of Shakespeare, actors, and teachers from all levels of education. One series of questions posed to us focused on the infatuation Americans have with Shakespeare: why do you teach Shakespeare? Why do you perform his works? Why is he of such significance to Americans? To which a teacher responded, "Shakespeare makes people moral," an assertion that received vigorous nods and words of affirmation. To some degree my work in the classroom—its focus on social justice—connects with my colleague's view.[11] We are both filled with a reservoir of hope, and we share a belief in the good that learning in a Shakespeare classroom can bring to our students and our communities today. While I do wholeheartedly believe that Shakespeare's works have the potential to help bring forth social change in pursuit of a more just and liberatory future, my faith in a classroom devoted to the study of Shakespeare's

---

[9] Ayanna Thompson explains that Shakespeare is reputed to be like eating one's "spinach.... He is good for you... universally good for you." And, although she hopes that in the twenty-first century we have collectively moved beyond this view, from my introductory sessions with students it is clear that this perception is still pervasive. Ayanna Thompson, "All that Glisters Is Not Gold," *Code Switch* (NPR), August 21, 2019, https://www.npr.org/transcripts/752850055.

[10] "Shakespeare on the Road: Celebrate William Shakespeare's 450th Birthday on a Road Trip to 14 Shakespeare Festivals all around North America in One Remarkable Summer." The University of Warwick and Shakespeare Birthplace Trust.

[11] The role of a humanities education and its desired effects to bring forth civic-minded members of a commonwealth is not new when one considers the incorporation of Shakespeare within US American high school curricula. Shakespeare became a crucial part of the American curriculum in the late nineteenth and early twentieth centuries, when he was presented as a moralizing force whose works like *Julius Caesar* and *The Merchant of Venice* could warn youths about the sins of sedition and propagate the glories of Christian compassion and mercy. These were also the two most commonly taught plays in American high schools and American colonial schools in the early twentieth century.

works is not the same as ceding agency to Shakespeare, which—in effect—disempowers us and, more importantly, prevents us from self-reflection and from recognizing the politics of knowledge creation. As teachers, students, audiences, performers, and directors, it is what *we* do with Shakespeare and not what he does to or for us. We are actively shaping what Shakespeare means to us now and what he will mean in our collective future.

Shakespeare and Whiteness

The Shakespeare seminar at UD is, at present, the only single-author-focused course that fulfills multiple general degree Common Academic Program, or CAP, requirements for undergraduate students (this is one of the reasons the Shakespeare seminar is extremely popular for a variety of students beyond those pursuing education and a degree in the humanities). And with Shakespeare's face carved onto the facade of the university's Humanities building along an area of heavy traffic across from the Kennedy Union—the community center of campus (a building with lounges, recreation, meeting spaces, student organization office spaces, and dining halls for students, faculty, and staff)—it is safe to say that both the curriculum and the physical space of the university attest to this early modern writer's privileged place in educational institutions. But in a university that is predominantly white, the fact that the Humanities building is adorned with the faces of primarily white male authors, theologians, philosophers, and musicians—the so-called fathers of the humanities—sends a message of exclusivity and reifies the association of Shakespeare with elitism, masculine privilege, and whiteness.

Our institutions of learning, Karen Buenavista Hanna has argued, are spaces that are founded upon "white heteropatriarchal ableist norms" that shape the differing experiences of our students in the classroom environment, and this is especially the case when Shakespeare is considered.[12] "In America," Arthur L. Little, Jr. argues, Shakespeare has been "thoroughly identified ... as white property."[13] The view of Shakespeare as white property goes hand

---

[12] Karen Buenavista Hanna, "Pedagogies in the Flesh: Building an Anti-Racist Decolonized Classroom," *Frontiers: A Journal of Women Studies* 40, no. 1 (2019): 234.

[13] Arthur L. Little, Jr., "Re-Historicizing Race, White Melancholia, and the Shakespearean Property," *Shakespeare Quarterly* 67, no. 1 (2016): 84–103.

in hand with the perception of the "early modern" as a period in which, as Ania Loomba and Jonathan Burton have underscored, "our modern world and some of its most cherished as well as problematic ideologies, institutions, and practices ... were engendered" *except* "when it comes to the question of race."[14] As I am one of five nonwhite faculty in a department of fifty instructors, my focus on constructions of race in the early modern period in a Shakespeare seminar has inevitably led to a few students articulating their concerns that such inquiries are anachronistic (and irreverent) impositions of a particular agenda onto subjects that are untouched by race-thinking.

For the vast majority of my students, our conversations on race formations in the early modern period have increased rather than hindered their interest in the sixteenth and seventeenth centuries. In particular, students have been drawn to the ways that the work of our classroom community calls into question the prior narratives they have been taught and the assumptions they had about England's early modern past generally imagined as a history that is exclusively *white*. Furthermore, the students who had been exposed to European history had been taught to take the lack of codified slave laws in England as definitive proof that—unlike the Iberian Peninsula—"England was too pure an air for Slaves to breathe in."[15] For those who had been "smuggled into the country," Noémie Ndiaye explains, the fact that England did not formally recognize slavery meant that they "found themselves in a legal limbo that, together with linguistic and cultural alienation, made them vulnerable to the whims of their clandestine buyers."[16] In London during the 1590s, the Afro-British population is estimated to have comprised 0.5 percent.[17] And, while the numbers of Black Tudors were certainly less than they were in Spain and Portugal, as Ndiaye has reminded us, their presence was noticeable to the point

---

[14] Jonathan Burton and Ania Loomba, "Introduction," in *Race in Early Modern England: A Documentary Companion* (New York: Palgrave, 2007), 2.

[15] Quoted in Susan Dwyer Amussen, *Caribbean Exchanges: Slavery and the Transformation of English Society, 1640–1700* (Chapel Hill: The University of North Carolina, 2009), 219. Amussen further explains how the lack of slave laws gave Afro-diasporic people brought into England ambiguous statuses that were exploited by those who imported and sold them.

[16] Noémie Ndiaye, *Scripts of Blackness: Early Modern Performance Culture and the Making of Race* (Philadelphia: University of Pennsylvania Press, 2022), 12.

[17] Gustav Ungerer, "The Presence of Africans in Elizabethan England and the Performance of *Titus Andronicus* at Burley-on-the-Hill, 1595/6," *Medieval and Renaissance Drama in England* 21 (2008): 20.

that Elizabeth issued three warrants of expulsion against the Afro-diasporic population.[18]

Although the Afro-diasporic population in Elizabethan England increased substantially due to diplomatic and commercial enterprises, as Imtiaz Habib's archival work has revealed, Afro-British people were already part of England even before Elizabeth came to the throne beginning predominantly with the initiatives of her grandfather, Henry VII, and the Scottish James IV.[19] Therefore while the Afro-diasporic population in England included those "of late ... brought into th[e] realm," there were certainly Black Tudors who were second- or third-generation men, women, and children born in England. According to Onyeka Nubia, "The Africans that lived in towns and rural communities in early modern England resided with Englishmen and women. Many of them would have considered themselves members of local communities, more than subjects of a nation state."[20] As part of my pedagogy, I share archival sources (generally legal records) with students, especially since doing so helps to expand students' understandings of who can be considered members of an English community.[21] It is not only the existence but the *belonging* of Black Tudors within the intimate relations of local, domestic English spaces that I underscore in order to challenge the general assumption that Black people were absent from England's early modern communities and, more broadly, from England's (white) history. As teachers we can push back against the assumption that Black Tudors either did not exist in the period or do not belong in our historical view of early modern England and the history of Europe more broadly. In doing so, we can help students interrogate how, if Black Tudors were members of local communities, Renaissance England became associated with *whiteness* alongside and through the exclusion, precarity, vulnerability, and vilification of targeted populations.

By drawing attention to the (damaging) cultural erasure of Black Tudors—a contemporary perception of their non-belonging within

---

[18] Ndiaye, *Scripts*, 12.
[19] Imtiaz Habib, *Black Lives in the English Archives, 1500–1677* (Aldershot: Ashgate, 2008), 65.
[20] Onyeka Nubia, *England's Other Countrymen: Black Tudor Society* (London: Zed Books, 2019), 31. See also David Olusoga, *Black and British: A Forgotten History* (London: Macmillan, 2016).
[21] The ERC-funded Travel, Transculturality, and Identity in England (TIDE) database, http://www.tideproject.uk/sample-teaching-resources/, provides excellent resources for educators who wish to provide students with archival sources on Black Tudors in London.

a shared early modern English past—educators can encourage students to consider thoughtfully and seriously how privilege, bias, and prejudice have shaped the narratives we tell, which are normalized and systemically perpetuated through institutions like education. Attention to the workings of systems and institutions invites educators to have difficult and candid conversations with colleagues and administrators about the institutional belonging of faculty of color within predominantly white universities. As one of the few faculty of color in the Department of English and one who teaches courses generally considered to be "white property," I often think about the ways that the departmental makeup confirms the association of "English" as a discipline with whiteness more generally. Simply stating that "diversity, equity, and inclusion are foundational Catholic principles" is not enough when students can complete a degree without once taking a course from a faculty member who does not readily "fit" preconceived ideas of who deserves authority in higher education.

Through Shakespeare, With Shakespeare, and In Shakespeare

It is worth mentioning that those who attend Catholic institutions are likely accustomed to the veneration of white/whitewashed male figures. Indeed, as the claim "Shakespeare makes us moral" indicates, Shakespeare can be viewed as a kind of secular religious symbol, and there are—to some—perceived similarities between Christ and Shakespeare. Despite the growing population of Catholics of color in the United States, the Catholic leadership—clergy and bishops—remain primarily white.[22] In this regard, lack of diversity among faculty and upper administration in Catholic religious institutions continues to confirm (perhaps unintentionally) the association of Catholicism with whiteness. Furthermore, the symbolism and art of the Catholic church are dominated by white people, despite the fact that one of the earliest Catholic regions included the Kingdom of Aksum in present-day Ethiopia and Eritrea; that not all saints were fair-skinned, blonde, and blue-eyed (e.g., consider the whitewashing of Augustine of Hippo, who was from Numidia); that angels, "which, theologically speaking, are immaterial creatures and therefore *do*

---

[22] See Daniel P. Horan, *A White Catholic's Guide to Racism and Privilege* (Notre Dame: Ave Maria Press, 2021), 100.

not have any color skin"; and, above all, that Christ was "an innocent man of color executed by state authorities in his time."[23] The presumption in the US of a "white church," Bryan N. Massingale provocatively argues, means that "*only* these ... particular cultural expressions are standard, normative, universal, and thus really 'Catholic.'"[24] Given the whitewashing of Catholic iconography and the predominantly white religious leadership of the Church in the US, Catholic Americans may be primed to accept without question the "natural" place of a white man—like Shakespeare—at the center of humanity and of morality.

By virtue of enrolling in a Shakespeare seminar, some students enter the classroom with the expectation that we will study the writings of a genius who wrote by candlelight with a quill in hand and whose works are his creation alone, his gift and sacrifice to us. This assumption hinders us from imagining a collaborative and experimental environment when we think of London's early modern theater scene. For this reason, it is not only important to convey that Shakespeare's works have multiple sources but also to share with students the interconnectedness of the early modern theater and the collaboration of multiple playwrights and players to produce not one particular text but a live performance subject to change and experimentation. Through doing so, we can help students to think beyond the exclusionary politics of authorial canons that have reified the narrative of the individual white man's genius through effacing the knowledge of the collaborative and innovative workings of early modern theater companies.[25] Such an emphasis on collaboration in Shakespeare's day matches the kind of ethos I try to foster in my classrooms, spaces of communal learning in which students are encouraged to value the meaningful knowledge we generate *together* over the ideas of one particular individual. A course that presents Shakespeare as the sole creator not only perpetuates the mythos of a white man's exceptionalism whose works are his and *his alone* (a belief that does not do justice to the workings of London's early modern theaters), but also undermines a sense of the strengths and benefits of collaboration.

---

[23] Horan, *White Catholic's Guide*, xiv, 97.
[24] Bryan N. Massingale, *Racial Justice and the Catholic Church* (Maryknoll, NY: Orbis Books, 2010), 79.
[25] See Peter Kirwan, *Shakespeare and the Idea of Apocrypha: Negotiating the Boundaries of the Dramatic Canon* (Cambridge: Cambridge University Press, 2015), for more on the exclusionary framework of authorial canons that prevent students from recognizing the collaborative networks of early modern theatrical companies.

As we unsettle and critique the conceptual ties that have turned the early modern period and Shakespeare into white property, we encourage students to reflect on a much larger issue—the politics of knowledge creation, which is perhaps one of the fundamental lessons students can take away from a course on Shakespeare.[26] We can have students consider how the association of the canon exclusively with Shakespeare has enabled the construction of him as an enduring and exemplary symbol of a white man's universal creative genius.

Shakespeare's canonization allows us to confront how our institutions of learning have been used to oppress the most disenfranchised members of our communities, to justify violence, and to construct and maintain white supremacy. Rather than give my students the early modern world they anticipate, one that romanticizes white heterosexism and ableism, I do what I can to be responsive, to reflect on my students' learning, and to structure my classes with early modern texts and secondary sources that critique and challenge the alignment of learning about Shakespeare, about England, and about the early moderns with the continued validation of racial and masculine superiority which continues to harm targeted populations.

In Ruben Espinosa's evocative call to action, he urges us to commit ourselves to antiracism and reminds us that our work offers students a way to understand the painful, complex, and divisive issues impacting our local, domestic, and global communities:

> It is *your* mountainish inhumanity that haunts me. And standing here amid that barbaric wall and the open wound of this borderland community, I urge you not just to stand with refugees, immigrants, and those dark of skin, but to stand *against* white supremacy by committing to antiracist efforts any time you sit to read, sit to write, or stand before your students who are seeking to make sense of the world around them.[27]

For some, the shift that undermines the perception of the early modern period as *white* and the recognition of the collaborative environment that was the early modern English theater can come

---

[26] Valerie Traub calls critical attention to our methodologies that shape the knowledge we create: "How do we know (what we think) we know?" Valerie Traub, *Thinking Sex with the Early Moderns* (Philadelphia: University of Pennsylvania Press, 2016), 49.

[27] Ruben Espinosa, "Shakespeare and Your Mountainish Inhumanity," *The Sundial*, August 16, 2019, https://medium.com/the-sundial-acmrs/shakespeare-and-your-mountainish-inhumanity-d255474027de.

with a sense of loss, but it can also offer students a chance to (re)connect with Shakespeare's corpus in inspiring and meaningful ways. Since the University of Dayton emphasizes the role of social justice as part of the university's identity as a Marianist institution, it is not uncommon for students who are pursuing an academic interest in education to be committed to social justice and antiracist pedagogy as they seek to give their future students a sense of belonging. As one would expect, many of the students who take the Shakespeare seminar plan to teach high school English courses. In conversation with my students, I have noticed that there is an increasing number of future educators who are beginning to question whether or not Shakespeare needs to be taught by them to ninth to twelfth graders. For some future teachers, Shakespeare's reputation is so entrenched in elitism, an aura of inaccessibility, and white heteropatriarchal exclusivity that they had never considered how Shakespeare could be compatible with a pedagogy that centers social justice and empowerment as a guiding principle.

The generation of students in my classrooms today, Gen Z, has been described as one of the most socially conscious generations, characterized by a commitment to making a positive impact. They are less likely, therefore, to readily accept Shakespeare as a necessary part of our curricula by virtue of his sacred place in the British (western/white) canon. In my classes, I hope to inspire students to see how teaching Shakespeare can be mobilized in pursuit of social justice. I demonstrate to students that one can be *passionate* about the early modern period and Shakespearean works, that we can *have fun* as a community of learners as we discuss and think deeply and meaningfully about sensitive and difficult topics like social inequality, power, privilege, violence, and oppression.

Students today are demanding more from their teachers and more from Shakespeare, more from their educational institutions and more from the Catholic church. Fortunately, Shakespeare—like Catholicism—is not a monolith, and we are shaping what both can and will mean to future generations. Many of my students embrace the social justice mission of the university as part of the Marianist Catholic identity of the institution, and they understand that meaningful learning through an ethically oriented approach that is politically responsive requires discomfort and a willingness to reckon with the histories of knowledge creation—not just the positives of Catholic educational institutions, but also the shortcomings and even harm that institutional spaces of learning have done and are continuing to do. While we are (re)learning and (re)creating what

Catholic education means in the United States, we are similarly revitalizing Shakespeare's works and making him accessible, exciting, and urgent to people who might not have thought that Shakespeare could mean anything to them. We are breathing meaning into Shakespeare, and we are making a place for him in our vision of a more just world.

Chapter 9

Shakespeare's Mixed Stock: Biracial Affect in the Field
Roya Biggie and Perry Guevara

With renewed urgency, the field of Shakespeare studies has turned its collective attention to race, not only to more fully understand a literary milieu characterized by British imperialism, the transatlantic slave trade, and emergent global capitalism, but also to critique the material conditions of a field that historically was built and maintained by white scholars and that ideologically buttressed the ascendance of the university as a settler colonial institution. The formation of the university, as a brick-and-mortar site of Indigenous displacement and cultural exclusion, necessarily involved the institutionalization of multiple and insidious racial anxieties within the canon, curriculum, and archive. For the past thirty or so years, the tendency in the field, in an effort to responsibly account for racial difference in Shakespeare, has been to center and study white anxieties about racialized others—fears of contamination, replacement, and miscegenation—that animated and continue to animate racial hostility in Anglophone societies. These anxieties abound, in part, due to the archive we have inherited: sermons, travelogues, epistolary correspondences, poetic and dramatic texts that evince deep worry, disgust, and fear, on behalf of European writers, of foreign bodies. The study of these affirms what we have always known: Shakespeare was never meant for most people. We have simply redistributed his texts to unintended readers. This fact, amplified by naysayers who not only doubt the presence of people of color in early modern England but also lodge accusations of anachronism, elicit *feelings* of unbelonging for these accidental readers.[1] Ambereen Dadabhoy

---

[1] See, for example, Patricia Parker and Margo Hendricks, eds., *Women, "Race" and Writing in the Early Modern Period* (London: Routledge, 1994), who in their introduction write against historicist objections to race and anachronism.

asks, "What happens when you read texts for whom you are not the intended audience, by writers who could not have imagined you as a reader?"[2] Moreover, what happens when a reader identifies with the racialized stranger, villain, or outcast because their sense of self misaligns with whiteness? Reading is an affective encounter, and these misalignments prove vexing at best and damaging at worst. In this chapter, we regard these frictions and their repetitions in higher education as *institutional,* if not as *institutionalized,* affect.

By affect, we refer to the range of feelings, sensations, sentiments, impressions, and atmospheres generated by and through relation, and we intend to register the ways in which affective experience is modulated, in large part, by race. In *Race and Affect in Early Modern English Literature,* Carol Mejia LaPerle queries, "What are the emotional experiences of racial formation and racist ideologies? How do feelings . . . come to signify race?"[3] These questions prompt us to ask what becomes possible if we set aside white anxieties about race to consider instead minority anxieties, what Kathy Park Hong identifies as "minor feelings," "the racialized range of emotions that are negative, dysphoric, and therefore untelegenic, built from the sediments of everyday racial experience and the irritant of having one's perception of reality constantly questioned or dismissed."[4] To show how "[r]ace informs affective experiences and vice versa," Mejia LaPerle points us to the work of cultural theorist Sianne Ngai, who argues that "emotional qualities slide into corporeal qualities in the case of racialized subjects, reinforcing the notion of race itself as a truth located, quite naturally, in the always obvious, highly visible body."[5] That is to say, race and affect are visceral, occurring at the interstices of skins, organs, and nerves, and "blur[ring] what is felt and what is embodied."[6] In *Shakespeare and the Cultivation of Difference,* Patricia Akhimie writes poignantly about the painful, lived experience of racism as "a persistent and particular kind of

---

[2] Ambereen Dadabhoy, "Imagining Islamicate Worlds: Race and Affect in the Contact Zone," in *Race and Affect in Early Modern English Literature,* ed. Carol Mejia LaPerle (Tempe: Arizona Center for Medieval and Renaissance Studies Press, 2022), 1, https://asu.pressbooks.pub/race-and-affect/chapter/1-imagining-islamicate-worlds-race-and-affect-in-the-contact-zone/.

[3] Mejia LaPerle, back cover of *Race and Affect in Early Modern English Literature.*

[4] Kathy Park Hong, *Minor Feelings: An Asian American Reckoning* (New York: One World, 2020), 55.

[5] Sianne Ngai, "'A Foul Lump Started Making Promises in My Voice': Race, Affect, and the Animated Subjects," *American Literature* 74, no. 3 (2002): 573, qtd. in Mejia LaPerle, "Introduction," *Race and Affect in Early Modern English Literature,* xix, https://asu.pressbooks.pub/race-and-affect/front-matter/introduction/.

[6] Mejia LaPerle, "Introduction," xx.

injustice, the signs of which are as fluid as they are injurious."[7] Visual "signs" of race, as materializations of disciplinary power, are somatic markers signifying beyond their raw physicality and thereby rationalizing the domination of one group of humans by another. The stakes are high, even in the study of literature. Mejia LaPerle admits:

> [A]ffect's power to cultivate and intensify belonging or exclusion, its ability to render visceral and thus naturalize machinations of control enacted on bodies, its influential yet unthinking priming towards how we treat people, in other words, affect's contributions to racial subjectivity and race relations are as formidable as they are understudied.[8]

As a beginning, we focus our attention on a related crux in Shakespeare: that of biracial affect—notably, as biracial scholars ourselves—and the ramifications for Shakespearean pedagogy.[9]

In this chapter, we reframe biraciality in early modern studies to show how the offspring of interracial couplings in Shakespeare reveal distinct structures of feeling rooted in uncertainty, ambivalence, and silence. We connect these representations in Shakespeare to not only the early modern archive, inclusive of travelogues, treatises, and natural histories, but also critical scholarship on early modern race. In so doing, we lay the groundwork for pedagogy that is attentive to racial affect and to the growing number of multiracial students in higher education. Moreover, we intend for this pedagogy to serve as a counterpoint to long-standing institutionalized affects engendered by settler colonial anxieties about racialized others and fortified across the history of the university. Finally, we end with a proposal for an advanced college-level course, Shakespeare's Mixed Stock, to not only explore biraciality through literature in the Shakespeare classroom but also model how university communities might confront racial inscrutability and thereby imagine institutional transformation.

What does it mean to be biracial in Shakespeare? First, we acknowledge that biraciality—much like race—is difficult to define in an early modern context. Shakespeare uses the term "race" a mere eighteen times across his body of work, and as Ania Loomba

---

[7] Patricia Akhimie, *Shakespeare and the Cultivation of Difference: Race and Conduct in the Early Modern World* (New York: Routledge, 2018), 9.
[8] Mejia LaPerle, "Introduction," xix–xx.
[9] In this chapter, we use "biracial, "mixed race," and "multiracial" interchangeably. Although we acknowledge that, to some, each might shade toward nuanced or different modes of identification, by and large, the terms easily slip into one another in our cultural lexicon on race.

observes, in ways that are "both distinct from" yet nonetheless ground "later deployments of the word and of the concept."[10] Shakespeare culled racialist tropes from a range of discourses including faith, lineage, natural history, and nationhood. In effect, what we find in Shakespeare is what Étienne Balibar calls "racism without race."[11] By that logic, we also seek to understand biraciality "without race"; that is, without reducing it to decontextualized skin color or physiognomy. Instead, we frame biraciality as a somatic and affective process of racialization shaped by overlapping discourses on difference and hybridity. According to Kerry Ann Rockquemore and David Brunsma, the term "biracial" is used inconsistently: "Some researchers use the term 'biracial' to describe ... specific racial combinations (e.g., those with one black parent and one white parent), while others use the term 'biracial' to make the distinction between first- and second-generation children of interracial couples."[12] Others regard biracial people as even smaller minorities within minorities: for example, *mulatto* as a subset of Black or *mestizo* as a subset of Hispanic. While these definitions are helpful in understanding how the term "biracial" is used sociologically, for the purposes of this chapter, we find more compelling Brigitte Fielder's articulation of race as primarily relational:

> Race is constructed in a maelstrom of social convergences, but it is also experiential, lived. To be racialized is to experience, to be subjected to forms of racial privilege and oppression—to live in racial relation.... Racial embodiment is a state of being in the world, not necessarily having racial materiality or performing race, although these are also involved in racial being. Race is identifying or being identified as a racial being, but it is not only individual. Race is collective.[13]

Racial identity—and biracial identity in particular—is not a mere matter of genealogical inheritance: the transmission of biological and cultural matter along patrilineal or matrilineal conduits. Rather, as Fielder argues, "race follows different lineages in narratives of interracial kinship, which themselves defy neat boundaries between

---

[10] Ania Loomba, *Shakespeare, Race, and Colonialism* (New York: Oxford University Press, 2002), 22.

[11] Étienne Balibar, "Is There a Neo-Racism?", in *Race, Nation, Class: Ambiguous Identities*, ed. Balibar and Immanuel Wallerstein, trans. Chris Turner (London: Verso, 1991), 23, qtd. in Loomba, *Shakespeare, Race*, 37.

[12] Kerry Ann Rockquemore and David Brunsma, *Beyond Black: Biracial Identity in America*, 2nd ed. (New York: Rowman and Littlefield, 2008), 18.

[13] Brigitte Fielder, *Relative Races: Genealogies of Kinship in Nineteenth-Century America* (Durham: Duke University Press, 2020), 10.

races and clear correlations of familial and racial identification."[14] In other words, biracial identity is perpetually under negotiation, especially when self-determination is prohibited or impossible. Rockquemore and Brunsma observe that "most mixed-race people fail to gain acceptance in white society," despite efforts to assimilate, and they instead construct their identities according to physical appearance and contextual factors such as family history and "intergroup relation."[15] Monoracial norms seek fixed identity, while simultaneously barring membership to not only dominant but also minoritized groups to those whose racial identities prove ambiguous. In her research, Theresa Williams found that people with racially "ambiguous appearances" were routinely confronted with the question "What are you?" by acquaintances and strangers alike.[16] The question is not benign; it is pointedly racial, seeking clear and unequivocal categorization. However, taken at its word, the question also registers as an ontological inquiry, as if the subject's humanness were inscrutable; their taxonomy, illegible; and their very being, up for debate.

How does inscrutability feel? And why ought we pay attention to biracial affect? We believe that such attention might avail new research methodologies and pedagogical approaches in support of a generation of students who increasingly identify as multiracial. Census data reveal that the multiracial population in the United States grew from approximately 9 million in 2010 to nearly 34 million in 2020, a 276 percent increase. Today, multiracial people make up over 10 percent of Americans. These numbers track with college enrollments, according to Kate Hermsmeyer, George Dou, and Kelsey Oberbroekling, who, in a recent essay for *Inside Higher Ed*, argue that colleges and universities have failed to meet the moment, neither devoting resources nor developing programming for multiracial students: "In higher education, students who identify as multiracial have been simultaneously oppressed and neglected as a result of societal and institutional practices that construct a monoracial-only view of race."[17] While biracial students might find support in organizations like a Black Student Union, such groups

---

[14] Fielder, *Relative Races*, 3.
[15] Rockquemore and Brunsma, *Beyond Black*, 24–25.
[16] Theresa Williams, "Race as Process: Reassessing the 'What Are You?' Encounters of Biracial Individuals," in *Racially Mixed People in America*, ed. Maria Root (Newbury Park: Sage, 1992), 15.
[17] Kate Hermsmeyer, George Dou, and Kelsey Oberbroekling, "When the Boxes No Longer Fit," *Inside Higher Ed*, November 23, 2021, www.insidehighered.com/views/2021/11/23/colleges-must-change-better-serve-multiracial-students-opinion.

"may not *feel* accommodating to students with multiracial identities" (emphasis ours).[18] Most campuses are "not structured in a way that supports the intersection of more than one identity," adhering too tightly to color binaries and ignoring the diverse experiences of racial mixture, hybridity, passing, not passing, self-determination, doubt, and unknowability that characterize biracial feeling.[19]

Students bring these experiences to the Shakespeare classroom because, as Dadabhoy reminds us, "Reading is an affective relation."[20] The readerly position determines with whom—that is, with which characters in the text—the reader connects. When encountering Muslim characters in early modern literature, Dadabhoy "experience[s] the stigma of demonization because I embody the identity of the antagonist in almost everything I read, study, and analyze. My identity challenges the canon's universalism .... I, then, must stand apart—or more accurately—be prohibited from the universal."[21] Whiteness depends on its capacity to project itself as the norm; it is universal and, therefore, invisible. How, then, might a biracial person experience a Shakespearean text? With which characters would they connect? European patriarchs? Maligned blackamoors? Passing references to ontological hybrids like mermaids and centaurs? We cannot say with certainty, but from personal experience, we suspect an impulse to "attend to that estranged other in whom [we] perceive a distorted reflection, a construction [we] can succor by illuminating the very many political, cultural, and ideological forces contouring [our] discursive being."[22] Although blatantly presentist, *this* is how the text is felt, with critical sympathy.

We recognize that some might allege conspicuous anachronism in applying the term "biracial" to early modernity. "Biracial" did not come into use until the middle of the twentieth century and then mostly within an American context.[23] However, we are convinced that Shakespeare's mixed characters signal something distinct about racial formation in the period and, therefore, present opportunities for reopening his plays to a growing number of biracial students.

---

[18] Hermsmeyer, Dou, and Oberbroekling, "When the Boxes." Nonetheless, we do not mean to discount the radical impact of BSUs and racial affinity groups and clubs that offer marginalized students a sense of belonging and community amidst academia's whitewashed walls.
[19] Hermsmeyer, Dou, and Oberbroekling, "When the Boxes."
[20] Dadabhoy, "Imagining Islamicate Worlds," 1.
[21] Dadabhoy, "Imagining Islamicate Worlds," 1.
[22] Dadabhoy, "Imagining Islamicate Worlds," 3.
[23] "biracial, adj.," *OED Online*, June 2022 (Oxford University Press), https://www.oed.com/view/Entry/19316 (accessed July 29, 2022).

Experiences of inscrutability and suspicions of ontological hybridity guide our analysis in this chapter, as we locate few-and-far-between biracial characters across Shakespeare's dramatic corpus, not simply to dwell on colonial anxieties about racial mixture, but more so to meditate on the affective lives of biracial people. What is peculiar about most of Shakespeare's mixed characters is that they are children: Aaron and Tamora's son in *Titus Andronicus*, the Indian Boy in *A Midsummer Night's Dream*, Cleopatra's bastard in *Antony and Cleopatra*, and the imagined offspring of miscegenation in such plays as *Othello* and *The Tempest*. The fact that they are children is telling: namely, that miscegenation, as a moral and social transgression in early modern England, not only fuels racialist anxieties in the plays, but also proves narratively generative—entertaining, even—both for Shakespeare and his audiences. In this context, the figure of the biracial child fails to emerge intact, hardly a fully realized human subject, and more of a plot device: a threat to social norms and established hierarchies. On the surface, they are stock characters, but they nonetheless manage to destabilize Shakespearean worlds from positions of silence and absence. The children never speak.

As we consider how best to teach biracial affect in the Shakespeare classroom, we argue that silence—what amounts to textual aphasia—is not simply a literary site of marginalization or deprivation. Rather, it is a densely affective experience, replete with not only uncertainty but also possibility. The affective capacities of silence signal the ambivalence of biracial feeling, especially as they hinge on experiences of partial inclusion, exclusion, and ongoing negotiations of selfhood. Often, Shakespeare's mixed children are regarded as objects, even as fetishes. For example, Anthony Guy Patricia says of the Indian Boy: "Titania holds onto the Indian prince, fetish-like, as a keepsake of his dead mother, pampering him in a precious, feminized world of flowers, sweets, and serenades."[24] This fetishistic objectivity, we contend, is suspect. What we are arguing for here is more akin to Fred Moten's articulation of the resistant art object. Moten analyzes the artist Adrian Piper's *Untitled Performance for Max's Kansas City* to understand the practice of "voluntary objectlike passivity" as a method of resistance and, thereby, recuperation of personhood in which, as Piper says, "My objecthood

---

[24] Anthony Guy Patricia, *Queering the Shakespeare Film: Gender Trouble, Gay Spectatorship, and Male Homoeroticism* (London: Bloomsbury Arden Shakespeare, 2017), 12.

became my subjecthood."[25] This deliberate passivity is an active and creative process undergirding "a lived critique of the assumed equivalence of personhood and subjectivity and, by extension, a force of resistance of objection that is always already in excess of the limits of subjection/subjectivity."[26] Silence may function similarly as an affective state of racialized feeling. How Shakespeare's mixed children emotionally inhabit their muteness is an open question. They could feel frustrated by their circumstances, resentful of their oppressors, exasperated by courtly politics, or forlorn in their isolation. Importantly, their reticence might be a choice rather than textual omission and a deliberate refusal to participate in emergent formations of race and racism on the early modern stage. The critical capacities of silence become more salient in performance than in text because theater artists have opportunities to mime quiet rebellions: giving the "silent treatment," so to speak. The children are not dumb; instead, they help us apprehend early modern racial mixture as relational, as Fielder argues of interracial kinship, and they reveal particular structures of feeling shaped by white anxiety but that do not belong to white people.

In the context of higher education, biracial silence serves multiple, critical functions, and as biracial scholars and teachers of Shakespeare ourselves, we understand these intimately. Sometimes silence is a mode of protection. As junior faculty at institutions where tenured faculty are predominantly white, becoming invisible in high-stakes situations safeguards our chances at promotion. Noncoincidentally, both of us were advised by senior colleagues not to "ruffle feathers" until granted tenure. That is not to mention the experience of constantly negotiating the status of our belonging or unbelonging in professional settings, determining whether we are "passing" in this moment or not. Sometimes silence is the practice of disengaging from the cramps and convulsions of the institution in the name of mental and emotional health. In these cases, withdrawal is more akin to self-care or meditation, a quiet respite at the margins of the institution. Sometimes silence is the consequence of abjection when humiliated by the avatars of the institution's colonial hierarchies, and sometimes silence is simply a symptom of exhaustion. Too often, faculty of color are called upon to helm institutional efforts at diversity, equity,

---

[25] Adrian Piper, *Out of Order, Out of Sight* (Cambridge, MA: MIT Press, 1996), 27, qtd. in Fred Moten, *In the Break: The Aesthetics of the Black Radical Tradition* (Minneapolis: University of Minnesota Press, 2003), 240.
[26] Moten, *In the Break*, 242.

and inclusion, which seem more like reputation management—what Amrita Dhar, in her chapter in this book, accurately identifies as "public-image-curation"—than the interpersonal and community-based labors that this work truly requires.[27] For many faculty of color, the pressing question remains: How can universities become more hospitable when commitments to diversity are confined to a single office or day, the online module or workshop?

These feelings, even before they rise from limbic to frontal-cortical cognition, signal something terribly amiss. Following Moten, we contend that the multifarious affects of silence sustain a lived critique of higher education's failure to responsibly reckon with its complicity in settler colonialism and racism. Furthermore, the institution's compulsion to publicly regard the presence of BIPOC students and faculty as evidence of institutional commitments to diversity, while bypassing infrastructure, programming, and curricula to support them, exacerbates the grating simultaneity of belonging and unbelonging. As Sara Ahmed in her study and extended theorization of institutional commitments to "diversity" comments, "This is why the very promise of inclusion can be the concealment and thus extension of exclusion."[28]

Where, then, do we begin to address these frictions? University administrations are the obvious place; however, it seems simple—perhaps naive, even—to recommend that administrations amplify the voices of students and faculty of color through, say, multicultural centers or initiatives that advance biracial inclusion, because we have seen at our own institutions how such efforts offload the intellectual, emotional, and practical labor of such work onto students and faculty of color, often untenured, and in so doing, further ghettoize their work from the "real business" of the university. Too often, these initiatives are meant to do the work of diversity for the entire campus, rather than university leadership positioning diversity at the forefront of all institutional decision-making.[29] Ahmed observes that

> "diversity" has been identified as a management term. Diversity becomes something to be managed and valued as a human resource.

---

[27] Amrita Dhar, "On Shakespeare, Anticolonial Pedagogy, and Being Just," this volume, 34.

[28] Sara Ahmed, *On Being Included: Racism and Diversity in Institutional Life* (Durham: Duke University Press, 2012), 183.

[29] We do not mean to suggest that universities adopt "color blind" policies or programs; such posturing, amongst other ills, fosters the harmful fictitious narrative that all members of the university community experience the institution in equitable ways.

Scholars have suggested that the managerial focus on diversity works to individuate differences and conceal the continuation of systematic inequalities within universities.[30]

At the risk of coming across as cynical, we are keenly aware that administrations are invested in the status quo and rarely imagine the university as anything other than what it has been. Ahmed further insinuates that the work of diversity might even be more insidious than previously thought: "Diversity could be understood as one of the techniques by which liberal multiculturalism manages differences by managing its more 'troublesome constituents.'"[31] Here, "troublesome" characterizes those who disrupt the presumed whiteness of the institution.

We recognize that our cynicism and doubt are caught up in "minor feelings" about the university as an institution and that these feelings are inevitably shaped by our own experiences of race in higher education. The affective experience of the university is not identical for all members of the university community, and for many, it is determined by structures of identity and categories of difference across race, gender, sexuality, class, age, and ability. We focus on biraciality not because we believe administrations necessarily ought to cater to biracial students with targeted diversity initiatives, but because an affective hermeneutics toward biraciality exposes the sutures of racial formation and recalls racial histories that might help us apprehend the racial politics of the university as a settler colonial institution. It is in the classroom and archive, therefore, where we insist this work begin.

As teachers, we can examine in our classes how the muffling of racial affect contributes to the maintenance of the institutional status quo, recognizing that pedagogy can be a step toward imagining how the institution might transform and what it could become. To that end, we ought to design courses attentive to the literary history of race in a period when more plastic concepts of geographic, religious, and ontological difference began to harden into what we now understand as modern racism. We can also attune our pedagogy to the affective experiences of racialization, acknowledging such processes not only in the texts we study but also in our academic disciplines. This entails recognizing silence as more than mere absence or deficit, especially in the classroom, and then intentionally creating space for it. Not every moment needs to be filled, when there is so much to be felt. Sometimes silence is the practice of giving attention, of more fully engaging.

---

[30] Ahmed, *On Being Included*, 53.
[31] Ahmed, *On Being Included*, 174.

We endorse a style of pedagogy that invites wonder into the silences. Because Shakespeare's biracial children never speak, we are left to wonder, to imagine, and to grow curious about their lives. Silence, therefore, is rife with interpretive possibilities for what biraciality means, not only in Shakespeare, but also in our institutional politics. Wonder, however, is not necessarily benign. Resulting largely from medieval and early modern travelers' fixation on foreign curiosities and their possession, the term is "associated increasingly with the manipulation of the colonized, the selling of the colony to backers back home, the exoticizing of whatever could be (or seem to be) subdued."[32] We recognize the challenge of dissociating "wonder"—both as inquiry and spectacle—from colonial projects of exploitation and marginalization, particularly in classroom conversations surrounding Shakespeare's silent and inscrutable mixed-race stock. The European market for natural histories, bestiaries, and travelogues reminds us that casting the nonwhite person as a wonder, as something to be wondered at, simultaneously feared and fetishized, was a matter of economic profit that rationalized colonial violence.[33] Concurrently, we also propose that wonder—that is, setting aside mastery and entering into the inquisitive mode—allows us to engage in what Eve Kosofsky Sedgwick refers to as "reparative reading."[34] In her study on the evolution of wonder, Mary Baine Campbell acknowledges the colonial underpinnings of wonder as a cognitive process of objectification, but also considers its reparative potential as practice for reading:

> Wonder might first be seen as a register opposed to that of 'paranoid reading'—one which embraces surprise, enjoys the excess and alteration which generate it, is constitutively open to the rewriting of the past as well as the future, the making of new worlds.[35]

What does it mean, then, to wonder in, with, and about silence? How do we imagine, more fully, the affective lives of characters for

---

[32] Mary Baine Campbell, *Wonder and Science: Imagining Worlds in Early Modern Europe* (Ithaca: Cornell University Press, 1999), 3.

[33] Lorraine Datson and Katharine Park, *Wonders and the Order of Nature 1150–1750* (Princeton: Princeton University Press, 2001), 21–66.

[34] Sedgwick defines the reparative reading position as one that "undertakes a different range of affects, ambitions, and risks. What we can best learn from such practices are, perhaps, the many ways selves and communities succeed in extracting sustenance from the objects of culture—even of a culture whose avowed desire has often been not to sustain them." Eve Kosofsky Sedgwick, *Touching Feeling: Affect, Pedagogy, Performativity* (Durham: Duke University Press, 2003), 150–51.

[35] Campbell, *Wonder and Science*, 3.

whom silence is choice, protection, necessity, or script? How can we meet silence with an ethical practice of wonder? Put differently, how do we divorce wonder from "exoticist projection" and "return it to its place as a subjective experience, an invitation to relation"?[36] We, in part, seize on wonder for its ambiguity, speculation, and magical thinking rather than more rigid techniques of formalist inquiry to assert that the traditional tools of literary analysis sometimes fail. Close reading cannot fully account for the resounding force of silence; likewise, the archive cannot fully reanimate lives that exist, for early modern Europeans, on the margins.

Our proposed course, Shakespeare's Mixed Stock, positions wonder not as untutored contemplation, but as a critical and political tool with which students can illuminate the affective lives of Shakespeare's biracial characters. Our goal is to cultivate the affective and intellectual capacities of wonder—say, as opposed to a "hermeneutics of suspicion," postulated by the French philosopher Paul Ricoeur—in an effort to understand what it means to be inscrutable and how it feels to live on the margins of racial legibility.[37] As a method, cognitive emotion, and artifact, wonder offers entry points into conversations surrounding not only Shakespeare's plays and characters, but also the limitations of the early modern archive, the colonialist legacies of English studies, and the lived experiences of those deemed "inscrutable"—wonders, we might say—by the academy today. Throughout the term, students will read plays that feature hybrid or mixed-race characters, whose ontology is up for debate. While plays such as Shakespeare's *Titus Andronicus*, *Othello*, and *The Tempest* allow us to imagine the ways in which white Europeans responded to the prospect of mixed-race progeny, as do excerpts from contemporaneous travel narratives, to wonder with these discourses means to ask, for instance: How might a mixed-race child feel when alienated from familial networks? What dangers and forms of violence might a mixed-race child perceive and encounter? These texts do not offer easy answers; yet, in wondering with them, we establish a form of "relation" and engage in practices of worldmaking; that is, we can entertain the possibility that "the past . . . could have happened differently," that "the future may be

---

[36] Mary Blaine Campbell, "Wonder," in *Keywords for Travel Writing Studies: A Critical Glossary*, ed. Charles Forsdick, Zoë Kinsley, and Kathryn Walchester (New York: Anthem Press, 2019), 294.

[37] Paul Ricoeur, *Freud and Philosophy: An Essay on Interpretation*, trans. Denis Savage (New Haven: Yale University Press, 1970), 33.

different from the present."³⁸ By pairing Shakespeare's plays with archival texts, we ask students to engage in constitutive openness, through Campbell's framework of wonder, an affective posture we believe is vital to a reparative future.

The representation of biracial individuals in Shakespeare as both strange yet somehow common is mirrored in the early modern archive, specifically in discourses that address miscegenation and interracial marriage. Class conversations on the sheer frequency of interracial relationships in Shakespeare's works and those of his contemporaries allow instructors to ask: Why do these relationships appear so often in the period's dramatic corpus? Does their frequency suggest that the English were invested in accommodating mixed-race families? Or does their frequency, and audiences' presumed fascination with such pairings, suggest their illicit nature? Following this initial discussion, instructors might then show students scholarship documenting the presence of nonwhite populations in England and excerpts from travelogues, parish records, legal documents, and medical discourses. In his seminal work, *Black Lives in the English Archives*, Imtiaz Habib documents five interracial marriages that appeared in parish records during the 1570s; the 1586 baptism of a mixed-race child; and from the turn of the sixteenth century, the christening and death records of children who were most likely mixed race.³⁹ More recently, Miranda Kaufmann has cited additional archival records that prove the presence of "lawful interracial families" and "illegitimate [mixed-race] children" in England during the sixteenth and seventeenth centuries.⁴⁰ Pairing archival evidence and critical work by scholars such as Habib and Kaufmann demonstrates to students that although archival evidence of mixed-race

---

[38] Sedgwick, *Touching Feeling*, 146.
[39] Imtiaz Habib, *Black Lives in the English Archives, 1500–1677* (Farnham: Ashgate, 2008), 95–96, 99–101. Habib points out that while these children are often given their English father's last name while marked as "baseborn" or "a Black mores Child," their mothers are confined to anonymity. Habib writes, "Such births may or may not be the products of illicit English sexual predation, but they mark the helplessness of black women confined to a silent chattel existence bereft of the protective structures of a normal civic life" (100).
[40] Miranda Kaufmann, "'Making the Beast with two Backs'—Interracial Relationships in Early Modern England," *Literature Compass* 12, no. 1 (2015): 26–27. Kaufmann's article provides useful evidence of the presence of biracial individuals; however, we are troubled by many of her claims, specifically her suggestion that miscegenation was socially more accepted than scholars, such as Habib, have suggested; that black women were not necessarily exploited by white English masters; and that the experience of white English female servants was likely comparable to their black counterparts (27–28).

relationships and individuals is scant, such mixings were neither common, nor were they entirely unusual.

In examining these discourses, students can consider how early modern figurations of biraciality interact with questions surrounding embodiment, race, and affect. Some archival sources, for example, betray an interest in the skin color of children born to interracial couples. A frequently cited passage from George Best's *A True Discourse*, relating the marriage of "an Ethiopian as black as cole" to "a faire English woman," fixates primarily on the reasons behind their child's dark skin.[41] As scholars have argued, this instance was of interest to Best's audience not solely because of the couple's atypical relationship, but also because the child's dark appearance disproved early modern climatological theories of somatic color. Such theories purported that those born in colder northern climes would have lighter skin while populations closer to the equatorial line would have darker complexions, a result of the sun's heat.[42] Examples such as Best's reassured readers who may have considered traveling abroad that their humoral dispositions would not be fundamentally altered by their new environment.[43] Instead, the newborn's complexion would have supported early modern theories of parthenogenesis, the assumption that a child would exhibit the physical traits of their father. For Best, the example of a dark-skinned, mixed-race, and English-born child allows him to conclude: ". . . this blackness proceedeth of some natural infection of the first inhabitants of that Country [Ethiopia], and so all the whole progeny of them descended are still polluted with the same blot of infection."[44]

Other travelogues focus on the complexion of mixed-race children born abroad, revealing anxieties surrounding the ontological effects of both racial mixture and unfamiliar atmospheric conditions. In another frequently cited example, the Dutch voyager Jan Huyghen van Linschoten comments on children born in India to Portuguese colonizers and Indian women:

> The Portingales in India, are many of them married with the naturall borne women of the countrie, and the children procéeding of them are called Mesticos, that is, half countrimen. These Mesticos

[41] George Best, *A True Discourse of the Late Voyages of Discoverie* (London, 1578), 29.
[42] See, for example, Mary Floyd Wilson, *English Ethnicity and Race in Early Modern Drama* (Cambridge: Cambridge University Press, 2003), 8–9; Kim F. Hall, *Things of Darkness: Economies of Race and Gender in the Early Modern World* (Ithaca: Cornell University Press, 1995), 11–12.
[43] Floyd-Wilson, *English Ethnicity*, 8; Hall, *Things of Darkness*, 12.
[44] Best, *A True Discourse*, 29.

are commonlie of yelowish colour, notwithstanding there are manie women among them, that are faire and well formed. The children of the Portingales, both boyes and gyrls, which are borne in India, are called Castisos, and are in all things like vnto the Portingales, onely somewhat differing in colour, for they draw towards a yealow colour: the children of those Castisos are yealow, and altogether like the Mesticos, and the children of Mesticos are of colour and fashion like the naturall borne Countrimen or Decaniins of the countrie, so that the posteritie of the Portingales, both men and womē[n] being in the third degrée, doe séeme to be naturall Indians, both in colour & fashion.[45]

Although differing significantly from Best's conclusions, van Linschoten similarly describes the reproductive consequences of non-European contact. His concern with and extended meditation on the complexion of *mestiços*, mixed-race children born in India, demonstrates an impulse to account for the potentially uncertain, hybrid, and mysterious physiologies of biracial children. Though emergent constructions of racial difference during the period were far more fluid than fixed, van Linschoten seems to write for an audience invested in conceptualizing a racial hierarchy that includes not only the Portuguese, Indians, *castiços*, and *mestiços*, but also the children of *mestiços*, whom van Linschoten claims "are of colour and fashion like the naturall borne Countrumen or Decaniins of the country [India]." Noteworthy as well is that the "yelowish" complexion of Portuguese children born in India, *castiços*, resembles that of their mixed-race *mestiço* counterparts; like the children of *mestiços*, the children of *castiços*, despite being born to Portuguese parents, also resemble "naturall Indians, both in colour & fashion." As Ivo Kamps argues, van Linschoten's depiction of these various groups "fits the racist logic of the Portuguese, who themselves discriminated against their hybrid offspring.... What seems foremost at issue here for the Portuguese is a form of cultural contamination. Van Linschoten's account, however, collapses the arguments about miscegenation and cultural contamination into a single story of racial degradation, and, ultimately, of racial erasure."[46]

While Best's and van Linschoten's racial taxonomies reflect European anxieties surrounding kinship ties and foreign contact,

---

[45] Iohn Huighen van Linschoten, *His discours of voyages into ye Easte & West Indies* (London: 1598), 52.
[46] Ivo Kamps, "Colonizing the Colonizer: A Dutchman in Asia Portuguesa," in *Travel Knowledge: European "Discoveries" in the Early Modern Period*, ed. Kamps and Jyotsna Singh (New York: Palgrave, 2011), 169.

they also allow students to glimpse the treatment and affective experiences of children whose racial identities were not self-determined, but constituted at least in part by discourses that champion white skin and endogenous ancestry. Best erases the biracial child's ties to their "faire English" mother and the country of their birth, proposing instead that their complexion affirms their ties to "polluted" kin and the country in which this "natural infection" took hold. In class conversations, instructors might lead students in wondering about how biracial children in Best's London experienced representations of their physiology that distanced them from their white mothers and fathers, and by extension, cultural and economic power. While van Linschoten allows for slightly more ambiguity than Best, we are again left to question how discourses such as van Linschoten's shaped the material and affective lives of biracial children in European colonies and outposts.[47] Instructors might point out that van Linschoten's theorization of the appearance and customs of India's "mestico" population seems to anticipate legal systems of racial classification, such as the United States' "one-drop rule," which align mixed-race children with the parent whose racial background is most disadvantaged.

These foundational engagements with the archive provide students with the texts and tools to imagine more fully the lives and livelihoods of biracial populations in Europe, and by extension the affective experiences of Shakespeare's mixed stock. When teaching biraciality in Shakespearean drama, we begin with Shakespeare's earliest tragedy, *Titus Andronicus*, a play in which racial mixture has murderous consequences and arguably one of the most disturbing scenes in any of the plays. In *Titus Andronicus*, Aaron's and Tamora's mixed-race son is condemned to death immediately following his birth, a murder Tamora herself sanctions. The play's white Goths and Romans want little to do with the biracial infant, referring to him as "a devil" and "a joyless, dismal, black and sorrowful issue," while insisting that Aaron "christen it with [his] dagger's point" (4.2.66, 67, 72).[48] Chiron and Demetrius, Tamora's children and the infant's half brothers, curse their mother and the child: "Woe to her chance and damned her loathed choice, / Accursed

---

[47] Descriptions of the "fairness" of non-European and non-Christian women were not uncommon. Dramatic examples include Jessica, Shylock's daughter in *The Merchant of Venice*, Quisara, the Moluccan princess of John Fletcher's *The Island Princess*, and Donusa, a Turkish princess in Philip Massinger's *The Renegado*.

[48] William Shakespeare, *Titus Andronicus*, ed. Jonathan Bate (London: Bloomsbury Publishing, 2018). Text references are to act, scene, and line of this edition.

the offspring of so foul a fiend, / It shall not live" (4.2.80–82). They recognize the infant's mixed parentage only in terms of the shame the child may cast on their family. The newborn, as they suggest, is aligned biologically and culturally with his father, claims that distance the infant from his white kin and the proximity to power that their racialized position and royal status grant. Similarly, the nurse's view of the child as "joyless" and "sorrowful" is rhetorically linked to the dark complexion he inherits from Aaron. Not only do these comments define and therefore limit the child's racialized personhood, but they also, as David Sterling Brown underscores, deny the infant the "innocence of (white) childhood" and associate him instead with "culpable adulthood."[49] In class conversations on these violent, derogatory remarks, instructors might ask students to consider the child's potential future as a mixed-race orphan, already deemed guilty, in *Titus*'s Rome. Students might also discuss the play's portrayals of mixed-race community and how the child's own self-determination might be impacted by such racialist commentary.

In *Othello*, mixed-race children—the imagined, half-human progeny of the play's interracial couple—do not materialize in the flesh on stage, but as the offspring of miscegenation, threaten to infect, as Best suggests, and degrade whiteness. Seeking to rouse Brabantio's paternalistic anxiety, Iago theriomorphizes interracial sex through the black-white color binary: "Even now, now, very now, an old black ram is tupping your white ewe" (1.1.87–88), an image distilled to the infamous "beast with two backs" (1.1.117–18) and intimated by the name of the inn where such intercourse takes place, the Sagittary, the mythic hybrid of human and horse (1.1.160).[50] Iago indulges such racialist illogic by further extending the equine metaphor, gulling Brabantio into the mistaken assumption that bestiality necessarily yields beasts: "[Y]ou'll have your daughter covered with a Barbary horse; you'll have your nephews neigh to you; you'll have coursers for cousins and jennets for germans" (1.1.113–15). Instructors might then turn to Loomba, who reminds us of "the deployment of 'race' as lineage, which often shows up in the context of horses" and which circulated in such zoographic texts as Edward Topsell's *Historie of Four-Footed Beastes and Snakes*

---

[49] David Sterling Brown, "'Is Black so Base a Hue?': Black Life Matters in Shakespeare's *Titus Andronicus*," in *Early Modern Black Diaspora Studies: A Critical Anthology*, ed. Cassander L. Smith, Nicholas R. Jones, and Miles P. Grier (New York: Palgrave Macmillan, 2017), 137–55 [144].

[50] William Shakespeare, *Othello*, ed. E. A. J. Honigmann (London: Bloomsbury Publishing, 2016). Text references are to act, scene, and line of this edition.

(1607).⁵¹ These metaphors converge with racist comparisons of African humans to simian nonhumans, an association made firm at least by the seventeenth century when Thomas Herbert wrote in his travelogue that they "have no better predecessors than monkeys."⁵² In discussions of the play, students might consider why the degradation of mother and child is figured in explicitly zoological terms; how such depictions are conversant with van Linschoten's hyper-focus on complexion, customs, and dress; and the children's potential treatment and social position in the Venetian court, given in particular Brabantio's racialist insults, as well as those of the Duke.

In *A Midsummer Night's Dream*, the changeling "Indian" boy offers a particular illustration of racialized hybridity. Early moderns typically employed the term "changeling" to describe someone of indeterminate origin, physiology, and character. In English folklore, fairies were thought to abduct infants, leaving fairy children, known as "changelings," in their place who, by all estimations, appeared to be entirely human. We learn from Puck, an admittedly untrustworthy source, that the boy's father was an Indian king; his mother, Titania tells us, was a votaress in her order. As instructors, we remind students that our goal is not to discern whether the boy may have mixed-race parentage, or whether he is a human or supernatural being. Rather, we lead students in theorizing *Midsummer*'s fairyland as a liminal space that lies ambiguously between Athens and India, causing the boy to undergo what Margo Hendricks suggests is a "particularized form . . . [of] ethnic (or racial) change that involves the forcible removal of a person from one culture to another."⁵³ Hendricks argues that the child, as well as Bottom, embody the Spanish conceptual term *mestizaje*, which was used to describe racial mixedness, crossbreeding, or adulteration. Bottom famously becomes a crossbred, equine-human hybrid while the boy presents "the possibility of human and fairy mixedness (the mestizo)."⁵⁴ In class, we point out that Titania wishes to care for the child because

---

⁵¹ Loomba, *Shakespeare, Race*, 23.
⁵² Thomas Herbert, *A Relation Of Some Years Travaile, Begunne Anno 1626* (London, 1634), 17.
⁵³ Margo Hendricks, "'Obscured by dreams': Race, Empire, and Shakespeare's *A Midsummer Night's Dream*," *Shakespeare Quarterly* 47, no. 1 (1996): 55. Hendricks argues that *Midsummer*, in bringing together older and emerging conceptions of race, presents a kind of conceptual borderland: "I believe a borderland also coalesces on an ideological level in the concept of race. This concept is neither wholly the older (and more feudal) idea based on class and lineage nor wholly the more modern idea based only on physical appearance (i.e. skin color, physiognomy)" (43).
⁵⁴ Hendricks, "'Obscured by dreams,'" 56.

of a promise made to his mother, and ask students to examine why exactly Oberon desires to possess the boy and make him a "henchman" or "Knight of his train" (2.1.124, 25).[55] These discussions often lead students to wonder whether the boy's perceived use is connected to his hybrid status, his being of the human and fairy worlds, of the "West" and the mercantile, "rich" "East" (2.1.139). Hendricks's article is particularly useful in guiding students through these questions; as she reminds us, "in another century or so Asian Indians would become the [English] household fashion."[56] Students might then question whether Titania plans to have the boy traverse the seas, as his mother once did, streamlining her access to exotic goods.[57] The boy's silence and, in some productions, absence on stage can lead to further questions surrounding the affective states he may have experienced as he observed two capricious faeries quarrel over his future. In teaching the play, we often ask our students: What may he have felt in knowing that his life was ultimately decided by a floral drug and an ass's head? Or, as Hendricks puts it, "What if he, rather than Puck, had been given the final word: what would the changeling child have said?"[58]

In Shakespeare's Mixed Stock, we hope that such wondering might also lead students to adaptation, what Adrienne Rich calls "re-vision": "the act of looking back, of seeing with fresh eyes, of entering an old text from a new critical direction . . . . Until we can understand the assumptions in which we are drenched we cannot know ourselves."[59] Our proposed course concludes with a final project that asks students to reimagine the life of one of Shakespeare's mixed-race characters, relocated to our current time and place, while taking into consideration more broadly representations of biraciality in the early modern archive. Having students adapt Shakespeare's narratives of racial mixture for performance in a new period and setting encourages them not only to apprehend the

---

[55] William Shakespeare, *A Midsummer Night's Dream*, ed. Sukanta Chaudhuri (London: Bloomsbury Publishing, 2017). Text references are to act, scene, and line of this edition.

[56] Hendricks, "'Obscured by dreams,'" 54.

[57] In associating the boy's and the votaress's bodies with foreign merchandise, Titania suggests that, much like the exotic goods imported from abroad, Europeans can generate profit from humans rendered as commodities. This moment alludes to the very real fetishization and exhibition of Native Americans and Africans in London, abusive practices that often led to the death of these individuals.

[58] Hendricks, "'Obscured by dreams,'" 60.

[59] Adrienne Rich, "When We Dead Awaken: Writing as Revision," *College English* 34, no. 1 (1972): 18.

ambivalence and inscrutability of his mixed-race characters, but also to confront the inscrutable aspects of themselves, those parts that are in flux, under development, and not so easily legible to cultural norms of identity. This work, Rich promises, enables "a radical critique of literature . . . a clue to how we live, how we have been living, how we have been led to imagine ourselves, and how our language has trapped as well as liberated us."[60]

By addressing the silences of biracial peoples through Shakespearean pedagogy, we bring racial affect to the surface, not only in our classrooms and academic fields, but also more widely in our institutions. As biracial faculty who are often called upon to do the institution's diversity work in all the ways the readership of this collection would expect, our engagement with racial affect does not end when we leave our classrooms. In the various roles we have occupied, much of our non-teaching work at our respective institutions has involved illuminating racial affect. Our professional experiences have been fraught—in part because they remind us of the ways in which we, as biracial scholars, occupy positions of belonging and exclusion, but also because such work reminds us that these "supplementary" and "optional" initiatives conceal the institution's commitment to certain kinds of affect, from certain kinds of bodies. It is because such initiatives can feel so unsatisfactory, can feel like lip service to the college's promotional brochures, that we feel it necessary to account for and keep an account of the other forms of labor faculty of color perform, the labor that does not appear on our curriculum vita, the labor we do not record when applying for promotion. Though deeply isolating, the unrecorded and sometimes never vocalized affective labor that faculty of color experience, "behind the scenes," as it were, is no less social, often occurring in situations in which our inclusion/exclusion is addressed and publicized. In regard to such moments—that, for instance, of being the only faculty member of color in a room and the only faculty member addressed by her first name—Ahmed argues, "Diversity work can involve an experience of hesitation, of not knowing what to do in these situations [of institutional non-belonging]. There is labor in having to respond to a situation that others are protected from, a situation that does not come up for those whose residence is assumed."[61] The labor of racial affect, as we show our students, can manifest in silence and retreat. This is the work of diversity.

---

[60] Rich, "When We Dead," 18.
[61] Ahmed, *On Being Included*, 176–77.

What we model in Shakespeare's Mixed Stock are responses to inscrutability, to the affective labor that accompanies the very liminality we describe. What might occur if the university were to meet inscrutability with wonder? What policies might change, what language might shift, what spaces might become more inclusive if racial affect were not ignored, but met by white faculty and administrators with humility, with a commitment to care, with an ethos of wonder that resists fear and fetishization? While it might seem that institutions are apathetic or would prefer to blithely ignore racial affect, we see in Shakespeare's Mixed Stock that too much is at stake: bodies, lives, and communities. In urging students to pause, to imagine otherwise, we uncover the emotional textures of silence. Rather than retreating to silence out of necessity or apathy, we come to understand silence as a source of critique, a mode of resistance, a place for rest, a space to wonder, and an affective prelude to the university that could be.

Chapter 10

Who Shot Romeo? And How Can We Stop the Bleeding? Urban Shakespeare, White People, and Education Beyond the Neoliberal Nightmare

Eric L. De Barros

In Jason Zeldes's *Romeo Is Bleeding*, a 2015 documentary about an urban adaptation of *Romeo and Juliet*, the two questions of my primary title are the governing, largely unspoken ones driving the narrative. Trapped within and traumatized by the drug-related gun violence plaguing Richmond, CA, Donté Clark, a co-founder of an after-school creative arts program, comes to see in *Romeo and Juliet* the possibility of an expressive way out. As both the play-adaptation (entitled *Té's Harmony*) and the film capture, Clark and his student collaborators engage in a hopeful process of adapting *Romeo and Juliet* into a lifesaving vehicle for the verbal and performative dexterity of spoken-word poetry, a dexterity the film highlights with an impressive combination of soulful music, dramatic sound effects, bold lighting, and extreme close-ups. In short, the film's representation of this Shakespearean adaptation, and particularly of Clark's performances, is nothing short of dazzling.

That dexterity, however, should come as no surprise, for performative lyricism in Black America is as old as the various manifestations of white oppression it was forged to combat. As if oblivious to that history, the film attempts to give us the impression that spoken-word poetry represents something sufficiently new, cool, and transformative to merit filming. Of course, the Shakespearean vehicle is central to that impression. But as with Black lyricism, there is nothing new about a film devoted to the pedagogical fantasy that Shakespeare possesses the power to save urban, Black and Brown lives. In fact, since 1994, in the wake of the socioeconomic devastation of the mid-1980s crack epidemic, there have been at least five such films.¹ In what follows, I examine Zeldes's *Romeo Is Bleeding* as a representative example, arguing that it fails to answer my titular questions, because the point of its pedagogical fantasy is not to offer any real answers. In other words, in the process of presenting my own answers, I will rudely or unpoetically argue that both Zeldes's film and Clark's play advance a self-serving pedagogy of figurative denial, what I term Shakespeare-as-poetry, to mystify and thereby perpetuate the ugly realities of embodied Black and Brown suffering.

As Ayanna Thompson usefully explains, these Shakespeare-based reform programs are so committed to Shakespeare's universality as well as his "authority, authenticity, and textual stability" that any critical discussions of race become irrelevant to the complexly racialized people they are supposedly intended to reform.² And while, for Thompson, one exception is the LA-based Will Power to Youth (WPY) program profiled in Lawrence Bridges's documentary *Why Shakespeare?*, I am unconvinced that that group's more creative, revisionary approach makes any transformative difference. The reason is that in both types of program Shakespeare is representing something more than Shakespeare. More fundamental than the privileging of authority and textual stability, Shakespeare is also representing highly aestheticized poetic language as a superior mode of expression. Simply stated, as an unidentified person in Bridges's film does, Shakespeare is "poetry."³ So, while WPY's approach may contain the potential to transform at-risk lives and distressed communities, its simultaneous acceptance of Shakespeare-as-poetry arguably limits, if not works against, the realization of that potential. For instance, when Ben Donenberg, WPY's artistic director, explains iambic pentameter as Shakespeare "asking your heart to sync up with [his characters]," or when Chris Anthony, the program's associate director, describes "the gift of Shakespeare,"⁴ we are left to wonder about the ethical implications

---

¹ Penny Marshall, dir., *Renaissance Man* (Touchstone Home Entertainment, 2003), DVD; Michèle Ohayon, dir., *Colors Straight Up* (Echo Pictures, 1997); Lawrence Bridges, dir., *Why Shakespeare?* (National Endowment for the Arts, 2004), *YouTube*, https://www.youtube.com/watch?v=Rt9n_uxWaBg; Michael Waldman, dir., *My Shakespeare* (Penguin Television, 2004); Mel Stuart, dir., *The Hobart Shakespeareans* (PBS, 2005); and Hank Rogerson, dir., *Shakespeare Behind Bars* (Philomath Films, 2006).
² Ayanna Thompson, *Passing Strange: Shakespeare, Race, and Contemporary America* (New York: Oxford University Press, 2011), 122.
³ Bridges, *Why Shakespeare?*
⁴ Bridges, *Why Shakespeare?*

of applying this understanding of poetry—of syncing hearts and a gift—to the lives of people oppressed by the most unpoetic of circumstances.

Theodor Adorno's "To write poetry after Auschwitz is barbaric"[5] is perhaps the most famous expression of this ethical skepticism. However, it is but one of the many instances that forced me over the course of my education to reflect on the relationship between highly aestheticized culture and brutality. There was Tadeusz Borowski's realization that oppression is the price of civilization and that the fate of the oppressed is that they will "be forgotten, drowned out by the voices of the poets, the jurists, the philosophers, the priests."[6] There was Joseph Conrad's *Heart of Darkness* and its representation of the power of Kurtzian eloquence—the gift of voice, expression, poetry—to obscure the ugly realities of European imperialism, "which mostly means the [violent] taking [of the earth] away from those who have a different complexion or slightly flatter noses."[7] There was Chinua Achebe's *Things Fall Apart* and its identification of the insidious, colonizing "poetry"[8] of Christianity. There was Ray Durem's "I Know I'm Not Sufficiently Obscure" and its rejection of the capacity of poetic language to represent the victimization of black people with the startling concluding address to white poets: "You deal with finer feelings, / very subtle—an autumn leaf / hanging from a tree—I see a body!"[9] There was Shakespeare's *Titus Andronicus* and its illustration of the failure of poetic language when Marcus awkwardly aestheticizes the blood flowing from the mouth of a raped and mutilated Lavinia as "a crimson river of warm blood, / Like to a bubbling fountain stirred with wind, / Doth rise and fall between thy roséd lips / Coming and going with thy honey breath."[10] While not specifically about poetry, there was Stephen Greenblatt's "Marvelous Possessions" and how the devastation of Amerindian peoples compels him to ask, "Should we not say then

---

[5] Theodor Adorno, "Cultural Criticism and Society," in *Prisms*, trans. Samuel and Shierry Weber (Cambridge, MA: The MIT Press, [1967] 1983), 34.

[6] Tadeusz Borowski, "Auschwitz, Our Home (A Letter)," in *This Way for the Gas, Ladies and Gentlemen*, trans. Barbara Vedder and Michael Kandel (London: Penguin Classics, 1976), 132.

[7] Joseph Conrad, *Heart of Darkness* (New York: Norton, [1899] 2017), 7.

[8] Chinua Achebe, *Things Fall Apart* (New York: Penguin, [1959] 2017), 147.

[9] Ray Durem, "I Know I'm Not Sufficiently Obscure," in *The Black Poets*, ed. Dudley Randall (New York: Bantam, 1971), 163.

[10] William Shakespeare, *Titus Andronicus*, in *The Norton Shakespeare*, ed. Stephen Greenblatt, Walter Cohen, Jean E. Howard, and Katherine Eisaman Maus (New York: W. W. Norton, [c. 1593–94] 1997), 2.4.22–25.

that words do not matter . . .?"¹¹ before concluding, "we are thus forced to abandon the dream of linguistic omnipotence."¹² And finally, in regard to the aestheticizing dangers of film, there was Robert Leventhal's critique of Steven Spielberg's *Schindler's List* for using romantic conventions of narrative to wipe away the horrific, material reality of the Holocaust.¹³ In short, what *Romeo Is Bleeding* and its play-adaptation fail to see is what these instances made it impossible for me to ignore: that the relationship between poetic language and the bodies of oppressed people is anything but obvious or obviously good.

Published by Red Beard Press, a publisher devoted to the voices of marginalized youth, the play's front matter celebrates the Shakespeare-as-poetry fantasy of urban reform at the heart of Clark's play.¹⁴ In the "Acknowledgments," Molly Raynor, the other co-founder of RAW Talent and Clark's teacher-mentor, thanks Clark "for all of the hard work, love, energy[,] and thought he put into the script,"¹⁵ before sharing,

> It was amazing to walk into work every day for three months and see Donte [*sic*] sitting at his desk, deeply engrossed in *Romeo & Juliet*. I could tell from the way he would smirk and chuckle to himself that he had overcome his initial disinterest in the play; that once he broke through the dense language and began making connections between Verona and Richmond, he came to truly appreciate the genius and humor of Shakespeare. He found a way to honor the original text without being confined by it.¹⁶

Although Raynor concludes that that breakthrough balance between textual respect and creative freedom results in an adaptation that "digs deeper into the roots of the conflict and challenges the reader to imagine a counter narrative to" Shakespeare's tragedy, the actual play does nothing of the sort.¹⁷ As I will detail shortly, Clark's adaptation doesn't so much dig deeper and challenge us as much as

---

[11] Stephen Greenblatt, "Marvelous Possessions," in *Marvelous Possessions: The Wonder of the New World* (Chicago: University of Chicago Press, 1991), 63.
[12] Greenblatt, "Marvelous Possessions," 63.
[13] Robert S. Leventhal, "Romancing the Holocaust, or Hollywood and Horror: Steven Spielberg's *Schindler's List*," *Holocaust Film; Film and the Holocaust*, 1995, http://www2.iath.virginia.edu/holocaust/schinlist.html.
[14] "Red Beard Press," https://neutralzone.myshopify.com/collections/red-beard-press (accessed August 25, 2023).
[15] Raw Talent, *Té's Harmony: A Story of Love at the Cross Roads* (Ann Arbor: Red Beard Press, 2013), 8.
[16] Talent, *Té's Harmony*, 8.
[17] Talent, *Té's Harmony*, 8.

it teases us with flashes of poetic brilliance before letting us off the hook with a questionable *deus ex machina* resolution. In that way, the play belies the bardolatrous privileging of Shakespearean expression at the heart of Raynor's hyperbolic claim, and, therefore, reveals that all Clark really needed to do to satisfy his Shakespeare-loving teacher was demonstrate a sufficient reverence for Shakespeare-as-poetry in both process and product.

For Raynor, the immediate inspiration for this thinking is actually not Shakespeare, but Luis J. Rodriguez, the poet, activist, and author of *Té's Harmony*'s foreword. As Raynor acknowledges, "[Rodriguez] is the model for what we are trying to accomplish with this play—creating social change through art—and we are so grateful for the work that he is doing around violence prevention and communal healing."[18] While I cannot speak to Rodriguez's work and assume he's well-meaning and that his work has made a positive difference, I am concerned with his articulation of a personal, neoliberal, even Oprah-Winfrey-style self-help understanding of creative expression.[19] "I am going to make a bold statement," he begins,

> A statement that may grate the ears of practical minded, cost-conscious and uninspired persons, usually, unfortunately, among those who run governments, schools, and corporations: The arts save lives. The arts are the best antidote for violence, disconnections, depressions and alienations.[20]

For Rodriguez, the arts have little, if anything, to do with the cultivation of a revolutionary critical consciousness that might inspire efforts to resist and/or dismantle the existing, neoliberal logic of "profit-driven structures of production and consumption."[21] In other words, for him, creative expression is not about the structural-institutional social change that, I think, Raynor is suggesting. On the contrary, it is about the reformation—really the salvation—of the individual from the physical and personal-emotional consequences of those structures, which Rodriguez also conveniently individualizes into the unimaginative, sellout bureaucrats that are so easy for us to blame. In that way, Rodriguez's creative expression effectively works on and through the bourgeois individual of its own creation

---

[18] Talent, *Té's Harmony*, 10.
[19] Nicole Aschoff, "Oprah Winfrey: One of the World's Best Neoliberal Capitalist Thinkers," *Guardian*, May 9, 2015, https://www.theguardian.com/tv-and-radio/2015/may/09/oprah-winfrey-neoliberal-capitalist-thinkers.
[20] Talent, *Té's Harmony*, 11.
[21] Aschoff, "Oprah Winfrey."

as the poetry of a secular religion with all of its neoliberal, colonizing potential.

There are at least two ways that Clark's play realizes that potential. The first, as indicated by the double entendre of Clark's title, is Té's assumption of the possessive position of a Petrarchan lover. For instance, after their initial masque-scene encounter, Té gazes at Harmony with a figurative copiousness to rival any Renaissance sonneteer:

> But I can hear it
> The eruption of her blood
> From volcanic times in Richmond
> That mold her obsidian
> Dark shades of hardened rock exterior
> Bruised and brittle, deep within
> With a sharpened shine that's fair
> A black stone, a jewel
> Fashioned for kings to wear.[22]

While a sympathetic attempt to represent her victimization by a patriarchal culture, this passage also ironically repeats that victimization with its objectification of her as a piece of jewelry "[f]ashioned" to be worn by a king—like Té presumably imagines himself to be. In the next scene, as if to translate that refined image of kingly jewelry into the lower register of present-day consumerism, Clark represents Té following—really stalking—Harmony into a Target department store. In the process of browsing her browsing clothing, he muses,

> From the outside you can tell
> You can smell that something died inside of her
> I wonder what it was that was left to rot in this vacant lot
> But if time permits
> These hands of my love will renovate
> This deserted shack behind her breast
> I'll build a mansion of all colors.[23]

Again, while well-intentioned, Clark represents Té further objectifying Harmony as a putrid, vacant lot or deserted shack in need of his renovating hands. The problem is that these instances of female objectification have little to do with Shakespeare as interpreted by more than thirty years of feminist and critical race scholarship. In other

---

[22] Talent, *Té's Harmony*, 1.5.36.
[23] Talent, *Té's Harmony*, 1.5.36.

words, they lack any critical or ethical awareness of Shakespeare's own complex representation of the violent, racialized, and imperialistic power implicated in the tradition of the Petrarchan love blazon that he inherited.[24] In the specific case of *Romeo and Juliet*, Clark is unaware that, by having Té engage in this voyeuristic cataloguing of Harmony's body, he is actually perpetuating the culture of violence he is attempting to end through creative expression. That is to say, in these instances, Clark is not simply positioning Té as a romantic, would-be lover; he is also positioning him as precisely the kind of man that violent and competitive patriarchal cultures produce. In short, he is simultaneously positioning him as a would-be rapist.[25]

Clark can't see any of this, because Shakespeare-as-poetry won't allow him to. As Laura Mulvey might argue, the point of Shakespeare-as-poetry, defined as it is by the pleasure and beauty of patriarchal creativity, is to deny such a destructive, ethically oriented analysis.[26] That's what I think also explains the second instance in Clark's play of Rodriguez's bourgeois philosophy of creative expression, when Clark turns Shakespeare's tragedy into the romance or tragicomedy of his spoken-word adaptation. As the Nurse/Narrator explains at the end of the play,

> But could there be another ending to this story?
> We know what you were expecting—a tragedy,
> The classic tale of star-crossed lovers who take their lives,
> The classic tale on Channel 5 News of Richmond youth,
> Ugly as the scarred backs of our ancestors
> Can you feel it?
> It's time to heal
> Time to reclaim the city of Pride and Purpose—our Richmond
> We know you were expecting us to choose death
> Narrator, Té & Harmony: [*Together*] But tonight, we choose life.[27]

---

[24] Kim F. Hall, *Things of Darkness: Economies of Race and Gender in Early Modern England* (Ithaca: Cornell University Press, 1995), 62–122; Patricia Parker, *Literary Fat Ladies: Rhetoric, Gender, Property* (London: Methuen, 1987); Nancy Vickers, "'The blazon of sweet beauty's best': Shakespeare's *Lucrece*," *Shakespeare and the Question of Theory*, ed. Patricia Parker and Geoffrey Hartman (New York: Methuen, 1985), 95–115; Katharine Eisaman Maus, "Taking Tropes Seriously: Language and Violence in Shakespeare's *Rape of Lucrece*," *Shakespeare Quarterly* 37, no. 1 (1986): 66–82.

[25] See Robert N. Watson and Stephen Dickey, "Wherefore Art Thou Tereu? Juliet and the Legacy of Rape," *Renaissance Quarterly* 58, no. 1 (2005): 127–56.

[26] Laura Mulvey, "Visual Pleasure and Narrative Cinema," in *Film Theory and Criticism: Introductory Readings*, ed. Leo Braudy and Marshall Cohen (New York: Oxford University Press, 1999), 833–44.

[27] Talent, *Té's Harmony*, 2.8.100–1.

This *deus ex machina* comes a few scenes after Clark's version of the Mercutio-Tybalt double homicide. After Té shoots and kills T-Y, the Tybalt character, for shooting and killing Gemini, the Mercutio character, he hides out in a nearby town. Soon after, he learns that a pregnant Harmony has been beaten and hospitalized and that rumor has it that he's responsible. He determines that he can no longer stay away, declaring to the friend who delivered the news, "I'm not running no more. I didn't do this—somebody lying on me / I'm tired of running. *Whatever happens, happens.* But I gotta go see / my girl and my seed."[28] Both families arm themselves after learning of his decision and converge on the hospital with every intention of continuing the tragic cycle of violence. This is where the tragedy ends, for Clark uses this point in the play to build up to the Nurse / Narrator's interruption and the closing image of everyone laughing and dancing. The only problem is that this choice of life depends on forgetting that earlier scene of death, and specifically that Té is still presumably wanted for T-Y's killing. Although Té's "Whatever happens, happens" indicates a willingness to accept the consequences of his actions, nothing ultimately happens and, more disturbingly, there's no sense that there will ever be a moral or judicial reckoning with the tragic loss of Black life. Much like Durem's imitation of the white poets' representation of a lynched black body, the Black bodies left by T-Y and Gemini evaporate within the romanticizing, spoken-word flourish that ends the play.

So, if there is any hope of answering my titular questions, it will require our courage to be rude, unpleasant, and, yes, unpoetic enough to reject Shakespeare-as-poetry and to call out all those committed to perpetuating it. In that spirit, it is now time for us to talk about white people.[29] Much like so much of today's social justice rhetoric, with so many white people all-of-a-sudden asserting "Black Lives Matter," another function of Shakespeare-as-poetry is to hide the role of white people through what Teju Cole usefully calls "The White-Savior Industrial Complex."[30] That complex has nothing to do with justice; it is about confirming white privilege through sentimental stories that always cast a "good" white person as the answer to Black and Brown suffering. As Matthew Hughey explains

---

[28] Talent, *Té's Harmony*, 2.7.95; my italics.
[29] See Arthur L. Little, Jr., *White People in Shakespeare: Essays on Race, Culture and the Elite* (New York: Bloomsbury, 2023).
[30] Teju Cole, "The White-Savior Industrial Complex," *The Atlantic*, January 11, 2013, https://www.theatlantic.com/international/archive/2012/03/the-white-savior-industrial-complex/254843/.

regarding the white-savior film genre, "these narratives help repair [especially in unsettled and racially charged times] what is truly the most dangerous myth of race—a tale of normal and natural white paternalism."[31] In this light, the dazzling lyricism of Clark's play renders invisible the "good" white people in control of it all: a white publisher, a white teacher, a white filmmaker, and a Latino poet with white friends.[32] Therefore, it is not just that the play's pedagogy of figurative denial is not about justice for Black people; equally disturbingly, it is also about the power-confirming sentimental needs of white people and the white-savior industrial complex that continues to produce them.

In contrast to the play, Zeldes's film must engage in a more complex process of showing and hiding its white people. As I stated at the beginning of the chapter, *Romeo Is Bleeding* is beautifully filmed. However, the story it tells is ultimately a tired, unpoetic one of a drug-dealing juvenile delinquent saved by a young white woman somehow deemed qualified enough to teach him eleventh-grade English. As Clark recounts how Raynor's recruitment of him opened his eyes to the tragedy of Black-on-Black violence, he also importantly exposes the limits of the neoliberal values of the charter-school college prep program that brought them together, when he eventually confesses, "I don't give a fuck about college."[33] Similar to the razzle-dazzle effect of the play and film, the charter school movement has been aggressively marketed by its own set of beautifully crafted films as the solution to a poetically fabricated educational crisis.[34] Indeed, as Diane Ravitch has convincingly argued, there is nothing so wrong with our 150-year system of public education that it couldn't be substantially addressed by a reinvestment of public funds into our public institutions. In that way, as Ravitch explains, the "reform" movement (of which charter schools are a part) "is really a 'corporate reform' movement, funded to a large degree by major

---

[31] Matthew W. Hughey, *The White Savior Film: Content, Critics, and Consumption* (Philadelphia: Temple University Press, 2014), 7 [15].

[32] The white friends are Michael Meade, quoted in the foreword, and Bruce Springsteen, as profiled online. See Luis J. Rodriguez, "Los Angeles Poet Laureate Luis J. Rodriguez on Bruce Springsteen," *Backstreet.com*, March 27, 2016, http://backstreets.com/rodriguez.html.

[33] *Romeo Is Bleeding*, DVD, directed by Jason Zeldes (Sausalito, CA: Roco Films, 2016), 0:07:15–0:07:16.

[34] Diane Ravitch, "The Myth of Charter Schools," *Brookings Institute*, November 11, 2010, https://www.brookings.edu/articles/the-myth-of-charter-schools/. I'd like to give a special thanks to Mohamed Elmaola, 82nd Airborne Division, US Army, for inspiring this section on the charter school movement.

foundations, Wall Street hedge fund managers, entrepreneurs, and the US Department of Education."[35] To these investors, education has nothing to do with the goal of preparing students with the critical consciousness necessary to participate intelligently and responsibly in a democratic society. Rather, it has to do with transferring public funds for the corporate purposes of managing or controlling students and teachers through the neoliberal, free-market principles of high-stakes testing and "no excuses" accountability. Under such a system, as is the case with the charter school employing Clark and Raynor, a white investment banker establishes a "school" where a principal becomes a CEO in charge of "quality control."[36]

In this regard, as a materialistic, lyrically skilled, education-hating young Black man, Clark is the perfect frontman for the kind of neoliberal agenda focused on beautifully representing Black suffering as a distraction from the desperate need for intelligent solutions. And although Zeldes's camera loves Clark, it also makes sure to contain his image, his words, and his story with Raynor, the loving white teacher who saved him from the mean streets of Richmond. Indeed, she's always somewhere on the margins of a shot, silently reminding us that Clark belongs to her.[37] And whenever she does speak, it is not to help Clark work through the limiting effects of his materialistic hatred of education, it is merely to express sentimental concern for his physical safety or to console him for having lost another friend to gun violence. Therefore, it is not surprising that, after their opening-night performance, after Zeldes's camera pans from the stage to a proud Raynor standing in the audience,[38] Clark sentimentally concludes, as he has been miseducated to conclude, that you can't stop gun violence and that "You just gotta have love."[39]

Please forgive me, but after two decades of struggling on the college level to undo this pedagogical damage, I must rudely and unpoetically conclude: that's bullshit.[40] Indeed, with a specific focus

---

[35] Diane Ravitch, *Reign of Error: The Hoax of the Privatization Movement and the Danger to America's Public Schools* (New York: Knopf Doubleday, 2013), 19.

[36] John H. Scully is the investment banker behind the Making Waves Program: https://making-waves.org/about/founding/; Making Waves Academy, "Our Approach," https://www.makingwavesacademy.org/about-us/approach.

[37] *Romeo Is Bleeding*, 0:11:58; 0:33:44; 0:35:29; 0:46:42; 0:47:50; 0:48:39; 0:50:37; 0:51:22; 1:07:15; and 1:19:40.

[38] *Romeo Is Bleeding*, 1:24:26.

[39] *Romeo Is Bleeding*, 1:28:43–44.

[40] For the inspiration of my unpoetic bluntness, see Christian Smith, "Higher Education Is Drowning in BS," *Chronicle of Higher Education*, January 9, 2018, https://www.chronicle.com/article/higher-education-is-drowning-in-bs/.

on embodied subjectivity, I have spent most of my time in the college classroom struggling to teach my students that social justice is not impossible or, worse than that, merely a matter of romanticized self-interest; on the contrary, social justice becomes possible when or if we commit ourselves to working together to identify the ugly material truth of oppression, which is structural-institutional and ideological in nature.

As discussed elsewhere, I have never managed to persuade more than a small percentage of those students.[41] One of the main reasons is an ironic reluctance on the part of teachers to have meaningful discussions about teaching. In all too many academic departments, such "complicated conversations,"[42] as the curriculum theorist William Pinar describes them, have been replaced by the uncritical sense of quantifiable certainty afforded by the fictions of various assessment measures of accountability. Drawing on psychoanalytic theory, Pinar explains that this logic of neoliberal values is rooted in the sexism and racism of our past. That is, the current obsession with the statistical management of the school as a business actually represents a deferred and displaced reaction to how the civil rights and feminist movements of the 1960s and 1970s threatened the radical transformation of educational spaces.[43] In this nightmarish present, the old sexist-racist functions as the new narrow-minded, sellout bureaucrat managing those spaces against transformative education for everyone.

This returns us to the question of whether it is possible to inspire more than a few students to resist this racist and sexist history bureaucratized in this way. Of course, the obvious answer is probably not. Like Clark's film-ending pessimism, I have often doubted my efforts to effect change through this kind of work. However, for those of us committed to pedagogical justice, for those of us unable to forget the suffering of our enslaved ancestors or compelled to confront and/or imagine the suffering of our children and/or our grandchildren, we have no choice but to teach; we have no choice but to fight.[44] And for me, this fight or, as Antonio Gramsci would term

---

[41] Eric L. De Barros, "Teacher Trouble: Performing Race in the Majority-White Shakespeare Classroom," *Journal of American Studies* 54, no. 1 (2020): 74–81.

[42] William F. Pinar, *What is Curriculum Theory?* (Mahwah: Lawrence Erlbaum Associates, 2004), 9.

[43] Pinar, *Curriculum Theory*, 54–67.

[44] As many will recognize, this statement is a critical reference to Walter Benjamin, "Theses on the Philosophy of History," in *Illuminations*, trans. Harry Zohn (New York: Schocken Books, 1968), XII: 260.

it, this "war of position" for a liberated future, has always centered on efforts to create space-based, classroom communities against the atomizing effects of the neoliberal practices that I have described.[45]

In this way, much like Terry Eagleton's suggestion that a return to rhetoric might move literary criticism and theory beyond the political evasiveness of liberal humanism, my tactical emphasis on community-building is radical because "thoroughly traditionalist."[46] That is, it is inspired by something as traditional as the Socratic dialogue of Plato's *Republic*, as introduced into the early modern period by Sir Thomas More's *Utopia*. While not explicitly stated in the book-one framing narrative, *Utopia*'s dialogue about the unjust societies of More's present and the possibilities of bringing about a justly ordered alternative is narratively premised on the privileged escape of the participant community from the corrupting demands of that unjust world. Specifically, it was an impasse in a diplomatic mission to Bruges that afforded More the time to travel to Antwerp, where he, Peter Giles, and Raphael Hythloday, a learned and well-traveled man already happily disconnected from worldly affairs, retired to More's house to learn from Hythloday's travels. As More describes the scene, "There in the garden [they] sat down on a bench covered with turf, to talk together."[47]

Perhaps a literalization of the gardening trope so central to the period's understanding of education as a creative but disciplined process of cultivation, More's garden is a perfect educational space in that it represents, as Wayne Rebhorn argues about Utopia, "an ideal environment to produce and suitably house ideal men."[48] In its separation from the corrupting influences of a postlapsarian world, the early modern garden was understood as "an ideally moral and intellectually stimulating environment" for humanity, despite its fallen nature, to strive for moral and intellectual perfection.[49]

Neoliberalism has significantly destroyed the potential of the school or university classroom to function as such a space. Nevertheless, it remains possible, as my limited success demonstrates,

---

[45] Antonio Gramsci, "The Transition from the War of Manoeuvre (Frontal Attack) to the War of Position," in *Selections from the Prison Notebooks*, trans. Quintin Hoare and Geffrey Nowell Smith (New York: International Publisher, 1971), 238.
[46] Terry Eagleton, "Conclusion: Political Criticism," in *Literary Theory: An Introduction* (Minneapolis: University of Minnesota Press, 1996), 179.
[47] Sir Thomas More, *Utopia: A Norton Critical Edition*, trans. George M. Logan (New York: Norton, [1516] 2011).
[48] Wayne Rebhorn, "Thomas More's Enclosed Garden: 'Utopia' and Renaissance Humanism," *English Literary Renaissance* 6, no. 2 (1976): 152.
[49] Rebhorn, "Thomas More's," 153.

to cultivate some of those students trapped within and oppressed by these anxiety-provoking laboratories of accountability. Indeed, as Nikki Giovanni and Tupac Shakur lyricize, it remains possible for something as beautiful as a rose to grow out of something as unnatural as concrete.[50] However, in keeping with my critique of Shakespeare-as-poetry, I realize that the potential to inspire a higher percentage of students demands that we move past that mystifying language of gardens and the isolated roses that somehow grow outside of them. In other words, I realized the need to focus in an unembellished way on the actual labor of transformative teaching and its unpoetic physical costs. In that way, what I'm suggesting is that our only hope of inspiring a critical mass of students just might be our sacrificial capacity to "out-teach"—to outfight—those sellout teachers and bureaucrats like the white people responsible for Clark's miseducation.

As with my emphasis on community-building dialogue, a pedagogical praxis I will soon detail, my understanding of the sacrificial nature of transformative teaching is radical because based on thoroughly traditional examples like that of Desiderius Erasmus. For instance, in his lengthy commentary on the "Labours of Hercules" adage, Erasmus vividly laments the unacknowledged physical consequences of scholarly labor:

> Here's your chance then, here's a splendid reward on offer for all those protracted nights of study, all those efforts, all those sacrifices. Cut yourself off from the pleasures of human life that all men share, neglect your worldly affairs, have no mercy on your appearance, sleep, or health. Never mind loss of eyesight, bid old age come before its time, think nothing of the life you've lost; and the result will be to arouse the dislike of very many people and the ill-will of even more.... Who would not be deterred by this from undertaking labour of the kind I speak of, unless he had the spirit of a true Hercules, and in his zeal to help others could "do and suffer anything."[51]

It is with that zealous spirit of a true Hercules that we must not be deterred by those physical and quality-of-life sacrifices, not even, as morbid as it sounds, by the possibility that our fight for pedagogical justice might be risking our lives. For me, for us, the bourgeois luxury of work-life balance does not apply, for, as bell hooks quotes

---

[50] Tupac Shakur, "The Rose That Grew from Concrete," ft. Nikki Giovanni (Amaru, 2000). https://www.youtube.com/watch?v=-ScYgXAUORI.

[51] Desiderius Erasmus, "Herculei labores/The labours of Hercules," in *Adages: Collected Works of Erasmus*, vol. 34 (Toronto: University of Toronto Press, 1992), 170–71.

Sweet Honey in the Rock to remind us, "We who believe in freedom cannot rest until it comes."[52]

So, in the past eight years, I have restlessly fought on and against that neoliberal "treadmill in the market-place" at four institutions spread over three countries to create inspirational extracurricular alternatives to that lost space of the classroom.[53] For the first four years, I developed a social justice approach to Shakespeare around the first institution's initiative to connect liberal education to "effective practice" in the hopes of establishing a social justice research center.[54] That idea fell short for two main reasons: first, it underestimated the extent to which such initiatives assume the inadequacy or even uselessness of the liberal arts in an ultimately superficial process of remarketing them in terms of a neoliberal return on economic investment; and second, related to that assumption, it underestimated the atomizing effects of neoliberalism on students by assuming that individual projects would naturally bring students together.

Over the next four years, I more fully recognized the oppositional nature of my vision and committed myself to fighting for its realization through the development of a student-centered, community-building discussion series called Shakespeare for Today.[55] At the third institution, despite the sudden traumatic shift to online instruction and the unethical increase in academic labor through the darkest days of the pandemic, I worked tirelessly with one dedicated student facilitator, Leah Onosato, on the conceptualization and promotion of five online gatherings focused on using Shakespeare to confront and solve—not magically escape or resolve, as Clark's Rodriguez-inspired play does—some of today's most pressing problems. Unfortunately, I suspect, in large part, due to the difficulty students experienced adjusting to COVID restrictions, those gatherings were minimally successful, with only about eight students attending on a regular basis.

[52] "A Public Dialogue Between bell hooks and Cornel West," https://www.youtube.com/watch?v=_LL0k6_pPKw&t=242s; Sweet Honey in the Rock, "Ella's Song," https://www.youtube.com/watch?v=Jv3JVUdotvY.
[53] Sir Thomas More, "499/From Thomas More," in *The Correspondence of Erasmus: Letters 446 to 593, 1516–1517* (Toronto: University of Toronto Press, [1516] 1971), 164.
[54] Eric L. De Barros, "'Shakespeare on his lips': Dreaming of the Shakespeare Center for Radical Thought and Transformative Action," in *Teaching Social Justice Through Shakespeare: Why Renaissance Literature Matters Now*, ed. Hillary Eklund and Wendy Beth Hyman (Edinburgh: Edinburgh University Press, 2019), 206–14.
[55] This series was inspired by the Philosophy for Lunch series at Montclair State University, founded by Tiger Roholt. I'd like to thank Naomi Liebler for bringing it to my attention.

So, by the time of the first ever in-person gathering at my current institution, I was pleased but not entirely surprised that something radical was beginning to happen, something qualitatively reminiscent of More's Utopian dialogue. Specifically, that first gathering was devoted to a discussion of Shakespeare's *The Rape of Lucrece* in relation to Afnan Albladi's "The Art of Destruction," an undergraduate visual arts project which Afnan described as representing "a [liberating] form of protest and a rebirth of painting ... which utterly opposes perfectionism in [artistic] technique."[56] That connection developed quite organically, when the University profiled Afnan's project at the same time that I was struggling to engage a characteristically grade-obsessed class in a discussion of *Lucrece*. So, once Afnan and Shivani Nair (my other student participant) agreed to work with me, we began to meet on a weekly basis to discuss the unpoetic present-day relevance of three relatively short passages from *Lucrece*. Indeed, by collaboratively reading our diverse embodied realities—the realities of a Christian African American man, a Muslim Saudi Arabian woman, and a Hindu Indian woman—in and through the poem over seven ninety-minute meetings, we managed to conceptualize a narrative structure for the gathering around the question: "Does Lucrece's violent and emotional attempt to add to the Fall of Troy painting suggest for us a model of critical, even destructive, engagement with a world that surrounds us with idealized or perfectionistic representations?"

In the course of our preparation, which suggested to us a genuinely decentered and creative pedagogical alternative to the neoliberal classroom, we decided to schedule the gathering as a catered, Iftar (fast-breaking) event.[57] To my delight, about forty-five students attended, with more than half not enrolled in any of my courses; and for nearly two hours on a Wednesday night during Ramadan, we were able to engage them in a solution-oriented discussion about the symbolic and physical dangers of today's media. This is all to say that this inaugural gathering was a wonderful success, with many students continuing the conversation well into the night. I was likewise delighted that, in the subsequent days, just as many students expressed interest in future gatherings.

---

[56] "AUS Students Earn International Honors at the Global Undergraduate Awards," September 23, 2021, https://www.aus.edu/media/news/aus-students-earn-international-honors-at-the-global-undergraduate-awards?utm_content=180966422&utm_medium=social&utm_source=linkedin&hss_channel=lcp-20988.

[57] It is important to note that the gathering took place at an American-style university in a majority-Muslim country over Ramadan, the holy month of fasting.

Unsurprisingly, outside of that community, it was as if the gathering never happened. Worse than Erasmus's experience of the ill-will of the many, no faculty or staff member attended the gathering or even acknowledged that it took place. It was as if all my efforts, which necessitated several visits to the doctor, were rendered invisible by those atomizing metrics of neoliberal accountability. Perhaps also suggesting a form of "know-your-place aggression," the only time I became visible was for the threat of institutional consequences to come, when the community-building efforts I continued in that lost space of the classroom provoked complaints from a small number of students frustrated by my deviation from the neoliberal norms that oppress them.[58] Despite all that, filled with that Herculean zeal, I am unafraid and undeterred, because the lifesaving, transformative potential of ethically oriented, politically responsive community-building is more than worth the risk. Indeed, if there is any hope of saving the Romeo of my titular questions, it will require that sacrificial willingness—that tireless and courageous willingness—to fight for his right to experience what my community of students experienced for a few hours that Wednesday night during Ramadan.

---

[58] Koritha Mitchell, "Identifying White Mediocrity and Know-Your-Place Aggression: A Form of Self-Care," *African American Review* 51, no. 4 (Winter 2018): 253–62. Mitchell defines know-your-place aggression "as the flexible, dynamic array of forces that answer the achievements of marginalized groups such that their success brings aggression as often as praise" (253).

Afterword
Wendy Beth Hyman

What if the future is unwritten? What if—despite the cascade of crises that have beset our fragile world for so many years, and have made doom seem all but inevitable—what if it is not actually over? What if we are actually uniquely positioned to make positive, even radical change?

This is the daring thought experiment of *Situating Shakespeare Pedagogy*, because its invitation is to imagine a world in which we still, despite everything, have a chance to change the future. It offers engaged teachers the radical possibility that we can make meaningful improvements to our world, and it proposes to do so through counterintuitive means: the Shakespeare classroom. This is as exciting a proposal as it is a controversial one, because Shakespeare's plays—whatever their undeniable artistic achievements—are not necessarily "liberating," nor are the ends to which they have historically been put anything but universally benign. At the same time, academic educators are in as beleaguered and defensive a position as at any point in history, by no means optimally empowered to enact their loftiest ideals (a task which one contributor, Eric De Barros, calls nothing short of "Herculean"). Nor are the changes we are called on to make merely ameliorative. If the lessons of the last several years have taught us anything, it is that the most devastating failures of our world—the shortcomings and injuries that matter most—are structural in nature. We know we must do nothing less than reimagine and reinvent a world worthy of living and teaching in. And yet, as the editors of the present volume observe, "The difficulty for a teacher who believes in education as the practice of freedom is that they cannot welcome their students to a liberated society that does not yet exist." In short, Renaissance scholars who prioritize social justice aim to change the world with an exhausted (if often ardent) workforce deploying problematic (if often magnificent) texts to educate underserved (if often hopeful) students studying in broken (if often well-intentioned) institutions. How do we make the most of this ambivalent opportunity, especially given that no possible blueprint exists that might speak across our otherwise heterogeneous, even divergent circumstances?

Enter this ambitious and inspired book, which addresses the very specific and situated ways in which our pedagogical practice can be mobilized toward effective change. To do so, it encourages that we aim to scale our ambitions, which means looking beyond merely changing individual minds (the liberal horizon) to changing the institutions whose policies have material effects on our lives. This is, admittedly, a challenging and decidedly postlapsarian endeavor. Many of us went into higher education with genuine conviction in the value of academia, of Renaissance literature, or at least of teaching as a "calling." We chose this profession, in many cases, as a form of resistance to more conventional career paths. Yet we have watched as all corners of academia have become interpolated within the apparatus of neoliberalism, and colleges and universities—which once seemed bastions of learning in an otherwise consumerist culture—have themselves become ever more effective bureaucracies for extracting our labor and maximizing their profit, replicating the larger society's structural injustices all the while. The great exodus of faculty from higher education is a testament to the ubiquity of exhaustion and disaffection. Yet for all of us who still long with De Barros to "out-teach" and to "outfight" the neoliberal status quo, there is a consolation for our lost idealism. In the terms of this book, it comes in the form of a reenergized classroom, alive with love, rage, protest, collaboration, creativity, passion, and risk.

The essays in this volume, explicitly chosen because they represent a wide array of institutional and geographical contexts mostly within the United States, of course do not all agree about every strategy. Some contributors to this volume celebrate how online learning during the pandemic "promoted sustained student engagement" (Muñoz) while others found it "disastrous" (De Barros). Some prioritize the radical potentiality of performance (Steele Brokaw, Gillen and Santos) while others attend more to textual hermeneutics (Mendoza) or even to what is unspoken altogether (Biggie and Guevara). Some essays propose unique exercises and forms of aesthetic engagement like costuming (Geng) or protest art (Oh); others focus more on classroom dynamics (Metzger, Dhar). The volume's hypothesis—that situatedness really *matters*—is borne out in this methodological diversity: we should take heart that the particularities of our diverse contexts may be mobilized toward simultaneously just and intellectually exhilarating ends. That is because, despite the many kinds of heterogeneity exhibited here, the essays in this volume illuminate several guiding principles that the justice-oriented teacher can turn to—whatever their circumstances. Here are what I see as some of the key takeaways.

First, the orientation of these essays is not only ethical but also epistemological. That is, they recognize that we won't get very far with vaguely advocating for what is "good" or "just." For one thing, that would frankly undervalue the rare and precious role we serve as scholar-teachers, not priests. Moreover, identifying Shakespeare with supposed moral truths has long been the purview of those with whom we may share very few values, including, as Kirsten Mendoza observes, "a particular kind of Americanized right-wing version of Christian faith." Instead, she insists, we must think in active ways *with* our students "about the politics of knowledge creation." A social justice imperative requires that we upend the model wherein knowledge is predominantly a top-down proposition, fed by texts or teachers to empty receptacles. Instead, we must "validate students' knowledges," making place for their own "epistemologies, languages, and practices" (Gillen and Santos). Social justice pedagogies, in other words, identify our "collaborative interdependence" (Metzger) in ways that disrupt conventional hierarchies of who counts as a knowledge creator. In turn, they demand that we put collaboration into action with techniques like "restorying" (Geng), protest art (Oh), and equitable course design to counter an "elitist academic monoculture" (Muñoz). By making our process transparent, moreover, we not only enact justice, but we also engage students in high-order metacognitive work through the very process of critique. To put it another way, in investigating the politics of knowledge creation, we teach thinking about thinking. From this foundation, students can readily analyze how power is appropriated even as they also construct practices of self-critique that will enable them to continually build upon their own learning process.

Much as these essays demand a kind of epistemological reckoning, they also give sincere attention to something far more marginalized in traditional academic discourse: feeling. The reader of this volume is positively struck by the extent to which its authors prioritize affect. Those feelings are not always "pretty"; as De Barros writes at one point, one must not be afraid to "rudely and unpoetically" call out "bullshit." The frustration of several authors at the kind of institutional neglect or racist erasure they have faced is as palpable as it is legitimate. These, and every other emotion pertaining to studying Shakespeare, find voice in these essays. For Mary Janell Metzger, it comes in the invitation to students to respond to two prompts on the first day: "In this class I hope . . ." and "In this class I fear . . . ." For Roya Biggie and Perry Guevara, it is about creating in the classroom "a space to wonder, and an affective prelude to institutional transformation." Katherine Steele Brokaw, too, hopes to "inspire confidence, spark creativity, and facilitate connection, rather than—as is too often the case—incite feelings of inadequacy." Mendoza energetically conveys that "we are similarly revitalizing Shakespeare's works and making him accessible, exciting, and urgent to people who might not have thought that Shakespeare could mean anything to them. We are breathing meaning into Shakespeare, and we are making a place for him in our vision of a more just world." And Amrita Dhar, again and again, speaks of love. Far from the desperately reductive view of social justice pedagogy promulgated by bad actors, what these authors bring to the teaching of Shakespeare is as beautifully complicated as the texts themselves. When we disrupt bardolatry, there is space in our classrooms for the whole range of feelings that our relationship to Shakespeare's plays elicit.

Third, these essays acknowledge labor. All of this work—emotional, intellectual, activist, creative—is demanding and often exhausting. The present circumstances of most academics mean that our work is regularly done *despite* rather than with the support of our institutions. This is a deeply frustrating and demeaning set of circumstances, sadly not unique to academia (one only need think of all the doctors trying to provide adequate health care despite big pharma, for instance), but certainly one that those of us working with vulnerable undergraduates feel poignantly. As Victoria Muñoz articulates, "in order for faculty to be able to meet minoritized students where they are, institutions must also meet faculty where they are," but all too often, that support never comes. It can leave many feeling, with De Barros, that all we have left is "our sacrificial capacity to 'out-teach'—to outfight—those sellout teachers and asshole bureaucrats." But in the face of institutional resistance, it is urgent that faculty organize. Indeed, I longed for more attention in these pages to unionization. Although not a legal option at many campuses (including mine), establishing union presence through the American Association of University Professors is a crucial way we can advocate for our rights as a class of workers. And beyond the union, we must pressure our extra-institutional organizations (RSA, SAA, MLA, SCSC, etc.) to keep these issues in the forefront. Those who care about social justice should seek to participate in leadership in these organizations. With *Measure for Measure*'s Isabella, faculty must "assay the power [we] have."[1]

Which brings me to the final takeaway from these essays: their needful, regenerative focus on futurity. Without falling sway to "cruel optimism" or the false consciousness of poisonous dreams, these essays make space for possibility.[2] As Dhar points out, this "rigorous-thinking-must-lead-to-responsible-and-meaningful-action" proposition really is implicit in all social justice pedagogy, undergirded by the conviction that things *can* be otherwise. The enactment of this possibility can take place in subtle but deeply meaningful ways, as in the humbling, energizing principle of non-closure that undergirds the classroom environment Metzger creates. It can be expressed as more explicit enactments of protest, which, as Oh rightly names, are also forms of "intellectual intervention with the urgent and future-oriented intent of improvement." Even sufficient "space to wonder" can be, as Biggie and Guevara put it, "affective prelude to institutional transformation." We can make choices, with Dhar, that foster "creating an academy that I can love enough to continue working within." I would point out that although our personal energies are not infinite, we do have in Shakespeare a wonderful model of what Brokaw rightly calls "a renewable cultural resource: we can plunder and adapt his texts for new purposes without diminishing them for future generations." When our local circumstances seem overwhelming or impossible, it can perhaps help us to remember that we are coparticipants across historical time and geographical space with almost countless others who have read, performed, adapted, collaborated with, responded to, critiqued, and been uplifted by Shakespeare's work. As Dhar reminds us, "The ground we are on is hallowed not because we are treading in the footsteps of a genius, but much more remarkably, because this is ground that has been traveled for hundreds of years by profoundly disparate peoples for an almost unimaginable range of purposes. To get to study the grain of these journeys, even a small selection of these journeys, is to travel in human history." We are not alone in history. We are not alone, even now.

Our influence, to say nothing of our organizing power, is sometimes greater than we think. Critiques about the "ivory tower" imply

---

[1] William Shakespeare, *Measure for Measure*, ed. A. R. Braunmuller and Robert N. Watson (London: Bloomsbury Arden Shakespeare, 2020), 1.4.76.

[2] Lauren Berlant, *Cruel Optimism* (Durham: Duke University Press, 2011). The editors of the present volume also recall Berlant in urging both the promise and precarity of our moment.

that academic work is insular, precious, and remote from the "real" world. It is true: there are countless millions who never think about the arcana of our field. But to demean our influence because of our scholarly specialization is a ubiquitous falsehood that disempowers and shames a cadre of professionals whose capacity is not trivial. Let's run the numbers. According to the Bureau of Labor Statistics, some 80,000 post-secondary teachers of literature and language work in the United States.[3] Even a faculty member with a fairly light teaching load is likely to have taught several thousand people by the conclusion of their career. Using some back of the napkin math, imagine the scholar with a 2/2 load and classes of twenty-five students each. That person will teach something approaching three thousand students after thirty years, depending on the percentage of repeat students. A single professor regularly teaching 100-person lecture courses might well teach as many as six or seven thousand people. And many of us—again depending on institutional context—may have a significant portion of our students go on to be teachers themselves. We need to stop believing in the lie of our powerlessness and irrelevance. An activated professoriate is actually in a remarkable position to have an outsized influence on the world around us.

For the last several years, we have been living through a global pandemic, a national uprising, a ruinous presidency, and a fraught election. We have also experienced escalating environmental crises, racist and gendered violence, economic upheaval, illness, and burnout. Academics in particular have shouldered the closure of many institutions and departments, extensive employment loss and contingency, staggering emotional and intellectual labor, cuts to salaries and benefits, institutional disenfranchisement and adjunctification, and a widespread loss of professional respect. These things are not "over"; many of us still live with fear, uncertainty, and trauma. I truly want to hope—as I write this at the beginning of 2023—that we are turning a positive corner, but I find little ballast for optimism. What history shows, instead, is that there have always been hard

---

[3] For 2021 the Bureau of Labor Statistics reported 58,480 faculty employed in post-secondary English language and literature, with 36,260 at colleges, universities, and professional schools, 21,950 at junior colleges; and 110 at technical and trade schools. They also report 19,640 post-secondary teachers of foreign language and literatures. See Bureau of Labor Statistics. Figures for Post-secondary English Language and Literature, [2021], https://www.bls.gov/oes/current/oes251123.htm?fbclid=IwAR0o2i0cSh3Nhg7wkaV4ANVqjOuVFzsUcYRVmGA1yPWwjGlfsopKSA_v_hM#st and https://www.bls.gov/oes/current/oes251124.htm?fbclid=IwAR2QqJMeCbWA476iW_ASz_XrxdMz8O0Gl_qGQVD2EH_dfjwCQ3KCKxE6feg#st (accessed January 27, 2023).

battles fought under great duress. Our foremost goal should be to bring the best of what we have to our classrooms and each other—to keep learning and fighting together—whatever version of our world we find ourselves in. There will always be challenges, but some of them will be not "dross to us, but allay."[4] The disruption this book promises is fertile, because transformative learning and social change thrive in the scrum.

---

[4] John Donne, "The Ecstasy," *John Donne: The Major Works*, ed. John Carey (Oxford: Oxford University Press, 2008), 121.

Bibliography

Achebe, Chinua. *Things Fall Apart*. 1959. New York: Penguin, 2017.
Adams, Brandi K., ed. "We Acknowledge Ours: Celebrating Kim F. Hall and *Things of Darkness* at 25." Special issue, *The Sundial*, March 30, 2021. https://medium.com/the-sundial-acmrs/we-acknowledge-ours-celebrating-kim-f-hall-and-things-of-darkness-at-25-5db6bd623f6b.
Adams, Joseph Quincy. "Shakespeare and American Culture." In *Shakespeare in America*, edited by James Shapiro, 418–35. New York: The Library of America, 2014.
Adorno, Theodor. "Cultural Criticism and Society." In *Prisms*, translated by Samuel and Shierry Weber, 17–34. Cambridge: The MIT Press, 1983.
Ahmed, Sara. *Complaint!* Durham: Duke University Press, 2021.
———. *Living a Feminist Life*. Durham: Duke University Press, 2017.
———. *On Being Included: Racism and Diversity in Institutional Life*. Durham: Duke University Press, 2012.
Akhimie, Patricia. *Shakespeare and the Cultivation of Difference: Race and Conduct in the Early Modern World*. Oxfordshire: Routledge, 2018.
Alexander, Kurtis. "How the Miwuk Tribe is Reclaiming Part of Yosemite Valley." *San Francisco Chronicle*, April 26, 2018. https://www.sfgate.com/science/article/How-the-Miwuk-tribe-is-reclaiming-part-of-12866845.php.
———. "Shakespeare as Community Practice." *Shakespeare Bulletin* 35, no. 3 (Fall 2017): 445–61.
———. "Text-Based/Concept-Driven." In *Shakespeare/Text: Arden Critical Intersections*, edited by Claire Bourne, 245–63. London: Bloomsbury, 2021.
Alexander, Michelle. *The New Jim Crow: Mass Incarceration in the Age of Colorblindness*. New York: The New Press, 2010.
Ambedkar, B. R. "Waiting for a Visa." In *Babasaheb Ambedkar: Writings and Speeches*, vol. 12, part 1, edited by Vasant Moon, 661–91. Bombay: Education Department, Government of Maharashtra, 1993.
American Museum of Natural History. "Addressing the Statue." https://www.amnh.org/exhibitions/addressing-the-statue.
Amussen, Susan Dwyer. *Caribbean Exchanges: Slavery and the*

Transformation of English Society, 1640–1700. Chapel Hill: The University of North Carolina, 2009.

Andom, Sofia. Interview by Randall Martin and Rebecca Salazar, May 30, 2021, https://www.cymbeline-anthropocene.com/article/17972-imogen-in-the-wild-interview-with-sofia-andom.

———. "Reflection on *Imogen in the Wild*." Unpublished essay, last modified May 8, 2021. Microsoft Word file.

Anzaldúa, Gloria E. *Borderlands/La Frontera: The New Mestiza*. 5th edition. San Francisco: Aunt Lute Press, 2022.

Aristotle. *Poetics*. In *Aristotle in 23 Volumes*, vol. 21, translated by H. Rackham. Cambridge, MA: Harvard University Press; London: William Heinemann Ltd., 1944. *Perseus Digital Library*. http://www.perseus.tufts.edu/hopper/text.jsp?doc=Perseus:text:1999.01.0056.

———. *Politics*. In *Aristotle in 23 Volumes*, vol. 23, translated by W. H. Fyfe. Cambridge, MA: Harvard University Press; London: William Heinemann Ltd., 1932. *Perseus Digital Library*. http://www.perseus.tufts.edu/hopper/text?doc=Perseus:text:1999.01.0058.

Aschoff, Nicole. "Oprah Winfrey: One of the World's Best Neoliberal Capitalist Thinkers." *Guardian*, May 9, 2015. https://www.theguardian.com/tv-and-radio/2015/may/09/oprah-winfrey-neoliberal-capitalist-thinkers.

Association of Art Museum Directors. "Latest Art Museum Staff Demographic Survey Shows Number of African American Curators and Women in Leadership Roles Increased." Press Releases & Statements, January 28, 2019. https://www.aam-us.org/2019/01/28/latest-art-museum-staff-demographic-survey-shows-increases-in-african-american-curators-and-women-in-leadership-roles/.

Augustine of Hippo. *The City of God*, book 1, translated by George E. McCracken. Loeb Classical Library. Cambridge, MA: Harvard University Press, 1957.

Ayres, Jackson, Katherine Bridgman, Scott Gage, Katherine Gillen, and Lizbett Tinoco. "Toward Decolonization: Integrating the English Studies Curriculum at Texas A&M University–San Antonio." Submitted to the *ADE Bulletin*.

Baker-Bell, April, et al. "This Ain't Another Statement! This is a DEMAND for Black Linguistic Justice!" *Conference on College Composition and Communication (CCCC)*, July 2020. https://cccc.ncte.org/cccc/demand-for-black-linguistic-justice.

Baldwin, James. *The Fire Next Time*. London: Penguin, 1964.

———. "A Talk to Teachers." 1963. In *Collected Essays*, 678–86. New York: Library of America, 1998.

———. "Why I Stopped Hating Shakespeare." 1964. In *The Cross of Redemption*, 53–56. New York: Pantheon, 2010.

"Bellingham Racial History Timeline." https://wp.wwu.edu/timeline/.

Benjamin, Walter. *Illuminations*. Translated by Harry Zohn. New York: Schocken, 1969.

Berlant, Lauren. *Cruel Optimism*. Durham: Duke University Press, 2011.
Bernstein, J. M. "Tragedy." In *Oxford Encyclopedia of Philosophy and Literature*, edited by Richard Eldridge, 71–94. Oxford: Oxford University Press, 2009.
Best, George. *A True Discourse of the Late Voyages of Discoverie*. London, 1578.
Bhardwaj, Vishal, dir. *Maqbool*. 2003.
———. *Omkara*. 2006.
Blake, Felice. "Why Black Lives Matter in the Humanities." In Crenshaw et al., *Seeing Race Again*, 307–26.
Bond, Anne, and Joshua F. Inwood. "Beyond White Privilege: Geographies of White Supremacy and Settler Colonialism." *Progress in Human Geography* (2015): 1–19.
The Booke of Sir Thomas More. 1601. British Library Harley MS 7368. https://www.bl.uk/collection-items/shakespeares-handwriting-in-the-book-of-sir-thomas-more.
Borowski, Tadeusz. *This Way for the Gas, Ladies and Gentlemen*. Translated by Barbara Vedder and Michael Kandel. London: Penguin Classics, 1976.
Bridges, Lawrence, dir. *Why Shakespeare?* National Endowment for the Arts, 2004. *YouTube*, https://www.youtube.com/watch?v=Rt9n_uxWaBg.
Brokaw, Katherine Steele, and Paul Prescott. "Applied Shakespeare in Yosemite National Park." *Critical Survey* 31, no. 4 (Winter 2019): 15–28.
———. "Reduce, Rewrite, Recycle: Adapting Shakespeare for the Environment." In *The Arden Research Companion to Shakespeare and Adaptation*, edited by Diana Henderson and Stephen O'Neill, 303–22. London: Bloomsbury, 2022.
———. "Saving the Earth Needs All Hands on Deck, Including Shakespeare's." *Modesto Bee* and *Merced Sun-Star*, April 11, 2018. https://www.modbee.com/opinion/article208648584.html.
Brown, Adrienne Maree. *Emergent Strategy: Shaping Chance, Changing Worlds*. Chico: A.K. Worlds Press, 2017.
Brown, David Sterling. "'Is Black So Base a Hue?': Black Life in *Titus Andronicus*." In *Early Modern Black Diaspora Studies*, edited by Cassander L. Smith, Nicholas R. Jones, and Miles P. Grier, 137–55. New York: Palgrave Macmillan, 2017.
———. "The 'Sonic Color Line': Shakespeare and the Canonization of Sexual Violence against Black Men." *The Sundial*, August 16, 2019. https://medium.com/the-sundial-acmrs/the-sonic-color-line-shakespeare-and-the-canonization-of-sexual-violence-against-black-men-ch166dca9af8.
Brown, David Sterling, and Arthur L. Little, Jr., "To Teach Shakespeare for Survival: Talking with David Sterling Brown and Arthur L. Little Jr." *Public Books*, November 5, 2021. https://www.publicbooks.org/to-teach-shakespeare-for-survival-talking-with-david-sterling-brown-and-arthur-l-little-jr/.

Bureau of Labor Statistics. Figures for Post-secondary English Language and Literature. [2021.] Accessed January 27, 2023. https://www.bls.gov/oes/current/oes251123.htm?fbclid=IwAR0o2i0cSh3Nhg7wkaV4ANVqjOuVFzsUcYRVmGA1yPWwjGlfsopKSA_v_hM#st and https://www.bls.gov/oes/current/oes251124.htm?fbclid=IwAR2QqJMeCbWA476iW_ASz_XrxdMz8O0Gl_qGQVD2EH_dfjwCQ3KCKxE6feg#st.

Burnham, Margaret A. *By Hands Now Known: Jim Crow's Legal Executioners*. New York: Norton, 2022.

Burton, Jonathan, project lead. *The Qualities of Mercy*. YouTube, https://www.youtube.com/playlist?list=PLEcX8YVMVUzMF3r3hUo2Kl8BGOqacYYZg.

Campbell, Mary Baine. "Wonder." In *Keywords for Travel Writing Studies: A Critical Glossary*, edited by Charles Forsdick, Zoë Kinsley, and Kathryn Walchester, 292–94. New York: Anthem Press, 2019.

———. *Wonder and Science: Imagining Worlds in Early Modern Europe*. Ithaca: Cornell University Press, 1999.

Carter, Mike. "Brothers' Lawsuit Against Olympia Police Officer Who Shot Them Can Move Forward, Judge Rules." *Seattle Times*, February 12, 2019. https://www.seattletimes.com/seattle-news/law-justice/federal-judge-allows-lawsuit-alleging-excessive-force-by-olympia-officer-in-2015-shooting-to-move-forward/.

Case, Zachary A., ed. *Encyclopedia of Critical White Studies in Education*. Leiden: Brill, 2021.

Castro, Erin, ed. *Understanding Equity in Community College Practice*. San Francisco: Jossey-Bass, 2015.

Chaganti, Seeta. "B-sides: Chaucer's House of Fame." *Public Books*, February 14, 2019. https://www.publicbooks.org/b-sides-chaucers-the-house-of-fame/.

Chakravarty, Urvashi. "The Renaissance of Race and the Future of Early Modern Race Studies." *English Literary Renaissance* 50, no. 1 (2020): 17–24.

Chakravarty, Urvashi, and Ayanna Thompson, eds. "Race and Periodization." Special issue, *New Literary History* 52, no. 3/4 (2021).

Chakravorty, Swapan. *Bangalir Ingreji Sahitya Charcha* [*The Study of English Literature by Bengalis*]. Kolkata: Anushtup, 2011.

———. "Imminent Ruin and Desperate Remedy: Calcutta and Its Fragments." *Eurozine*, May 25, 2007. https://www.eurozine.com/imminent-ruin-and-desperate-remedy-calcutta-and-its-fragments/.

Chandler, Jennifer L. S., and Erica Wiborg. "Whiteness Norms." In Case, *Encyclopedia*, 714–21.

Chaudhuri, Sukanta. "Development vs Environmental Security: How to Kill an Ecosystem." *Economic Times*, July 12, 2016. https://economictimes.indiatimes.com/blogs/et-commentary/development-vs-environmental-security-how-to-kill-an-ecosystem/.

———. "Knowledge Seekers: The Pursuit of Knowledge for HUMAN WELFARE." *Telegraph* (India), July 4, 2022. https://www.telegraphindia.com/opinion/knowledge-seekers-the-pursuit-of-knowledge-for-human-welfare/cid/1873033.

———. *View from Calcutta*. New Delhi: Chronicle Books, 2002.

Chaudhuri, Supriya. "Day and Life in the City." *Telegraph* (India), December 4, 2010. https://www.telegraphindia.com/opinion/rolling-in-the-stuff-of-magic/cid/891864.

———. "Rolling in the Stuff of Magic." *Telegraph* (India), August 26, 2000. https://www.telegraphindia.com/opinion/day-and-night-in-the-city/cid/456115.

Cobb, Keith Hamilton. *American Moor*. London: Methuen, 2020.

Cohen-Cruz, Jan. *Engaging Performance: Theatre as Call and Response*. London: Routledge, 2010.

Cole, Teju. "The White-Savior Industrial Complex." *The Atlantic*, January 11, 2013. https://www.theatlantic.com/international/archive/2012/03/the-white-savior-industrial-complex/254843/.

Coles, Kimberly Anne, Kim F. Hall, and Ayanna Thompson. "BlacKKKShakespearean: A Call for Action for Medieval and Early Modern Studies." *The Profession*, November 2019. https://profession.mla.org/blackkkshakespearean-a-call-to-action-for-medieval-and-early-modern-studies/.

Connon, Irena Leisbet Ceridwen, and Archie W. Simpson. "Critical Geography: An Introduction." In *International Relations Theory*, edited by Stephen McGlinchey. E-International Relations Publishing, 2018. https://www.e-ir.info/2018/01/21/critical-geography-an-introduction/.

Conrad, Joseph. *Heart of Darkness*. 1899. New York: Norton, 2017.

Corces-Zimmerman, Chris, Elizabeth Collins, Devon Thomas, and Nolan L. Cabrera. "Ontological Expansiveness." In Case, *Encyclopedia*, 432–38.

Coronado, Jorge. "On Entrenched Inequalities in the Research University: Activism and Teaching for Tenured Faculty Members." *PMLA/Publications of the Modern Language Association of America* 136, no. 3 (2021): 441–46.

Corrin, Lisa G., ed. *Mining the Museum: An Installation by Fred Wilson*. New York: New Press, 1994.

Craig, W. J., ed. *The Complete Works of William Shakespeare*. London: Oxford University Press, 1914; Bartleby.com, 2000. www.bartleby.com/70/.

Crenshaw, Kimberlé. "Demarginalizing the Intersection of Race and Sex: A Black Feminist Critique of Antidiscrimination Doctrine, Feminist Theory and Antiracist Politics." *University of Chicago Legal Forum*, Article 8 (1989): 139–66. http://chicagounbound.uchicago.edu/uclf/vol1989/iss1/8.

———. "Why Intersectionality Can't Wait." *Washington Post*, September 24, 2015. https://www.washingtonpost.com/news/in-theory/wp/2015/09/24/why-intersectionality-cant-wait. [https://perma.cc/HGD7-TKCP].

Crenshaw, Kimberlé Williams, Luke Charles Harris, Daniel Martinez HoSang, and George Lipsitz, eds. *Seeing Race Again: Countering Colorblindness across the Disciplines*. Oakland: University of California Press, 2019.

"Cymbeline in the Anthropocene." cymbeline-anthropocene.com.

Dadabhoy, Ambereen. "Imagining Islamicate Worlds: Race and Affect in the Contact Zone." In *Race and Affect in Early Modern English Literature*, edited by Carol Mejia LaPerle. Tempe: Arizona Center for Medieval and Renaissance Studies Press, 2022. https://asu.pressbooks.pub/race-and-affect/chapter/1-imagining-islamicate-worlds-race-and-affect-in-the-contact-zone/.

Darpinian, William. "Reflection on *Imogen in the Wild*." Unpublished essay, last modified May 1, 2021. Microsoft Word file.

Das, Nandini, João Vicente Melo, Haig Smith, and Lauren Working. *Keywords of Identity, Race, and Human Mobility in Early Modern England*. Amsterdam: Amsterdam University Press, 2021.

Datson, Lorraine, and Katharine Park. *Wonders and the Order of Nature 1150–1750*. Princeton: Princeton University Press, 2001.

Davis-Secord, Sarah, ed. "Teaching a Diverse and Inclusive Premodern World." Special issue, *Studies in Medieval and Renaissance Teaching* 27, no. 2 (2020).

DC Historic Preservation Office. "Civil Rights Tour: Protest—Howard University." *DC Historic Sites*. https://historicsites.dcpreservation.org/items/show/1009.

De Barros, Eric L. "'Shakespeare on his lips': Dreaming of the Shakespeare Center for Radical Thought and Transformative Action." In Eklund and Hyman, *Teaching Social Justice*, 206–14.

———. "Teacher Trouble: Performing Race in the Majority-White Shakespeare Classroom." *Journal of American Studies* 54, no. 1 (2020): 74–81.

Demeter, Jason. "African-American Shakespeares: Loving Blackness as Political Resistance." In Eklund and Hyman, *Teaching Social Justice*, 67–75.

———. "'To appropriate these white centuries': James Baldwin's Race-Conscious Shakespeare." In *The Routledge Handbook of Shakespeare and Global Appropriation*, edited by Christy Desmet, Sujata Iyengar, and Miriam Jacobson, 59–68. London: Routledge, 2020.

Desai, Adhaar Noor. "Topical Shakespeare and the Urgency of Ambiguity." In Eklund and Hyman, *Teaching Social Justice*, 27–35.

Dhar, Amrita. "*The Invention of Race* and the Postcolonial Renaissance." *The Cambridge Journal of Postcolonial Literary Inquiry* 9, no. 1 (2022): 132–38. https://doi.org/10.1017/pli.2021.38.

———. "When They Consider How Their Light Is Spent: On Intersectional Race and Disability Theories in the Classroom." In *Race in the European Renaissance: A Classroom Guide*, edited by Matthieu Chapman and

Anna Wainwright, 161–83. Tempe: Arizona Center for Medieval and Renaissance Studies Press, 2023.

Diaz, Natalie. *Postcolonial Love Poem*. Minneapolis: Graywolf Press, 2020.

Dixon, Alisha. "Western's First Black Student, Alma Clark." *The Western Front*, February 21, 2019. https://cpb-us-e1.wpmucdn.com/wp.wwu.edu/dist/0/3143/files/2019/11/Alma-Clark.pdf.

Donne, John. *John Donne: The Major Works*, edited by John Carey. Oxford: Oxford University Press, 2008.

Dozier, Raine. "Experiences of Faculty of Color at Western Washington University: For the President's Taskforce on Equity, Inclusion, and Diversity." 2019. https://crtc.wwu.edu/files/2019-11/ExperiencesofFacultyOfColorAtWWU.pdf.

"Draft declaration on the expulsion of 'Negroes and Blackamoors', 1601." 1601. British Library Historical Manuscripts Commission, Salisbury MSS, xi, 569. Hatfield Cecil Papers 91/15. https://www.bl.uk/collection-items/draft-proclamation-on-the-expulsion-of-negroes-and-blackamoors-1601.

Du Bois, W. E. B. "Strivings of the Negro People." *The Atlantic*, August 1897. https://www.theatlantic.com/magazine/archive/1897/08/strivings-of-the-negro-people/305446/.

Durem, Ray. "I Know I'm Not Sufficiently Obscure." In *The Black Poets*, edited by Dudley Randall, 163. New York: Bantam, 1971.

Dyer, Richard. *White*. New York: Routledge, 1997.

Eagleton, Terry. *Literary Theory: An Introduction*. Minneapolis: University of Minnesota Press, 1996.

"EarthShakes Alliance." earthshakes.ucmerced.edu.

Edgar, Thomas. *Lawes Resolution of Women's Rights*. London, 1632.

Eklund, Hillary. "Shakespeare, Service Learning, and the Embattled Humanities." In Eklund and Hyman, *Teaching Social Justice*, 187–96.

Eklund, Hillary, and Wendy Beth Hyman, eds. *Teaching Social Justice Through Shakespeare: Why Renaissance Literature Matters Now*. Edinburgh: Edinburgh University Press, 2019.

Erasmus, Desiderius. "Herculei labores/The labours of Hercules." 1508. In *Adages: Collected Works of Erasmus*, vol. 34, translated by R. A. B. Mynors. Toronto: University of Toronto Press, 1992.

Erickson, Peter, and Kim F. Hall. "'A New Scholarly Song': Rereading Early Modern Race." Special issue, *Shakespeare Quarterly* 67, no. 1 (2016): 1–13.

Espinosa, Ruben. "Chicano Shakespeare: The Bard, the Border, and the Peripheries of Performance." In Eklund and Hyman, *Teaching Social Justice through Shakespeare*, 76–84.

———. "A 'nation of such barbarous temper': Beyond the White Savior of *Sir Thomas More*." *Shakespeare Bulletin* 39, no. 4 (2021): 683–94.

———. "Postcolonial Studies." In *The Arden Handbook of Contemporary Shakespeare Criticism*, edited by Evelyn Gajowski, 159–72. London: Bloomsbury Arden, 2020.

———. "Shakespeare and Your Mountainish Inhumanity." *The Sundial*, August 16, 2019. https://medium.com/the-sundial-acmrs/shakespeare-and-your-mountainish-inhumanity-d255474027de.

———. "Stranger Shakespeare." *Shakespeare Quarterly* 67, no. 1 (2016): 51–67.

———. "Traversing the Temporal Borderlands of Shakespeare." *New Literary History* 52, no. 3–4 (2021): 605–23.

European Research Council. "Travel, Transculturality, and Identity in England, c. 1550–1700." https://www.tideproject.uk/.

Fielder, Brigitte. *Relative Races: Genealogies of Kinship in Nineteenth-Century America*. Durham: Duke University Press, 2020.

Findlay, Polly, dir. *The Merchant of Venice*. Royal Shakespeare Company, 2015. https://www.rsc.org.uk/the-merchant-of-venice/past-productions/polly-findlay-2015-production.

Fischel, Anne, Zoltan Grossman, and Lin Nelson. "Another Side of the Evergreen State College Story." *Huffington Post*, August 11, 2017. https://www.huffpost.com/entry/evergreen-state-college-another-side_b_598cd293e4b090964295e8fc.

Flaherty, Colleen. "Calling It Quits." *Inside Higher Ed*, July 5, 2022, https://www.insidehighered.com/news/2022/07/05/professors-are-leaving-academe-during-great-resignation.

Flood, Alison. "Yale English Students Call for End of Focus on White Male Writers." *Guardian*, June 1, 2016. https://www.theguardian.com/books/2016/jun/01/yale-english-students-call-for-end-of-focus-on-white-male-writers#:~:text=Undergraduates%20at%20Yale%20University%20have,might%20read%20only%20white%20male

Franklin, Jonathan. "Howard University Students Reach an Agreement with Officials after a Month of Protest." *NPR*, November 15, 2021. https://www.npr.org/2021/11/15/1055929172/howard-university-students-end-protest-housing-agreement.

Freire, Paolo. *Pedagogy of the Oppressed, 50th Anniversary Edition*. Translated by Myra Bergman Ramos. New York: Bloomsbury, 2018.

Fricker, Miranda. *Epistemic Injustice: Power and the Ethics of Knowing*. Oxford: Oxford University Press, 2007.

García, Gina Ann. "Decolonizing Hispanic-Serving Institutions: A Framework for Organizing." *Journal of Hispanic Higher Education* 17, no. 2 (2018): 132–47.

George Mason University. *Open Source Shakespeare*. https://www.opensourceshakespeare.org/.

Gillen, Katherine. *Chaste Value: Economic Crisis, Female Chastity and the Production of Social Difference on Shakespeare's Stage*. Edinburgh: Edinburgh University Press, 2019.

———. "Language, Race, and Shakespeare Appropriation on San Antonio's Southside: A Qualities of Mercy Dispatch." *The Sundial*, August 19, 2020. https://medium.com/the-sundial-acmrs/language-race-and-shakespeare-appropriation-on-san-antonios-southside-a-qualities-of-mercy-9baed8e93599.

Gillen, Katherine, and Lisa Jennings. "Decolonizing Shakespeare? Toward an Antiracist, Culturally Sustaining Practice." *The Sundial*, November 26, 2019. https://medium.com/the-sundial-acmrs/decolonizing-shakespeare-toward-an-antiracist-culturally-sustaining-praxis-904cb9ff8a96.

Global Shakespeares Video & Performance Archive. MIT. https://globalshakespeares.mit.edu/.

"Globe4Globe Presentations." *The EarthShakes Alliance*. earthshakes.ucmerced.edu/globe4globe-videos.

Gonsalez, Marcos. "Caliban Never Belonged to Shakespeare: What Shakespeare's 'Thing of Darkness' Tells us about Gatekeeping and Language." *Literary Hub*, July 26, 2019. https://lithub.com/caliban-never-belonged-to-shakespeare/.

———. "Recognizing the Enduring Whiteness of Jane Austen." *Literary Hub*, December 11, 2019. https://lithub.com/recognizing-the-enduring-whiteness-of-jane-austen/.

Gonzalez, Arlyne. "Reflection on *Imogen in the Wild*." Unpublished essay, last modified May 1, 2021. Microsoft Word file.

Gonzalez, José Cruz. *Invierno*. In *The Bard in the Borderlands: An Anthology of Shakespeare Appropriations en La Frontera*, vol. 2, edited by Katherine Gillen, Adrianna M. Santos, and Kathryn Vomero Santos. Tempe: ACMRS Press, forthcoming 2024.

Gopal, Priyamvada. *Insurgent Empire: Anticolonial Resistance and British Dissent*. London: Verso, 2019.

Grady, Kyle. "'The Miseducation of Irie Jones': Representation and Identification in the Shakespeare Classroom." *Early Modern Culture* 14 (2019): 26–43.

Gramsci, Antonio. "The Transition from the War of Manoeuvre (Frontal Attack) to the War of Position." In *Selections from the Prison Notebooks*, translated by Quintin Hoare and Geffrey Nowell Smith, 238–39. New York: International Publisher, 1971.

Grande, Sandy. "Refusing the University." In *Toward What Justice? Describing Diverse Dreams of Justice in Education*, edited by Eve Tuck and K. Wayne Yang, 47–65. New York: Routledge, 2018.

Granderson, LZ. "Nikole Hannah-Jones Became a Political Target: What She's Learned from the 'Hurtful' Attacks." *Los Angeles Times*, November 14, 2021. https://www.latimes.com/entertainment-arts/books/story/2021-11-14/nikole-hannah-jones-the-1619-project-book.

Green, Neisha-Anne. "Moving beyond Alright: And the Emotional Toll of This, My Life Matters Too, in the Writing Center Work." *The Writing Center Journal* 37, no. 1 (2018): 15–34.

Greenberg, Marissa. "Podcast Pedagogy." *The Sundial*, January 12, 2021. https://medium.com/the-sundial-acmrs/podcast-pedagogy-5185e1c1016e.

———, host. *Promiscuous Listening: A John Milton Podcast*. https://marisagreenberg.com/promiscuous-listening-a-john-milton-podcast/.

Greenberg, Marissa, and Elizabeth Williamson. "Caucusing in the Online Literature Classroom." In *Teaching Literature in the Online Classroom*, edited by John Miller and Julie Wilhelm, 124–39. New York: The Modern Language Association of America, 2022.

Greenblatt, Stephen. "Marvelous Possessions." In *Marvelous Possessions: The Wonder of the New World*, 52–85. Chicago: University of Chicago Press, 1991.

Gumbs, Alexis Pauline, "Daily Bread: Nourishing Sustainable Practices for Community Accountable Scholars." *Brilliance Remastered*, July 31, 2012.

Gupta, Abhijit. "Only Connect." *Telegraph* (India), 2004–6.

Habib, Imtiaz. *Black Lives in the English Archives, 1500–1677: Imprints of the Invisible*. New York: Routledge, 2008; rpt. 2020.

Hall, Kim F. "Beauty and the Beast of Whiteness: Teaching Race and Gender." *Shakespeare Quarterly* 47, no. 4 (1996): 461–75.

———. "Introduction" to *American Moor* by Keith Hamilton Cobb, ix–xi. London: Methuen, 2020.

———, ed. *Othello: Texts and Contexts*. New York: Bedford/St. Martin's, 2006.

———. "Othello Was My Grandfather: Shakespeare in the African Diaspora," Shakespeare's Birthday Lecture at the Folger Shakespeare Library. June 27, 2016. https://folgerpedia.folger.edu/Shakespeare%27s_Birthday_Lecture:_%22Othello_Was_My_Grandfather:_Shakespeare_in_the_African_Diaspora%22.

———. "'These bastard signs of fair': Literary Whiteness in Shakespeare's Sonnets." In *Post-Colonial Shakespeares*, edited by Ania Loomba and Mark Orkin, 64–83. London: Routledge, 1998.

———. *Things of Darkness: Economies of Race and Gender in Early Modern England*. Ithaca: Cornell University Press, 1995.

Hall, Stuart. *Familiar Stranger: A Life Between Two Islands*. Durham: Duke University Press, 2017.

Hanna, Karen Buenavista. "Pedagogies in the Flesh: Building an Anti-Racist Decolonized Classroom." *Frontiers: A Journal of Women Studies* 40, no. 1 (2019): 229–44.

Harris, Cheryl I. "Reflections on *Whiteness As Property*." *Harvard Law Review Forum* 134 (2020): 1–10.

———. "Whiteness as Property." *Harvard Law Review* 610, no. 8 (1993): 1707–91.

Harris, Jonathan Gil. *Masala Shakespeare: How a Firangi Writer Became Indian*. New Delhi: Aleph, 2018.

Hartman, Saidiya. "Venus in Two Acts." *Small Axe* 12, no. 2 (2008): 1–14.

Hendricks, Margo. "Coloring the Past, Considerations on Our Future: RaceB4Race." *New Literary History* 52, no. 3/4 (2021): 365–84.

———. "'Obscured by dreams': Race, Empire, and Shakespeare's *A Midsummer Night's Dream*." *Shakespeare Quarterly* 47, no. 1 (1996): 37–60.

Herbert, Thomas. *A Relation Of Some Years Travaile, Begunne Anno 1626*. London, 1634.

Hermsmeyer, Kate, George Dou, and Kelsey Oberbroekling. "When the Boxes No Longer Fit." *Inside Higher Ed*, November 23, 2021. www.insidehighered.com/views/2021/11/23/colleges-must-change-better-serve-multiracial-students-opinion.

Hollins, Caprice, and Ilsa Govan. *Diversity, Equity, and Inclusion: Strategies for Facilitating Conversations on Race*. Guilford, CT: Rowman and Littlefield Press, 2013.

hooks, bell. *Black Looks: Race and Representation*. Boston: South End, 1992.

———. *Teaching Critical Thinking: Practical Wisdom*. New York: Routledge, 2010.

———. *Teaching to Transgress: Education as the Practice of Freedom*. New York: Routledge, 1994.

Horan, Daniel P. *A White Catholic's Guide to Racism and Privilege*. Notre Dame: Ave Maria Press, 2021.

de Hostos, Eugenio María. *Eugenio María de Hostos, Promotor of Pan Americanism*, edited by Eugenio Carlos de Hostos. Madrid: Juan Bravo, 1953.

Hsy, Jonathan. *Antiracist Medievalisms: From "Yellow Peril" to Black Lives Matter*. Amsterdam: ARC, 2021.

Hughey, Matthew W. *The White Savior Film: Content, Critics, and Consumption*. Philadelphia: Temple University Press, 2014.

Hylton, Jeremy, creator. *The Complete Works of William Shakespeare*. MIT. http://shakespeare.mit.edu/.

Hyman, Wendy Beth, and Hillary Eklund. "Introduction: Making Meaning and Doing Justice with Early Modern Texts." In Eklund and Hyman, *Teaching Social Justice*, 1–23.

Ignatiev, Noel. *How the Irish Became White*. New York: Routledge, 2009.

"Inclusive Pedagogy." Shakespeare Association of America. https://shakespeareassociation.org/resources/inclusive-pedagogy/. Accessed January 26, 2023.

Jaffee, Annie. "Probationary Whiteness." In Case, *Encyclopedia*, 505–12.

Jarvis, Jonathan, and Destry Jarvis. "The Great Dismantling of America's National Parks is Under Way." *Guardian*, January 10, 2020. https://www.theguardian.com/environment/2020/jan/10/us-national-parks-dismantling-under-way.

Jowett, John, ed. *Sir Thomas More*. Arden Shakespeare. London: Bloomsbury, 2011.

Judson, Phoebe Goodell. *A Pioneer's Search for an Ideal Home: A Book of Personal Memoirs*. Bellingham: Union Printing, Binding and Stationary Co., 1925. https://www.sos.wa.gov/legacy/publicationsviewer/?title=Pioneer%27s%20search%20for%20an%20ideal%20home&ID=21.

Kajikawa, Loren. "The Possessive Investment in Classical Music: Confronting Legacies of White Supremacy in US Schools and Departments of Music." In Crenshaw et al., *Seeing Race Again*, 307–26.

Kamps, Ivo. "Colonizing the Colonizer: A Dutchman in Asia Portuguesa." In *Travel Knowledge: European "Discoveries" in the Early Modern Period*, edited by Kamps and Jyotsna Singh, 160–83. New York: Palgrave, 2011.

Kaphar, Titus. "Can Art Amend History?" *TED: Ideas worth spreading*, August 1, 2017. https://www.ted.com/talks/titus_kaphar_can_art_amend_history?language=en.

Kaufmann, Miranda. "'Making the Beast with two Backs'—Interracial Relationships in Early Modern England." *Literature Compass* 12, no. 1 (2015): 22–37.

Kendi, Ibram X. *Antiracist Baby*. New York: Kokila, 2020.

———. *How to Be an Antiracist*. New York: Random House, 2019.

———. *Stamped from the Beginning: The Definitive History of Racist Ideas in America*. New York: Nation Books, 2016.

Kershaw, Baz. "Performance Practice as Research: Perspectives from a Small Island." In *Mapping Landscapes for Performance as Research: Scholarly Acts and Creative Cartographies*, edited by Shannon Rose Riley and Lynette Hunter, 1–13. London: Palgrave Macmillan, 2009.

King, Stephen. *On Writing: A Memoir of the Craft*. New York: Scribner, 2000.

Kirwan, Peter. *Shakespeare and the Idea of Apocrypha: Negotiating the Boundaries of the Dramatic Canon*. Cambridge: Cambridge University Press, 2015.

Knauf, Ana Sofia. "'Go Back to the Zoo': How Evergreen State College Became a Target for Right-Wing Trolls." *The Stranger*, June 14, 2017. https://www.thestranger.com/news/2017/06/14/25216539/go-back-to-the-zoo-how-evergreen-state-college-became-a-target-for-right-wing-trolls.

Kovach, Margaret. "Epistemology and Research: Centring Tribal Knowledge." In *Indigenous Methodologies: Characteristics, Conversations, and Contexts*, edited by Margaret Kovach, 55–74. Toronto: University of Toronto Press, 2010.

La Force, Thessaly, Zoë Lescaze, Nancy Hass, and M. H. Miller. "The 25 Most Influential Works of American Protest Art Since World War II." *New York Times*, October 15, 2020. https://www.nytimes.com/2020/10/15/t-magazine/most-influential-protest-art.html.

Lara-Bonilla, Inmaculada. "Crafting a Latina/o Higher Education Rights Discourse in New York: The Founding and 'Saving' of Eugenio María de Hostos Community College." *New York History* 97, no. 2 (2016): 187–228.

LaRosa, Mahea. "Reflection on *Imogen in the Wild*." Unpublished essay, last modified May 8, 2022. Microsoft Word file.

Lavezzo, Kathy. "New Ethnicities and Medieval 'Race.'" *Addressing the Crisis: The Stuart Hall Project* 1 (2019): 1–5. https://doi.org/10.17077/2643-8291.1003.

Lee, James Kyung-Jin. "Multiculturalism." In *Keywords for Asian American Studies*, edited by Cathy J. Schlund-Vials, K. Scott Wong, and Trinh Vo, n.p. New York: New York University Press, 2015. Credo Reference.

Letterman, David. "Cardi B," *My Next Guest Needs No Introduction with David Letterman*. Netflix Corporation, 2022.

Leventhal, Robert S. "Romancing the Holocaust, or Hollywood and Horror: Steven Spielberg's *Schindler's List*." *Holocaust Film; Film and the Holocaust*, 1995. http://www2.iath.virginia.edu/holocaust/schinlist.html.

Little, Arthur L., Jr. "Re-Historicizing Race, White Melancholia, and the Shakespearean Property." *Shakespeare Quarterly* 67, no. 1 (2016): 84–103.

———. *Shakespeare Jungle Fever: National-Imperial Re-Visions of Race, Rape, and Sacrifice*. Stanford: Stanford University Press, 2000.

———, ed. *White People in Shakespeare: Essays on Race, Culture and the Elite*. New York: Bloomsbury, 2023.

Loftis, Sonya Freeman. *Shakespeare and Disability Studies*. Oxford: Oxford University Press, 2021.

Loomba, Ania. *Shakespeare, Race, and Colonialism*. New York: Oxford University Press, 2002.

Loomba, Ania, and Jonathan Burton, eds. *Race in Early Modern England: A Documentary Companion*. London: Palgrave Macmillan, 2007.

Lorde, Audre. *Sister Outsider*. Berkeley: Crossing Press, 1984.

Marimow, Ann E., Aadit Tambe, and Adrian Blanco. "How the Supreme Court Ruled in the Major Decisions of 2022." *Washington Post*, June 21, 2022. https://www.washingtonpost.com/politics/interactive/2022/significant-supreme-court-decisions-2022/.

Marshall, Penny, dir. *Renaissance Man*. 2003; DVD, Touchstone Home Entertainment.

Martin, Randall, and Evelyn O'Malley, "Eco-Shakespeare in Performance: Introduction," *Shakespeare Bulletin* 36, no. 3 (Fall 2018): 377–90.

Martin, Randall, and Rebecca Salazar. Interview with Sofia Andom. May 30, 2021. https://www.cymbeline-anthropocene.com/article/17972-imogen-in-the-wild-interview-with-sofia-andom.

Massingale, Bryan N. *Racial Justice and the Catholic Church*. Maryknoll, NY: Orbis Books, 2010.

Maus, Katharine Eisaman. "Taking Tropes Seriously: Language and

Violence in Shakespeare's *Rape of Lucrece*." *Shakespeare Quarterly* 37, no. 1 (1986): 66–82.

May, Theresa J. "*Tú eres mi otro yo*—Staying with the Trouble: Ecodramaturgy and the AnthropoScene." *Journal of American Drama and Theatre* 29, no. 2 (2017): 1–18.

Mejia LaPerle, Carol, ed. Introduction to *Race and Affect in Early Modern English Literature*. Tempe: Arizona Center for Medieval and Renaissance Studies Press, 2022. https://asu.pressbooks.pub/race-and-affect/front-matter/introduction/.

Meyerhoff, Eli. *Beyond Education: Radical Studying for Another World*. Minneapolis: University of Minnesota Press, 2019.

miller, joan. "Raceplay: Whiteness and Erasure in Cross-Racial Cosplay." In *Fandom, Now in Color: A Collection of Voices*, edited by Rukmini Pande, 65–78. Iowa City: University of Iowa Press, 2020.

Milsom, Alexandra L. "Assessing and Transgressing: On the Racist Origins of Academic Standardization." *Nineteenth-Century Gender Studies* 17, no. 1 (2021): n.p.. http://ncgsjournal.com/issue171/milsom.html.

Mintz, Susannah B. *Love Affair in the Garden of Milton: Loss, Poetry, and the Meaning of Unbelief*. Baton Rouge: Louisiana State University Press, 2021.

Mitchell, Koritha. "Identifying White Mediocrity and Know-Your-Place Aggression: A Form of Self-Care." *African American Review* 51, no. 4 (Winter 2018): 253–62.

Monument Lab. "National Monument Audit." September 2021. https://monumentlab.com/monumentlab-nationalmonumentaudit.pdf.

More, Sir Thomas. *Utopia: A Norton Critical Edition*. 1516. Translated by George M. Logan. New York: Norton, 2011.

Morgan, Jennifer L. *Reckoning with Slavery: Gender, Kinship, and Capitalism in the Early Black Atlantic*. Durham: Duke University Press, 2021.

Morrison, Toni. "The Site of Memory." In *Inventing the Truth: The Art and Craft of Memoir*, edited by William Zinsser, 83–102. Boston: Houghton, 1995.

Morrison, Toni, and Rokia Traoré. *Desdemona*. London: Oberon Books, 2012.

Moten, Fred. *In the Break: The Aesthetics of the Black Radical Tradition*. Minneapolis: University of Minnesota Press, 2003.

Moten, Fred, and Stefano Harney. *The Undercommons: Fugitive Planning and Black Study*. Brooklyn: Minor Compositions, 2013.

Mowat, Barbara, et al. *Shakespeare's Plays, Sonnets and Poems*. Washington, DC: Folger Shakespeare Library, n.d. https://shakespeare.folger.edu.

Mulvey, Laura. "Visual Pleasure and Narrative Cinema." In *Film Theory and Criticism: Introductory Readings*, edited by Leo Braudy and Marshall Cohen, 711–21. New York: Oxford University Press, 2009.

Muñoz, José Esteban. *Disidentifications: Queers of Color and the Performance of Politics*. Minneapolis: University of Minnesota Press, 1999.

Muñoz, Victoria. *Spanish Romance in the Battle for Global Supremacy:*

Tudor and Stuart Black Legends. Anthem World Epic and Romance. London: Anthem, 2021.

Natanson, Hannah. "'It's all white people': Allegations of White Supremacy Are Tearing Apart Prestigious Medieval Studies Group." *Washington Post*, September 19, 2019. https://www.washingtonpost.com/education/2019/09/19/its-all-white-people-allegations-white-supremacy-are-tearing-apart-prestigious-medieval-studies-group/.

National Native American Boarding School Healing Coalition. https://boardingschoolhealing.org.

National Public Radio. "Uvalde Elementary School Shooting." Special series, May 24, 2022–September 10, 2022. https://www.npr.org/series/1101183663/uvalde-elementary-school-shooting.

Ndiaye, Noémie. *Scripts of Blackness: Early Modern Performance Culture and the Making of Race*. Philadelphia: University of Pennsylvania Press, 2022.

New York State Higher Education Services Corporation. *NYSHESC*. https://www.hesc.ny.gov/.

Nicholas V. "The Bull Romanus Pontifex (Nicholas V), January 8, 1455." *Papal Encyclicals Online*. https://www.papalencyclicals.net/nichol05/romanus-pontifex.htm.

Nubia, Onyeka. *England's Other Countrymen: Black Tudor Society*. London: Zed Books, 2019.

O'Brien, Luke. "The Making of an American Nazi." *The Atlantic*, December 2017. https://www.theatlantic.com/magazine/archive/2017/12/the-making-of-an-american-nazi/544119/.

O'Dair, Sharon, and Timothy Francisco, eds. *Shakespeare and the 99%: Literary Studies, the Profession, and the Production of Inequity*. Switzerland: Palgrave Macmillan, 2019.

OED Online. www.oed.com.

Ohayon, Michèle, dir. *Colors Straight Up*. 1997; Echo Pictures.

The Ohio State University, Anti-Hate Resources and Action Network. "Campus Attacks." https://u.osu.edu/fighthate/assault-on-u-s-campuses/.

The Ohio State University Office of Compliance and Integrity. "Stauss Investigation." https://compliance.osu.edu/strauss-investigation.html.

The Ohio State University Office of Diversity and Inclusion, https://odi.osu.edu/.

The Ohio State University Office of Institutional Equity, https://equity.osu.edu/.

The Ohio State University Office of the President. "A Message from President Drake: Strauss Investigation Report." May 17, 2019. https://president.osu.edu/story/strauss-investigation-report.

Olson, Rebecca, and Stephanie Pietros, eds. "First-Generation Shakespeare." *Early Modern Culture* 14 (2019): articles 2–13.

Olusoga, David. *Black and British: A Forgotten History*. London: Macmillan, 2016.

Painter, Nell Irvin. *The History of White People*. New York: W. W. Norton, 2010.
Palfrey, Simon, and Tiffany Stern. *Shakespeare in Parts*. Oxford: Oxford University Press, 2011.
Pande, Rukmini. *Squee from the Margins: Fandom and Race*. Iowa City: University of Iowa Press, 2018.
paperson, la. *A Third University Is Possible*. Minneapolis: University of Minnesota Press, 2017.
Paris, Django. "Culturally Sustaining Pedagogy: A Needed Change in Stance, Terminology, and Practice." *Educational Researcher* 41, no. 3 (2012): 93–97.
Paris, Jamie. "On Teaching *The Tempest* in the Shadow of Unmarked Indian Residential School Graves." *The Sundial*, November 15, 2022. https://medium.com/the-sundial-acmrs/on-teaching-the-tempest-in-the-shadow-of-unmarked-indian-residential-school-graves-f6803fecbdda.
Park Hong, Kathy. *Minor Feelings: An Asian American Reckoning*. New York: One World, 2020.
Parker, Patricia. *Literary Fat Ladies: Rhetoric, Gender, Property*. London: Methuen, 1987.
Parker, Patricia, and Margo Hendricks, eds. *Women, "Race" and Writing in the Early Modern Period*. London: Routledge, 1994.
Patricia, Anthony Guy. *Queering the Shakespeare Film: Gender Trouble, Gay Spectatorship, and Male Homoeroticism*. London: Bloomsbury Arden Shakespeare, 2017.
Patterson, Wendy. "1871–2021: A Short History of Education in the United States." Buffalo State, The State University of New York, 2021. https://suny.buffalostate.edu/news/1871-2021-short-history-education-united-states.
Pinar, William F. *What is Curriculum Theory?* Mahwah: Lawrence Erlbaum Associates, 2004.
Price, Margaret. *Crip Spacetime*. Durham: Duke University Press, 2024 forthcoming.
PSC CUNY. "Fight for Full State Funding of CUNY FY 2023." https://psc-cuny.org/issues/statebudgetcampaign2022.
Puttenham, George. *The Art of English Poesy: A Critical Edition*, edited by Frank Whigham and Wayne A. Rebhorn. Ithaca: Cornell University Press, 2007.
Puwar, Nirmal. *Space Invaders: Race, Gender, and Bodies Out of Place*. Oxford: Berg [Bloomsbury], 2004.
Rancière, Jacques. *Dissensus: On Politics and Aesthetics*. Translated by Steven Corcoran. New York: Continuum, 2010.
Ravitch, Diane. *Reign of Error: The Hoax of the Privatization Movement and the Danger to America's Public Schools*. New York: Knopf Doubleday, 2013.
Raw Talent. *Té's Harmony: A Story of Love at the Cross Roads*. Ann Arbor: Red Beard Press, 2013.
Rebhorn, Wayne. "Thomas More's Enclosed Garden: 'Utopia' and

Renaissance Humanism." *English Literary Renaissance* 6, no. 2 (1976): 140–55.

Red Bull Theater. *Exploring Othello in 2020*. October 7, 14, 21, and 28, 2020. https://www.redbulltheater.com/exploring-othello-2020.

Rich, Adrienne. "When We Dead Awaken: Writing as Revision." *College English* 34, no. 1 (1972): 18–30.

Richie, Beth E. *Arrested Justice: Black Women, Violence, and America's Prison Nation*. New York: New York University Press, 2012.

Ricoeur, Paul. *Freud and Philosophy: An Essay on Interpretation*. Translated by Denis Savage. New Haven: Yale University Press, 1970.

Rockquemore, Kerry Ann, and David Brunsma. *Beyond Black: Biracial Identity in America*, 2nd edition. New York: Rowman and Littlefield, 2008.

Rodriguez, Luis J. "Los Angeles Poet Laureate Luis J. Rodriguez on Bruce Springsteen." *Backstreet.com*, March 27, 2016. http://backstreets.com/rodriguez.html.

Rogerson, Hank, dir. *Shakespeare Behind Bars*. 2006; Philomath Films, DVD.

Romeo Is Bleeding. DVD. Directed by Jason Zeldes. Sausalito, CA: Roco Films, 2016.

Romey, Kristin. "Decoding the Hate Symbols Seen at the Capitol Insurrection." *National Geographic*. January 23, 2021. https://www.nationalgeographic.co.uk/history-and-civilisation/2021/01/decoding-the-hate-symbols-seen-at-the-capitol-insurrection.

Ruiter, David, ed. *The Arden Research Handbooks of Shakespeare and Social Justice*. London: Bloomsbury, 2021.

Santos, Kathryn Vomero. "¿Shakespeare para todos?" *Shakespeare Quarterly* 73, no. 1 (2022): 49–75.

Saxena, Akshya. *Vernacular English: Reading the Anglophone in Postcolonial India*. Princeton: Princeton University Press, 2022.

Sayet, Madeline. "Interrogating the Shakespeare System." *HowlRound*, August 31, 2020. https://howlround.com/interrogating-shakespeare-system.

———. *Where We Belong*. London: Bloomsbury, 2022.

Schatz, Shasta. "I'll Make This Brief." *Green Linen Shirt* (blog), April 19, 2021. https://greenlinenshirt.com/2021/04/29/ill-make-this-brief/#more-3490.

Schneider, Gregory. "Virginia to Dismantle Pedestal where Robert E. Lee Statue Stood in Richmond." *Washington Post*, December 5, 2021. https://www.washingtonpost.com/dc-md-va/2021/12/05/lee-statue-richmond-virginia-monument-avenue/.

Schuessler, Jennifer. "Medieval Scholars Joust with White Nationalists. And One Another." *New York Times*, May 5, 2019. https://www.nytimes.com/2019/05/05/arts/the-battle-for-medieval-studies-white-supremacy.html.

Schwarz, Kathryn. "Chastity, Militant and Married: Cavendish's Romance, Milton's Masque." *PMLA* 118, no. 2 (2003): 270–85.

Scott, Dread. "A Man Was Lynched by Police Yesterday." 2015. https://www.dreadscott.net/portfolio_page/a-man-was-lynched-by-police-yesterday.

Sedgwick, Eve Kosofsky. *Touching Feeling: Affect, Pedagogy, Performativity*. Durham: Duke University Press, 2003.

Sefa Dei, George J., and Meredith Lordan. "Introduction: Envisioning New Meanings, Memories and Actions for Anti-Colonial Theory and Decolonial Praxis." In Anti-Colonial Theory and Decolonial Praxis, edited by Sefa Dei and Lordan, vii–xxi. New York: Peter Lang, 2016.

Sen, Manu, dir. *Bhrantibilash*. 1963.

Seymour, Laura. *Shakespeare and Neurodiversity*. Forthcoming.

Shakespeare, William. *Measure for Measure*. Edited by A. R. Braunmuller and Robert N. Watson. London: Bloomsbury Arden Shakespeare, 2020.

———. *The Merchant of Venice*. Edited by John Drakakis. London: Bloomsbury, 2010.

———. *A Midsummer Night's Dream*. Edited by Sukanta Chaudhuri. London: Bloomsbury, 2017.

———. *Othello*. Edited by E. A. J. Honigmann. London: Bloomsbury, 2016.

———. *Othello*. In *The Norton Shakespeare: Tragedies*. 3rd edition. Edited by Stephen Greenblatt, Walter Cohen, Suzanne Gossett, Jean E. Howard, Gordon Mcmullan, and Katharine Eisaman Maus. New York: Norton, 2015.

———. *The Rape of Lucrece*. In *The Norton Shakespeare*, edited by Stephen Greenblatt, Walter Cohen, Jean E. Howard, and Katherine Eisaman Maus. New York: W. W. Norton, 1997.

———. *The Riverside Shakespeare*. Boston: Houghton Mifflin, 1974.

———. *Titus Andronicus*. Edited by Jonathan Bate. London: Bloomsbury Publishing, 2018.

———. *Titus Andronicus*. In *The Norton Shakespeare*, edited by Stephen Greenblatt, Walter Cohen, Jean E. Howard, and Katherine Eisaman Maus. New York: W. W. Norton, 1997.

Shakespeare, William, and Katherine Steele Brokaw, Paul Prescott, and Billy Wolfgang. *Imogen in the Wild*. Directed by Katherine Steele Brokaw. Merced, CA: Shakespeare in Yosemite, 2021. Available on *YouTube* and at https://yosemiteshakes.ucmerced.edu/films/imogen-wild-film-2021.

"Shakespeare in Yosemite." yosemiteshakes.ucmerced.edu.

Shakespeare Unlimited (podcast). Folger Shakespeare Library. https://www.folger.edu/shakespeare-unlimited.

Shakespeare's Globe. "Teaching Resources." https://www.shakespearesglobe.com/learn/teaching-resources/.

Shakur, Tupac. "The Rose That Grew from Concrete ft. Nikki Giovanni." Amaru, 2000. https://www.youtube.com/watch?v=-ScYgXAUORI.

Sharpe, Christina. *In the Wake: On Blackness and Being*. Durham: Duke University Press, 2016.

Singh, Jyotsna. *Colonial Narratives/Cultural Dialogues: 'Discovery' of India in the Language of Colonialism.* London: Routledge, 1996.

———. "Different Shakespeares: The Bard in Colonial/Postcolonial India." *Theatre and Hegemony* 41, no. 4 (1989): 445–58.

———. *Shakespeare and Postcolonial Theory.* London: Bloomsbury, 2019.

Smith, Christian. "Higher Education Is Drowning in BS." *Chronicle of Higher Education*, January 9, 2018. https://www.chronicle.com/article/higher-education-is-drowning-in-bs/.

Smith, Emma. *Portable Magic: A History of Books and Their Readers.* London: Penguin, 2022.

———, ed. "Shakespeare and Education." Special issue, *Shakespeare Survey* 74 (2021).

———. "Was Shylock Jewish?" *Shakespeare Quarterly* 64, no. 2 (2013): 188–219.

Smith, Ian. *Black Shakespeare: Reading and Misreading Race.* Cambridge: Cambridge University Press, 2022.

———. "We are Othello: Speaking of Race in Early Modern Studies," *Shakespeare Quarterly* 67, no. 1 (2016): 104–24.

Smith, Linda Tuhiwai. *Decolonizing Methodologies: Research and Indigenous Peoples.* 2nd edition. London: Zed Books, 2012.

Spicer, Joaneath, ed. *Revealing the African Presence in Renaissance Art.* Baltimore: Walters, 2012.

Spivak, Gayatri Chakravorty. *The Post-Colonial Critic: Interviews, Strategies, Dialogues.* London: Routledge, 1990.

———. *Thinking Academic Freedom in Gendered Post-Coloniality.* Cape Town: University of Cape Town, 1992.

Stevenson, Bryan. *Just Mercy: A Story of Justice and Redemption.* New York: Spiegel & Grau, 2014.

Stoler, Ann. *Carnal Knowledge and Imperial Power: Race and the Intimate in Colonial Rule.* Berkeley: University of California Press, 1995; 2010.

"The Stranger's Case: Refugee Week." *Shakespeare's Globe.* June 20, 2018. https://www.shakespearesglobe.com/discover/blogs-and-features/2018/06/20/the-strangers-case-refugee-week/.

Stuart, Mel, dir. *The Hobart Shakespeareans.* 2005; PBS, DVD.

Sullivan, Shannon. *Revealing Whiteness: The Unconscious Habits of Racial Privilege.* Bloomington: Indiana University Press, 2006.

Sunada-Tate, Remy. "Reflection on *Imogen in the Wild.*" Unpublished essay, last modified May 2, 2021. Microsoft Word file.

Tagore, Rabindranath. "35" ("Where the Mind Is without Fear"). *Gitanjali*, 1912.

Táíwò, Olúfẹ́mi. *Against Decolonisation: Taking African Agency Seriously.* London: Hurst, 2022.

Taylor, Matthew, and Jessica Murray. "'Overwhelming and terrifying': The Rise of Climate Anxiety." *Guardian*, February 10, 2020. https://

www.theguardian.com/environment/2020/feb/10/overwhelming-and-terrifying-impact-of-climate-crisis-on-mental-health.

Taymor, Julie, dir. *The Tempest*. 2010.

Thakur, Vikram Singh. *Shakespeare and Indian Theatre: The Politics of Performance*. New Delhi: Bloomsbury India, 2020.

wa Thiong'o, Ngũgĩ. *Decolonising the Mind: The Politics of Language in African Literature*. Portsmouth: Heinemann, 1986.

Thomas, Elizabeth Ebony. *The Dark Fantastic: Race and the Imagination from Harry Potter to the Hunger Games*. New York: New York University Press, 2019.

Thompson, Ayanna. "An Afterword About Self/Communal Care." In Eklund and Hyman, *Teaching Social Justice Through Shakespeare*, 235–38.

———, guest. "All That Glisters is Not Gold." *Code Switch* (NPR), August 21, 2019. https://www.npr.org/transcripts/752850055.

———, ed. *The Cambridge Companion to Shakespeare and Race*. Cambridge: Cambridge University Press, 2021.

———. Introduction to Shakespeare, *Othello*, edited by Honigmann.

———. *Passing Strange: Shakespeare, Race, and Contemporary America*. New York: Oxford University Press, 2011.

Thompson, Ayanna, and Laura Turchi. *Teaching Shakespeare with Purpose: A Student-Centred Approach*. London: Bloomsbury, 2016.

Tolia-Kelly, Divya P. "Rancière and the Re-distribution of the Sensible: The Artist Rosanna Raymond, Dissensus and Postcolonial Sensibilities within the Spaces of the Museum." *Progress in Human Geography* 43, no. 1 (2019): 123–40.

Toppled Monuments Archive. "Archive Map." https://www.toppledmonumentsarchive.org/.

Traub, Valerie. *Thinking Sex with the Early Moderns*. Philadelphia: University of Pennsylvania Press, 2016.

Ungerer, Gustav. "The Presence of Africans in Elizabethan England and the Performance of *Titus Andronicus* at Burley-on-the-Hill, 1595/6." *Medieval and Renaissance Drama in England* 21 (2008): 19–55.

University of Victoria. *Internet Shakespeare Editions*. https://internetshakespeare.uvic.ca/.

van Linschoten, Iohn Huighen. *His discours of voyages into ye Easte & West Indies*. London: 1598.

Vickers, Nancy. "'The blazon of sweet beauty's best': Shakespeare's *Lucrece*." In *Shakespeare and the Question of Theory*, edited by Patricia Parker and Geoffrey Hartman, 95–115. New York: Methuen, 1985.

Viswanathan, Gauri. *Masks of Conquest: Literary Study and British Rule in India*. New York: Columbia University Press, 1989.

Vives, Juan Luis. *A Very frutefull and pleasant boke called the Instruction of a Christen Woman*. London, 1529.

Vizenor, Gerald. *Fugitive Poses: Native American Indian Scenes of Absence and Presence*. Lincoln: University of Nebraska Press, 1998.
Waldman, Michael, dir. *My Shakespeare*. 2004; Penguin Television.
Watson, Robert N., and Stephen Dickey. "Wherefore Art Thou Tereu? Juliet and the Legacy of Rape." *Renaissance Quarterly* 58, no. 1 (2005): 127–56.
Way, Geoffrey, ed. "*The Qualities of Mercy* Dispatches." *The Sundial*, August 12, 2020. https://medium.com/the-sundial-acmrs/introducing-the-qualities-of-mercy-dispatches-3a2682f98585.
Wherry, Timothy Lee. *The Librarian's Guide to Intellectual Property in the Digital Age: Copyrights, Patents, and Trademarks*. Chicago: American Library Association, 2002.
Wiggins, Grant, and Jay McTighe. *Understanding by Design*. Alexandria: Association for Supervision and Curriculum Development, 2005.
Wilkerson, Isabel. *Caste: The Origins of Our Discontent*. New York: Random House, 2020.
Williams, Patricia. *The Alchemy of Race and Rights: Diary of a Law Professor*. Cambridge, MA: Harvard University Press, 1991.
Williams, Theresa. "Race as Process: Reassessing the 'What Are You?' Encounters of Biracial Individuals." In *Racially Mixed People in America*, edited by Maria Root, 191–210. Newbury Park: Sage, 1992.
Wilson, Mary Floyd. *English Ethnicity and Race in Early Modern Drama*. Cambridge: Cambridge University Press, 2003.
Witmore, Michael, host. "Farewell, Master, Farewell, Farewell." Featuring Madeline Sayat. *Shakespeare Unlimited* (podcast), episode 170. Folger Shakespeare Library. June 22, 2021. https://www.folger.edu/shakespeare-unlimited/where-we-belong-sayet.
———. "Freedom, Heyday! Heyday, Freedom!" *Shakespeare Unlimited* (podcast), episode 20. Folger Shakespeare Library. February 11, 2015. https://www.folger.edu/shakespeare-unlimited/african-americans-shakespeare.
Wolfe, Patrick. "The Settler Colonial Complex: An Introduction." *American Indian Culture and Research Journal* 37, no. 2 (2013): 1–22.
Young, Helen. "Why the Far-Right and White Supremacists Have Embraced the Middle Ages and Their Symbols." *The Conversation*, January 13, 2021. v.
Yuen, Nancy Wang. "'The Chair' Is a Surprisingly Accurate—If Farcical—Reflection of Issues Facing Women, People of Color in Academia." *Los Angeles Times*, August 23, 2021.

Index

ableism, 6, 30, 61, 151, 156
accessibility, 105, 116, 117, 123, 157
activism, 1, 3, 13, 15, 19, 25, 29, 35n, 49–50, 51, 56, 58, 61, 63–4, 68, 82, 105, 107, 111, 114, 123, 125, 137–8, 184, 199
aesthetic matching, 126–30, 135–6, 142–3
affect, 20, 45, 86, 87, 145, 159–70, 172, 174, 177–9, 198–200; *see also* Berlant, Lauren
Ahmed, Sara, 8–10, 11, 21, 89–90, 128, 167–8, 178
African American, 15, 44, 47, 50, 51, 54, 59–60, 85, 135, 139n, 194; *see also* Brown, David Sterling; Hall, Kim F.; Hendricks, Margo; Little, Arthur L., Jr.
Africans, presence of in early modern Europe, 152–3, 177n
Akhimie, Patricia, 88n, 160–1
alienation, 19, 64–5, 80, 130, 152, 170, 184
American National Parks (Yosemite), 19, 94–110
anticolonial (pedagogy), 23, 26, 32–4, 68, 167n; *see also* decolonization; postcolonialism; settler colonialism
antiracism *see* racism and racists: antiracism
antisemitism, 57, 88
Anzaldúa, Gloria E., 111, 119
Aristotle, 86–7
Asian American, 6, 47, 126, 127, 131, 139, 143n; *see also* Hong, Kathy Park; Hsy, Jonathan
assimilation, 142–3, 78n, 80, 106, 163

Augustine of Hippo, St., 147–9, 154
  The City of God, 147–9

Baldwin, James, 9–12, 18, 21–2, 45
  "A Talk to Teachers," 10–11
  "Why I Stopped Hating Shakespeare," 12, 18, 22, 27n, 47–8
Balibar, Étienne, 162
bardolatry, 116, 184, 199
belonging, 8, 13–16, 19, 21, 27, 33, 36, 43, 71, 79–80, 103, 114, 149, 153–4, 157, 161, 164n, 166, 167, 178
  lack of (exclusion, non-belonging, unbelonging), 4, 8–9, 42, 81–2, 89, 92, 153, 159, 161, 165–7, 178
Benjamin, Walter, 135, 190
Berlant, Lauren, 7–9, 200
Best, George, 172
BIPOC (Black, Indigenous, and Persons/People of Color), 15, 41n, 95, 121, 134, 139; *see also* African American; Asian American; biracial; immigrant; Indigenous; Latin(e)x
biracial, 161–78
Black feminism, 122, 185
Black Lives Matter (BLM), 2, 51, 59, 137, 187
Black Tudors *see* Africans, presence of in early modern Europe
Book of Sir Thomas More, The, 37–8, 69
Borderlands, 4, 19, 111, 113–25, 156, 176n; *see also* Anzaldúa, Gloria E.; US–Mexico border
British literature survey class, 29, 46n, 129–30, 135, 140, 142
Brown, Adrienne Maree, 82–3

Brown, David Sterling, 66–7, 175
Burton, Jonathan, 4, 66, 118, 152

Campbell, Mary Blaine, 169–70
"cancel culture," 45, 47
canonicity, 1, 11, 19, 44, 46–7, 53, 61, 99, 113–14, 119, 121–2, 123, 127, 129–30, 135n, 142, 144, 150, 155–7, 159, 164
capitalism, 24, 102, 159
Cardi B, 62–3
Catholicism, 84, 144–5, 147, 149, 154–5, 157–8
caucusing, viii–ix, 14, 16; *see also* Day of Absence
Césaire, Aimé, 26–7
Chaganti, Seeta, 53
Chair, The, 127–8, 137
Chakravarty, Urvashi, viii, 66–7
Chicanx theater, 113–14, 116–17; *see also* Latin(e)x
Christianity, 69, 78, 87, 88, 115, 147–50, 174n, 182, 194, 198
classism *see* elitism
Cobb, Keith Hamilton, 41, 90–2
Community Engaged Scholarship (CES), 98–9; *see also* Gumbs, Alexis Pauline
Coronado, Jorge, 1–3, 7
cosplay, 130–1, 134; *see also* fan culture; hobby costumers
COVID-19 pandemic, viii, 2, 13, 17, 73–4, 95, 97, 130, 193, 197, 201
Crenshaw, Kimberlé, 6n, 35n, 120–1; *see also* intersectionality
critical geography, 19, 79, 80, 93n
critical race theory (CRT), 42, 112
critical university studies (CUS), 7
cultural knowledge, 12, 49; *see also* epistemology; knowledge creation and co-creation
curricula and curricular design, 18, 24, 25–6, 44, 46, 59–60, 64n, 65, 73n, 75–6, 77, 79, 111–13, 120–1, 144, 150n, 151, 157, 159, 167, 190

Dadabhoy, Ambereen, 159–60, 164
Datson, Lorraine, and Katharine Park, 169
Day of Absence, 14–16
decolonization, 18, 24, 32n, 33, 44, 46, 61, 81, 111–14, 119, 120–2;

see also anticolonial (pedagogy), postcolonialism, settler colonialism
deficit thinking, 12, 65–6, 168
Dei, George J. Sefa, and Meredith Lordan, 112–13
Demeter, Jason, 9, 12, 48
Desai, Adhaar Noor, 9–10
Devi, Mahasweta, 26–7
Disability Studies, 35, 41n
diversity, equity, and inclusion
  university and college offices and statements, 8, 21, 34, 62, 144n, 154, 166–8, 178
  organizational programs, 17n
DuBois, W. E. B., 48

economic inequality, 20, 61, 65, 70, 73, 112, 180, 201
  historical, 169, 174
ecodramaturgy, 98–9
EarthShakes Alliance, 104, 107n
Eklund, Hillary, 99
  and Wendy Beth Hyman, 32, 144
elitism, 65, 71, 151, 157, 198
environmental justice, 94–5, 100, 103–5
equity, 34, 97, 107; *see also* diversity, equity, and inclusion
  in higher education, 2, 21, 62–4, 73, 75
epistemology, 45, 112, 114, 116, 129, 198; *see also* cultural knowledge; knowledge creation and co-creation
Erasmus, Desiderius, 192–3, 195
Espinosa, Ruben, 38n, 113, 119, 156
Eurocentrism, 32n, 119, 121
Evergreen State College, The, ix, 13–16; *see also* Day of Absence

fan culture, 19, 130, 137, 142; *see also* cosplay; hobby costumers
Floyd, George, 17, 51, 129–30
Floyd Wilson, Mary, 172
Folger Shakespeare Library, 17n, 28, 74, 123
  Folger Digital Texts, 71
  Shakespeare's Birthday Lecture *see* Hall, Kim F.
  Shakespeare Unlimited, 38, 41n
Freire, Paulo, 45, 65, 67

Gillen, Katherine, and Lisa Jennings, 81, 120

Gonsalez, Marcos, 48
Grande, Sandy, 5
Green, Neisha-Anne, 65
Gumbs, Alexis Pauline, 117

Habib, Imtiaz, 66, 171
Hall, Kim F., 3, 28, 32n, 36, 42, 66, 93
Hanna, Karen Buenavista, 151; *see also* whiteness: white spaces
Harris, Cheryl I., 128–9
Hendricks, Margo, 3, 66, 176–7
heteronormative patriarchy, 30, 95, 151, 157; *see also* misogyny; sexism
Hispanic Serving Institution (HSI), 1, 13, 63, 112, 116n, 122
Historically Black College or University (HBCU), 1, 19, 45, 47, 81n
historical costuming *see* hobby costumers
hobby costumers, 130–1, 134–40, 142, 197
Hostos, Eugenio María de, 63–4, 75
    "An Essay on 'Hamlet,'" 68
hooks, bell, 34n, 45, 84n, 130, 134, 141, 192–3
Hong, Kathy Park, 160, 168
Hsy, Jonathan, 126n, 131; *see also* restorying
Hyman, Wendy Beth, and Hillary Eklund *see* Eklund, Hillary, and Wendy Beth Hyman

immigrant, 20, 23, 28–9, 32, 38n, 42, 69–70, 79–80, 82, 84–5, 106–7, 112, 119, 141, 156
India
    higher education in, 25–6
    historical, 165, 172–3, 176–7
Indigenous
    genocide, 23
    lands and peoples, 78, 81, 96, 102, 111
    normal schools, 78–80
interdisciplinarity, 120, 122
intersectionality, 6, 17, 18, 35, 44, 48, 120–2, 139
Islam *see* Dadabhoy, Ambereen

justice *see* environmental justice; reparative justice; social justice

Kaphar, Titus, 53–6
Kajikawa, Loren, 129

Kamps, Ivo, 173
Karim-Cooper, Farah, 4
Kaufmann, Miranda, 171
knowledge creation and co-creation, 67, 116, 125, 135, 144, 151, 156–7, 198; *see also* cultural knowledge; epistemology

Little, Arthur L., Jr., 35n, 67, 129, 151
LaPerle, Carol Mejia, 160–1
Latin(e)x, 6, 63, 64, 70, 79, 96, 106, 118, 122, 188
LGBTQ+/LGBTQIA2+, 2, 8, 15, 50, 95, 106, 112, 118
Loomba, Ania, 66, 152, 161–2, 175
Lorde, Audre, 25n, 89

Martin, Randall, 106
    and Evelyn O'Malley, 99
mesticos, mestizaje, mestizos, 162, 172–3, 176
MeToo, 2, 40
Mignard, Pierre, 55
miller, joan, 134
Milton, John, 25, 28, 30, 38n
minor feelings *see* Hong, Kathy Park
misogyny, 100, 102, 103, 146–8; *see also* heteronormative patriarchy; sexism
mixed race *see* biracial
monuments, 22, 51–3, 57–8, 67
More, Thomas, 191
morality, 47, 155
Moten, Fred, 165, 167
    and Stefano Harney, 91
multiracial *see* biracial
Mulvey, Laura, 186
Muñoz, José Esteban, 134, 143n

Ndiaye, Noémie, 152–3
neoliberalism, 184–5, 188–91, 193–5, 197
Nubia, Onyeka, 153

online teaching, 13, 17, 39, 43n, 46n, 73, 74n, 100, 106, 129, 167, 193, 197
Open Educational Resources (OER), 71–2, 74
oppression, 10, 39, 48, 53, 65, 67, 119, 145, 157, 162, 182, 190
    poetry as tool of, 180

Oluo, Ijemoa, 84
Oxford English Dictionary (OED), 39

Painter, Nell Irvin, 84
pandemic *see* COVID-19 pandemic
Patricia, Anthony Guy, 165
Performance as Research *see* Practice as Research (PaR)
pleasure, 24, 90, 137, 139, 142, 145, 146–7n, 186
podcasts and webinars, 38, 41n
postcolonialism, 26, 28–9, 31–2, 41–3, 46, 119; *see also* anticolonial (pedagogy); decolonization; settler colonialism
Practice as Research (PaR), 98
Predominantly White Institution (PWI), 48, 58, 82–3, 112, 127, 142, 144, 151, 154
Premodern Critical Race Studies (PCRS), 3
Prescott, Paul, 94, 99, 100
professional development, 123
protest art, 49–52, 56–8, 61, 197, 198
Puttenham, George, 6–7
Puwar, Nirmal, 128

queer *see* LGBTQ+/LGBTQIA2+

race, 6, 29, 30, 33, 41, 44, 49, 56, 59, 66–7, 77, 84, 88, 89n, 126, 128–9, 135, 142, 159–63, 166, 172, 181, 188; *see also* biracial; racism and racists; whiteness
  race-conscious pedagogy, 17, 24, 31, 48, 81, 85, 111–12, 131, 152, 168
  raceplay, 134
racism and racists, 6, 10, 11n, 23n, 30, 31n, 35–6n, 38n, 44, 46–7, 52–4, 59, 61, 65, 69, 84, 88, 89n, 91, 102, 111–12, 128–9, 137–8, 160, 162, 166–7, 168, 173, 176, 190, 198, 201
  antiracism, 10, 19, 23n, 77, 80, 92, 113, 119, 121, 127, 129, 156–7
  anti-Black racism, 51, 57, 59
Ravitch, Diane, 188–9
restorying, 57, 80, 126n, 130–1, 133, 140–1, 142–3, 198
reparative justice, 23, 86
Rich, Adrienne, 177

Rodriguez, Luis J., 184, 186, 193
Roy, Arundhati, 43

"safe place" / "safe space," 30, 137–8
Sayet, Madeline, 37, 116–17
Schatz, Shasta, 126n, 130–1, 133–41, 142
Scott, Dread, 50
Sedgwick, Eve Kosofsky, 169, 171
settler colonialism, 4, 24, 28, 29, 52n, 77–81, 85–6, 92–3, 159, 161, 167–8; *see also* anticolonial (pedagogy); decolonization; postcolonialism
sexism, 6, 57, 69, 137, 149, 150, 190; *see also* heteronormative patriarchy; misogyny
Shakespeare Association of America (SAA), viii–ix, 16–17, 199
Shakespeare, William – adaptations, collections
  Bard in the Borderlands: An Anthology of Shakespeare Appropriations en La Frontera, The, 117, 123
  MIT Global Shakespeares, 37
  Qualities of Mercy, The, 118
Shakespeare, William – adaptations, film
  Bhrantibilish, dir. Sen, 37
  Maqbool, dir. Bhardwaj, 40–1
  Omkara, dir. Bhardwaj, 37
  Romeo is Bleeding, dir. Zeldes *see* Zeldes, Jason
  Tempest, The, dir. Taymor, 37
Shakespeare, William – adaptations, stage
  American Moor see Cobb, Keith Hamilton
  Desdemona, by Morrison and Traoré, 37, 41
  El Henry, by Siguenza, 114, 117
  Harlem Duet, by Sears, 41
  Imogen in the Wild, by Shakespeare in Yosemite, 95, 100–7
  Invierno, by González, 114, 120
  Kino and Teresa, by Lujan, 114, 117, 120–1
  Language of Flowers, The, by Villarreal, 114, 120–1
  Love's Labors Lost, by Shakespeare in Yosemite, 97–8, 102, 104–5, 107–8, 110
  Midsummer Night's Dream, A, by Shakespeare in Yosemite, 97, 102

Shakespeare, William – adaptations, stage (*cont.*)
  Ofélio, by Inocêncio, 114, 118, 120–1
  Red Velvet, by Chakrabarti, 41
  Té's Harmony, by Clark, 180–1, 184–90, 192–3
  Tragic Corrido of Romeo and Lupe, The, by Magaña, 114–16, 120
  Where We Belong see Sayet, Madeline
Shakespeare, William – performances; *see also* Practice as Research (PaR)
  Merchant of Venice, The, dir. Findlay, 69
Shakespeare, William – plays and poems
  Antony and Cleopatra, 165
  As You Like It, 97, 105, 109
  Comedy of Errors, The, 6, 37
  Cymbeline, 95, 100
  Hamlet, 67–8, 118
  Henry IV, Part II, 6, 117
  Henry V, 6
  King Lear, 39, 88
  Love's Labors Lost, 109
  Merchant of Venice, The, 40, 69, 88, 118–19, 150n, 174n; *see also* Shakespeare, William – adaptations, collections: *Qualities of Mercy, The*
  Midsummer Night's Dream, A, 165, 176–7
  Measure for Measure, 40, 200
  Othello, 35, 41–2, 46, 50, 59, 88, 90–1, 165, 170, 175
  Rape of Lucrece, The, 88, 145–6, 148–9, 194
  Romeo and Juliet, 88, 114, 115, 116–17, 180, 186
  Sonnet 128, 6
  Tempest, The, 28, 46, 145, 165, 170
  Titus Andronicus, 46n, 59, 88, 165, 170, 174–5, 182
  Winter's Tale, The, 114
Singh, Jyotsna, 26, 43n
situation, viii, 1, 4, 5–9, 10, 12, 13, 16–21, 43, 63–4, 65, 70, 76, 124, 166, 178, 197
slavery, 10, 23, 77n, 84–5, 152
Smith, Ian, 48
Smith, Linda Tuhiwai, 122
social justice, 1, 3–5, 7–8, 9–10, 13–14, 16, 17–18, 20–1, 45–6, 49–50, 53–4, 56, 60, 63–4, 69, 95, 125, 135, 137, 143, 144n, 149–50, 157, 187, 190, 193, 196, 198–200
social justice movements *see* Black Lives Matter (BLM); MeToo
Stoler, Ann, 88

tenure and promotion, 2, 16, 21, 75, 81n, 112, 127, 166–7
testimony, 83, 89, 91
Thomas, Ebony Elizabeth, 80n, 131; *see also* restorying
Thompson, Ayanna, 61n, 66, 95, 150n, 181
  and Laura Turchi, 36n, 45, 68
TIDE Project, 42, 153n

unions and unionization, 75, 199
US–Mexico border, 4, 19, 111, 121

van Linschoten, John Huighen, 172–4, 176
visual rhetoric and analysis, 49, 50, 53, 59
Vives, Juan Luis, 147

webinars *see* podcasts and webinars
Wilkerson, Isabel, 84–5
wonder, 169–70, 179, 199–200
whiteness, 13–15, 17–19, 27, 29, 33, 39, 44, 46–50, 54–5, 77–81, 84–5, 87–93, 95–6, 107, 112, 113–14, 116–19, 121, 126–9, 131, 134–5, 138, 141, 142–3, 144, 150–7, 159–60, 162–4, 166, 170, 171n, 174–5, 179, 182, 187–9, 192
  "fairness," 47, 174n
  white property, Shakespeare as, 12, 20, 31, 36, 46–7, 77–8, 91, 93, 115–16, 121, 127, 151–2, 154, 156
  white saviorism, 66, 187–8
  white spaces, 14–15, 28–30, 82–3, 86, 90, 93, 106, 136–7, 139, 143, 168
  white supremacy, 3, 6, 9–11, 14, 29, 31, 31n–32n, 45, 48, 51–2, 54, 82, 88–9, 92, 111–12, 122, 156, 180
whitewashing, 131, 139, 148n, 154–5, 164n

YouTube, 97, 99, 100, 104

Zeldes, Jason, 180–1, 188–9

EU representative:
Easy Access System Europe
Mustamäe tee 50, 10621 Tallinn, Estonia
Gpsr.requests@easproject.com

www.ingramcontent.com/pod-product-compliance
Lightning Source LLC
Chambersburg PA
CBHW070344240426
43671CB00013BA/2398